CAPITALISM AND INFANCY

CAPITALISM
AND
INFANCY

Essays on
Psychoanalysis and Politics

Edited by Barry Richards

FAB
Free Association Books
London 1984

Humanities Press
New Jersey 1984

First published in Great Britain in 1984 by
FREE ASSOCIATION BOOKS
26 Freegrove Road
London N7

and in the USA by
HUMANITIES PRESS, INC.
Atlantic Highlands, NJ 07716

British Library Cataloguing in Publication Data
Capitalism and infancy.
1. Social psychology. 2. Psychoanalysis
I. Richards, Barry
302 HM251

ISBN 0-946960-09-7
ISBN 0-946960-10-0 Pbk

Humanities Press Inc.
ISBN 0-391-03205-4
ISBN 0-391-03210-0 Pbk

Printed in Great Britain by SRP Ltd., Exeter
Cover printed by Doveton Press Ltd., Bristol

Cover by Carlos Sapochnik

CONTENTS

INTRODUCTION

Barry Richards

The title of this book may cause some perplexity. If it seems to echo Erikson's *Childhood and Society*, this would not be entirely inappropriate, insofar as Erikson's widely read book is an attempt to combine a psychoanalytic account of individual development with some social commentary. The similarity probably ends there, however, for Erikson's psychoanalytic framework is a 'neo-Freudian' one and his social account somewhat untheorised. It was Marcuse who pointed out that the neo-Freudians' characteristic stress on 'adaptation' – on the functional relations between psyche and society – involved a turning away from the damage done to individuals in our present social order[1] and so blunted psychoanalysis as a tool for social critique, preparing it instead for incorporation into optimistic schemes for the consolidation of democracy. Erikson's book has become a key text for students and practitioners of the psychologically-minded liberalism that has prevailed in much subsequent social science and welfare practice. Apparent within this consensus are both considerable resources of interpersonal sensitivity and altruism, and a general lack of feeling for the systematic effects of social structure and economic life.

This book aims to recognize both personal interiority and the systematic social contexts within which inner dramas are defined. To do this involves examining both existing forms of unhappiness, and possibilities for resistant and transcendent creativity within the limits of, and on the basis of, psychic need.

To these ends the two terms of the title are a little more specific than Erikson's, although they both still suffer from formidable breadth of reference. The term 'capitalism' suggests that the basic perspective of the book is a socialist and oppositional one, cognisant of our present society as organised around a particular mode of economic production and extensively constituted by market relations. 'Infancy', perhaps more puzzling, refers to the focus in much post-Freudian psychoanalytic work on the very early period of life. In particular the concerns of this book are with Kleinian and object-relational theories in psychoanalysis, and their stress upon earliest experience and phantasy, and upon the nurture of infants. Some implications of this shift from a primary concern with the Oedipal organisation of sexuality, i.e. from the classical Freudian emphasis on the later events of childhood, are explored in depth in the book.

Before introducing the different chapters in more detail, it may be helpful to offer some further clarification and situation of the book's project. The title might suggest it to be a work of psychohistory, in the sense of historical studies of the social specificity of modes of psychological development (see, for example, de Mause, 1974).[2] A psychohistorical study of capitalism and infancy would seek to trace the provisions for infant care as they have been shaped within the capitalist period, both within family relations and in public welfare; and to investigate the meanings and customs concerning the definition, care and growth of infants. Important topics for such a study would include developments in post-natal care, the emergence of health visiting and the general pedagogy of mothering, feeding practices, the development of psychoanalysis, and of the developmental psychology of infancy, the rise of 'attachment theory', and the impact of feminism.

This book contains no research of this kind. The purpose here is rather to effect some political arguments as to why a student and critic of contemporary capitalism should take a serious interest in the questions that post-Freudian psychoanalysis poses. This is mainly done by example – by examining the potential and the problems of psychoanalytically-based approaches to gender, the family, creativity, popular culture, and aggression.

Even with this definition of the book's project there are omissions, which some readers will feel to be weaknesses. For example, a significant precursor of the current work in this area is that of the early Laing who based *The Divided Self* on a phenomenological approach but was also influenced by the Kleinian and object-relational theories being developed in Britain in the 1950's. A study of this early convergence between radical social critique and a psychological perspective drawing on those theories, would have been an appropriate and interesting chapter for this book.[3]

Another absence is a specific treatment of the relations between Lacanian developments of psychoanalysis, and those under consideration here. Substantial, quite critical observations on the former are made in various chapters, and those sympathetic to the Lacanian approach may feel it has been given short shrift. It is worth saying that although there are major differences between the structuralist rediscovery of Freud and the psychoanalytic work examined here, some common ground can be suggested. For example, the post-Freudian theories are characterised by a *relational* conception of the basis of psychic life, and one major attraction of Lacan for Marxists has been the fit of his theory to Marx's notion of the individual as consisting of the ensemble of social relations of which s/he is a part. Lacan's work is a critique of the notion of the essential individual and an examination of the fractures, the 'lack', and the 'misrecognition' at the centre of personal being. Its political appeal has included far-reaching rejections of authoritarianism, hierarchy and institutional power, and its contribution to May 1968 may be underestimated in Britain. Lacan has also spoken powerfully to the subversive, poetic impulse in psychoanalysis as opposed to the scientific style which has facilitated the stultifying assimilation of psychoanalysis into empiricist social science.

These are substantial offerings, and consistent with central themes in both the British object-relations school and the New Left; but Sherry Turkle's *Psychoanalytic Politics*, a study of French psychoanalysis, shows that more needs to be said. Despite the rejection of institutional certification of analysts, a particularly autocratic system of qualification appears to have been established at Lacan's Ecole. The poetic concerns were eclipsed by mathematical ones and, above all, there was from the start an overbearing intellectualism and snobbish elitism. It is hard not to feel that Lacan's 'radical indifference to cure', as Turkle calls it – the occasion for some of his conflicts with the psychoanalytic establishment and for some of his celebration by the Left – is close to a radical indifference to suffering. Insistence on the inevitable fragmentation of the ego and the search for truth do not, for object-relations writers, mean an abandonment of therapeutic work or a disdain for caring. In their work researching and nurturing efforts are closely interwoven.

These are my own thoughts; the book as a whole does not seek to articulate a critique of Lacanianism, on which subject the authors have quite diverse views. It is for the reader to assess the work here in relation to that of Lacan and various others.

In the case of feminism, though, or at least certain currents within it, one major engagement is central to the purposes of several chapters. Background discussion here would in any case account in part for the original idea of the book, which was in the work of a reading group studying various psychoanalytic texts, and socialist and feminist appropriations of psychoanalysis.[4]

Two works were particularly important for that group and have been widely influential in Britain and the U.S.: Christopher Lasch's *The Culture of Narcissism*, and Dorothy Dinnerstein's *The Rocking of the Cradle and the Ruling of the World*. The work on narcissism I discuss in Chapter Six; Dinnerstein's book is referred to in Chapter One and more extensively discussed by Elshtain in Chapter Three. In her indebtedness to Klein, Dinnerstein is of particular relevance to the project of the whole book; she seeks to combine the psychoanalytic rendering of infancy, the broadest analysis of contemporary society, and imperatives for radical change. For Dinnerstein, the crucial social arrangement is the more or less exclusive female monopoly of infant care: for everyone, the first 'Other' is a woman. The infant's first experiences of the other (the mother) force upon it the knowledge of its individuality and mortality. As a defence against this unbearable knowledge, the realm of experience embodied by the mother is fiercely rejected in favour of worldly activity, of striving for achievement in the social world in the effort to transcend or deny individual separateness and mortality. Hence the split between heart and head, intimacy and achievement, bodily abandon and rational activity, emotional life and worldly business. And also between femininity and masculinity, since it is woman, as the infant's first other, who is continually invested and reinvested with the first half of the split, the inner realm of infantile experience and intensity and sensuality for which we all feel both yearning and terror. And hence also the pervasive ambivalence of femininity in culture – its charms and dangers. Masculinity, and men, are invested with the struggle in and with the world, with the denial or transcendence of vulnerability through outward achievement.

Dinnerstein tries to ground an account of massive cultural processes on a sensitivity to the particularities of subjective experience, to the different ways in which men and women experience the primary otherness of woman. In this she differs from the other American work which puts forward a similar thesis (and has perhaps been more widely read) – Nancy Chodorow's *The Reproduction of Mothering*. A far more academic text, this does not attempt to evoke infantile experience, but does identify women's mothering as the crucial site of social reproduction and it adopts a partly psychoanalytic approach for understanding the significance and effects of this arrangement. Chodorow suggests that the girl's pre-Oedipal mother-love persists in a way that the boy's does not, because the mother's narcissistic sense of oneness with her daughter is likely to be stronger, while the son is more likely to be cathected as a sexual *other*. Thus trapped by her mother's narcissistic love, the girl may be helped to separate by her Oedipal attachment to her father, but love for the father can never completely replace primary love for the mother. While men are driven into a separateness in which their affectional resources and relational capacities are severely curtailed, women are held in dependent attachments to their mothers. Both genders pay a terrible price for being thus mothered.

There are very serious difficulties with this approach, which conflicts with other implications one may draw from the psychoanalytic study of infancy and parenting, and Jean Bethke Elshtain's critique (Chapter Three) exposes its shortcomings at a number of levels. However, Dinnerstein's attempt to interweave the cultural and the infantile remains important for the development of the book's project. Again, it is for the reader to draw his or her conclusions from various chapters regarding the critique of mothering, and other feminist positions, although below I suggest directions in which I think the different chapters point.

Some of the book focusses upon questions raised *within* psychoanalytic theory, where these have implications for critical social theory; some is more attentive to questions *about* psychoanalysis; and some is less directly concerned with psychoanalysis *per se* but develops lines of argument drawing upon it. It is assumed throughout that psychoanalysis is historically produced and limited, as both theory and practice; and that if there is to be, for example, a psychoanalytic psychopathology of culture, there must also be a cultural history of psychoanalysis. In fact only Peter Barham's chapter is an explicit address to this matter; elsewhere the reader will need to bear in mind the research that largely remains to be done on the historical conjunctures which have called forth psychoanalytic discourse, and within which its concepts, techniques and priorities have been negotiated.

The first chapter, 'Family and Authority', is in two parts: an extract from a paper by Christopher Lasch, and excerpts from a discussion that followed a reading of the paper in London. Together they define a range of theoretical and political concerns central to the book as a whole. In his paper Lasch appraises a major thesis of both Freudo-Marxism and psychoanalytic feminism: the choice of patriarchal authority as the primary target for cultural revolution. He finds a crucial similarity between the more simplistic polemics, with patriarchy as a fountainhead of multiple oppressions, and the more informed statements such as those of Mitchell, Dinnerstein and Chodorow, with patriarchy as a point of anchorage and refraction for a complex of oppression. Even though the latter two base their work on post-Freudian explorations of pre-Oedipal development and of mothering, their conclusions conform to the consensual denigration of the family and of gender-based parenting roles. Recognition of the importance of mothering, and consequently of the *secondary* nature of patriarchy, do not lead to a reconsideration of the attack upon *fathering*. Rather it compounds with it the attack upon mothering. Mothering is assimilated into the critique of patriarchy. Indeed it is put at the centre of its reorganisation, rather than that critique being assimilated within an alternative set of concerns about the emotional development of babies and children.

Of course, Dinnerstein and Chodorow argued at length why the former should happen; some of those arguments are addressed in this book by Jean Bethke Elshtain. Lasch's main emphasis here is on the way in which the Left, locked in combat with images of patriarchy, has failed to register a deep collapse of patriarchal authority, and to expound a positive philosophy of authority. It has also, Lasch goes on to argue in the discussion, misinterpreted the relationship of patriarchal authority to capitalism. He is challenged from two directions. One is from the reiteration of feminist arguments, and the other from an empirical standpoint; have the structures of authority, at least in Britain, disintegrated to the extent that Lasch believes?

Lasch's book *The Culture of Narcissism* (see Chapter 6) had, by the time of this seminar, been quite widely read, and in the discussion responses to his paper were conflated, inevitably, with those to his book. The result illustrates some of the debates which underpin socialist attempts to clarify desirable forms of domestic and political life.

Peter Barham suggests that socialists might see psychoanalysis, especially Kleinian and object-relational theory, as offering important, perhaps necessary, contributions to the thinking through of the socialist project and its requirements for action in a capitalist world. The theory of 'cultural materialism', as developed in the work of Raymond Williams, calls for explorations of individual internalisations of the social order. However, cultural materialism also clearly demands that those explorations be continually located within changing historical scenarios, and are conducted in ways that embody reflection on the contexts of exploration, and on the choices made in the development of explorative techniques. Barham applies this requirement to one area of psychoanalytic practice, and he finds such reflexive capacities to be absent.

The area is the work with small groups developed at the Tavistock Centre in London where, especially in W.R. Bion's practice, Kleinian theory has strongly influenced the development both of group psychotherapy, and of groups for less easily apprehended purposes –

groups convened to study themselves for the improvement of participants' interpersonal and professional sensitivities, and for their greater self-knowledge. Barham focusses on the self-consciousness possible within the terms of such a 'study group', one form of the 'group relations' work elaborated within the Tavistock's contribution to post-war reconstruction. This contribution centred upon the translation of war-time practices into wide-ranging civil objectives to reform capitalism by applying theoretical insights into the infantile dimension of adult psychology to practices in welfare and industry; in short to humanise capitalism according to psychoanalytic principles. However, the institutional and conceptual definitions within which the 'study group' activity was performed did not accommodate questions about these definitions; indeed they explicitly sought to eliminate the world outside the room within which the group took place. This generates a deep tension between the group's potential for critical study of interpersonal events, and its mystification about itself. The tension is expressed in ambivalence towards the 'consultant', the paid expert in the group, and in the image of the room as the setting and boundary of the group. Barham likens this image to that of the 'living room' in naturalistic drama, discussed by Williams as both the focal scene of personal life and a place of isolation from, though vulnerability to, the important processes in society.

The chapter concludes with observations on an attempt within the particular institutional form of the small group to reassert the autonomy from wider social pressures it felt it once possessed and so project the crisis within the dramatic form of the group onto the external world. Barham's conceptualisation of psychoanalytic activities as dramatic forms in historical crisis establishes an additional dimension to that provided by the discussion with Lasch and one within which the rest of the book is to be read. The dimension is the historicity of psychoanalytic theories and practices, which need to be seen as expressions of institutional and professional interests, at the same time as we recruit them into our programmes of inquiry and opposition.

The American political theorist Jean Bethke Elshtain sets forth another contextual and cautionary argument, this one concerning the ease with which appropriations of psychoanalysis can lead to schematic and narrow views of the world, especially unwelcome for the political styles and strategies which they propose. Her critique is of three very influential, psychoanalytically-based feminist analyses of gender. Elshtain begins by setting out her conception of psychoanalysis as an interpretive endeavour, able to produce 'thick' descriptions of the subjective world and its dense networks of meaning. Juliet Mitchell's formalist, positivistic analysis in *Psychoanalysis and Feminism*, by contrast, is found to be stiff, impoverished and teleological. Elshtain finds Dinnerstein's notion of 'normal psychopathology' to be problematic.[5] Her use of the psychoanalytic concept of splitting lacks regard for the complexities of the term in psychoanalysis; and her interlocking of the dynamics of splitting with the development of gender identity is a most questionable leap. Dinnerstein, Elshtain suggests, has uncritically absorbed a nature-culture distinction bequeathed to feminism by bourgeois thought and, like de Beauvoir, mapped it straight onto gender. Chodorow's work owes more to Parsonian functionalism but makes the same *a priori* assumption as Dinnerstein: that gender difference necessarily entails inequality and sexism. Anthropological evidence does not support this assumption, Elshtain observes; in many cultures the specific activities of women are the basis for particular forms of their power and authority. Advocacy of gender 'symmetry', therefore, tends to be linked to ethnocentric and unidimensional conceptions of power and authority.

In all three writers the support for androgynous ideals (see Elshtain, 1981) embodies a simplistic, 'abstracted' theory and utopian politics, displaced from larger dimensions of cultural crisis. The conflation of gender difference with male dominance precludes alternative conceptions of difference as interdependence and complementarity; it flows from and gives support to the market-based precepts of contemporary 'narcissistic' culture. All three works seek to encompass the whole of human history, and their *a priori*, universalising style is, at least potentially, affiliated with the coercive, manipulative politics associated particularly with vanguardist prescriptions for social transformation.

Elshtain indicates an alternative approach, which would give more weight to the agency and creativity of the developing child, would recognise the basis of personal identity in the *body*-ego, and so see the sense of self as being fundamentally gendered. Her work is not only an input to debates around psychoanalytic understandings of gender but more generally signals a major reassessment of much feminist polemic on gender difference.

In six chapters there is some reflection of the authors' experience of various forms of clinical practice. The most extensive use of clinical material is made by Sue Holland and Ray Holland, who show how early experiences of parents may later be elaborated into particularly painful ways of choosing a sexual partner and rearing children. In the cases they discuss, the elaboration may be seen, perhaps more clearly than is often the case, as the work of identifiable historical processes – the racism and enforced migrations of colonialism.

The Hollands begin with general observations on the links between depression and the loss of close others, and the impression given by some depressed working-class women that they have never had, and can never have, stable relations with intimate others. Their object-relations account of this phenomenon is richly illustrated in cases involving white working-class women with black men, where the woman's ambivalence towards her father is re-enacted in her relationship with the black father of her children. Deeply dissatisfied with her partner, rejected both by her children and, for different reasons, by her original family, pitied by black women, this woman exists in a specially blasted region in the current geography of loneliness. But the more 'independent' black woman has another principal difficulty: her hatred of the mother who left her in the Caribbean is the source of a fierce self-hatred, layered with self-hatred derived from the internalisation of earlier relationships between, for example, black overseers and underlings. These historical dramas provide numerous roles or vantage points from which the black can look upon him/herself with contempt.

Migrant populations have long been objects of socially concerned and sometimes radical study in and around psychiatry (see, e.g. Haugsgjerd, 1981); the Hollands' work suggests how the study of mixed-race couples can help define objectives for a therapeutic practice explicating the historical context of failures in parenting.

Joel Kovel is an American writer and psychoanalyst, well known in Britain for his *Complete Guide to Therapy*. His 'Rationalization and the family' first appeared in *Telos*, an American radical philosophy journal, in 1978. The paper asks questions about the *psychological* nature of bureaucratically and rationally administered capitalism, and the relationship of that to family life. Kovel's imaginative style moves energetically across wide tracts of history and culture, while requiring us to consider closely the emotional stances of individuals in the present, to whom Kovel as an analyst is engaged in listening.

Along with Lasch, Kovel rejects the claim that the family as such is in some essential way implicated in domination, and his formulation, by contrast, is that 'the family supplies a transhistorical substructure for the possibilities of domination.' Such a notion of the transhistorical offers a way of reconceptualising the problems of biology and instinct so that full weight can be given to the limits of bodily existence – to nutritional, excretory and homeostatic requirements – without recourse to biologism. These limits and requirements, to which Elshtain and Robinson here address themselves, and with which Peter Fuller's work as another example has been concerned (see, e.g., his *Art and Psychoanalysis*), are in an abstract sense constants of human existence, but are not in any concrete sense a- or supra-historical.

In keeping with Lasch, and with the general perspective of the book, Kovel stresses the distinction between Oedipal and pre-Oedipal levels of development. While the production of that distinction within psychoanalytic theory is not yet accounted for in historical terms, we can nonetheless appreciate the decisiveness of the pre-Oedipal in both cultural and psychic spheres. For instance, following Kovel's analysis, we must come to view the struggle against patriarchy as misplaced. Patriarchal forms are like pagan adornments to the clean functional lines of the administrative style and are potent only in local contingencies. It is rational administration which now answers the deepest calls from the individual psyche, which objectifies the most primitive sense of 'necessity', as Kovel describes it, and which thrives on the pre-Oedipal phantasies now released in the social and psychic spaces where traditional authorities once stood.

Kovel pursues implications of this broad analysis in relation to the concept of the ego, the strategic assessment of social policy, and potentials for resistance. He enables us, too, to glimpse some of the inner modes of surviving in this rationalised world – our compulsive engagement with it, and our defensive embrace of its false objects.

These 'inner modes' are also the primary concerns of my chapter on psychopathology in culture, which I approach through a review of some recent psychoanalytic writing on schizoid, borderline and narcissistic personalities. The shift in developmental theory to a concentration on early stages of development has been accompanied by corresponding changes in psychoanalytic practice and its conceptualisation of clinical problems, many of which are now seen as rooted in the infant's earliest experiences, described by Klein as the 'paranoid-schizoid' position (see pp. 170–172).

This 'position' is constituted by a process of 'splitting' and, in the work of the object-relations writers that I consider, is seen to be elaborated in adult life as schizoid and pathological yet somehow 'normal' ways of relating to the world defensively and falsely, designed to camouflage a split-off inner core of weakness.

We can use this framework to consider not only the borderline and narcissistic conditions – descriptions of which are closely related to the accounts of schizoid processes – but also the deployment of psychoanalytic theory as a whole, as the more systematic of the object-relations writers intend. I attempt to map out parts of our present cultural landscape using this framework: this involves a concern with the dynamics of withdrawal and aborted or pseudo-engagement – the 'in-out dilemma' of the schizoid, as Guntrip referred to it, and with the impoverishment of reparative activities. I am particularly concerned with some of the psychological forms of rationality generated by the market and the State, with 'silent pathologies' in everyday experience, and with the vicissitudes and survivals of authentic affectivity.

The core of Ștephen Robinson's paper is an examination of the problem of how to conceive of the relationships between 'inner' and 'outer' worlds, reviewing their treatment in Freud's work, and in Kleinian and object-relations writings. Considering the way Kleinians have used 'unconscious phantasy', he argues for a reformulation of the notion of the 'environment'. Kleinian theory in this area is, he suggests, Kantian in its insistence upon innate origins of unconscious phantasies. Phantasies are seen as modifiable by the experience of external reality, but even this limited action of the external world is achieved only negatively, through its absences and failures. A conception of the outer world as positively formative is, Robinson argues, undeveloped in psychoanalytic writings.

The makings of one exist, however, and he goes on to elaborate a theory of a 'corporeal ego' as the most adequate conceptualisation of earliest psychic life, and of the developmental relationship between internal and external factors. (He is very close to Jean Bethke Elshtain here.) The first ego-activity is 'oral judgement' – the acceptance or rejection of substances presented at the mouth; even primitive introjection is secondary to 'in-corporealisation'. Accepted substances are digested, and it is these physical exchanges between body and environment which are the prototypes of psychic processes, the foundation of self-other differentiation, and of a sense of agency. As Robinson points out, this conception undercuts that which seeks the origin of subjectivity in language. Linguistic elaborations of selfhood occur *after* the emergence of psychic structure from the neo-natal 'psyche-soma' (Winnicott's idea of the inseparability of early mental and physical process). That is, the infant is 'parent' to the child.

In his final section Robinson returns to his opening theme: the problem of understanding the meanings of 'aggression'. Recording the value of 'aggressive' differentiation of self from other, he notes the difficulty Marxists have had in doing this in relation to Marx's work itself; having considered the complexities surrounding a theoretical location of both constructive aggression and destructive rage, he raises questions about their inner and outer determinants.

The final chapter, by Margaret Rustin and Michael Rustin, is at odds, at some levels, with others in the book. Unlike the chapters by Kovel, Sue Holland and Ray Holland, and myself, it does not set out to use psychoanalytic theory as a means of delineating the forms of psychological damage characteristic of contemporary capitalism. On the contrary, it seeks to advance a conception of psychoanalysis as a source of positive models for the management of a wide range of affairs, both in any future conditions of socialism and in those areas of current practice where economic and ideological forces permit. In this the Rustins are making a different political assessment from that offered by Peter Barham of the influence of Kleinian and subsequent developments in psychoanalysis upon the reformism embodied within the British Welfare State. Barham stresses the tendency towards mystification; the Rustins' argument focusses instead upon the relief which can be brought to distressed individuals through the establishment of local cultures of sensitivity and care, and the positive implications of this for the development of welfare policies.

Their paper extends some of the points raised in the 'Discussion' section of the chapter on 'Family and Authority' and conflicts with the analyses made by Christopher Lasch, Russell Jacoby, Philip Rieff and others of the significance of the growth of the welfare and therapeutic professions and of associated cultural changes. For the Rustins these are on balance and in principle welcome developments, which prefigure much of what we may hope to see in a society less dominated by the capitalist exchange principle. The better examples of these welfare interventions demonstrate the extent to which capitalist social policy has conceded the importance of early needs for nurture and their psychological persistence later in life.

Thus this final chapter brings together three related issues. Firstly, there is the difference (perhaps mainly one of mood) amongst socialist explorations of psychoanalysis between those which concentrate upon 'diagnostic' work and the development of a moral psychopathology of capitalism, and those which are oriented towards the identification in theory and in practical interventions of a positive psychological morality. Secondly, there are divergent evaluations of the ways in which psychoanalytic work, especially the 'British' psychoanalysis of infancy, has informed technologies of intervention. Thirdly, there is the broader question of how the influence of psychoanalysis within welfare practices is related to changes in family life, or rather (assuming that psychoanalysis *has* been a major element in the development of more expressive and child-centred styles of family interaction) of how we assess the latter changes. Here again the Rustins are optimistic that the loosening of family structures represents a beneficial development.

However, underlying these differences between contributions to this collection there is some important commonality of intellectual preoccupation and political objective. This is indicated in the Rustins' discussion of the socialist tradition and its strengths and problems. Psychoanalysis, as a sophisticated and practical theory of *individual* need and possibility, can contribute substantially to the construction of socialist outlooks which are able to confront the cultural and psychological achievements of bourgeois individuality without collapsing into an ahistorical humanism or taking refuge in dogmatic re-assertions of collective values.

All in all, then, this collection invites the reader to juxtapose and intermingle two discourses, realms of theory, kinds of response to the problem of making sense of living in a world of distress: the psychoanalytic, specifically 'Kleinian' and 'object-relational', and the socialist, specifically a range of political perspectives sharing a broad analysis of capitalism, a sense of complexity, and at least a modicum of hope.

The long tradition of affiliation between psychoanalysis and radical socialism seems now to be in a new phase of vigour and influence. But the direction of this development is as uncertain as ever: both psychoanalysis and socialism are complex, ambivalent and negotiable traditions, and the product of their intercourse is highly vulnerable to subtle recuperations into the existing order. We confront hegemonic processes of great weight and intricacy; they impel us towards psychoanalysis for illumination of their sources of strength and points of weakness and contradiction; but they also prepare a multitude of paths which keep us within their universe, even when we think we have encompassed them. As the restructuring of State welfare and educational provisions proceeds, the prospects for a *socialist* appraisal of what is wrong with welfare capitalism diminish. Popular feelings are now articulated more skilfully and comprehensively by the politicians and ideologists of the fundamentalist Right than has been achieved by any other propaganda force for some considerable time, perhaps (in Britain) since 1945. For example, there is a quality of hopelessness about the shouts of 'Maggie out!', however loud and angry, when these are set against the seamless confidence of Thatcher's style. One component of that style is the contrivance, in the tradition of authoritarianism, to be both leader and rebel at the same time. Thus Thatcher leads the British people in a 'war' against 'national weakness', a popular uprising in which nationalistic militarism is equated with 'strength' and 'authority', any more pacific or compassionate attitude with ineptitude and dishonesty. This style is creative, in one sense of the word, and can thrive on the inarticulate exasperation of its opponents.

Thatcher's style also elicits much sado-masochistic excitement, which does at least point up the relationship of electoral demagogy to primitive emotional processes in the individual and the group. These are rather more obscured in the rationalistic social-democratic consensus, and social investigators have hitherto had the leisure to examine them in the (for some of us) more remote context of Europe between the wars. But the new situation can be turned to our advantage only if radical critique is able to explore that relationship and suggests how oppositional politics might *differently* address primitive needs.

To do so does not imply a behavioural engineering approach to social transformation. Rather it means the attempt to characterise the psychic meaning of alternatives to politics of domination and manipulation (within which we must include the autonomy-owning democracy of the neo-Freudians). Distinctions need to be made and analysed historically, for instance between authority and authoritarianism, or moral leadership and moralistic demagogy. At times such distinctions prove to be matters of subtle, unconscious emotional nuance: hence the particular value of some theoretical understanding of unconscious mental life.

Yet despite feminist and radical Left interest in psychoanalysis, opposition to the fundamentalist Right is often only productive of clichés and negativity. The Rightists' proposition that it is not capitalism, but the Left, that seeks to destroy remaining hopes for a secure life is all too easily plausible when the radical Left offers little in crucial areas of social policy other than critique – for instance its continuing attacks upon the 'family'.

Psychoanalytic thought – in the form of Reichian and Lacanian doctrines of the ills of repression – is implicated in this failure of opposition to the degree that it fails to help make necessary emotional distinctions and to register human needs for nurture. The schools of contemporary psychoanalysis represented in this book seem to me to have more to offer in the task of clarifying the social conditions by which we could hope to achieve the greatest possibilities for emotional security and happiness. At present, the Right is hardly challenged in its attention to these matters, even as it threatens us with unthinkable deaths. It is hoped that the intellectual work presented here can be influential within what must in the present circumstances of authoritarian and militarist offensives be a far-reaching reconsideration of the Left's programmes and reconstruction of its alliances.

Notes

1. Erikson makes this clear in the Foreword to the First Edition of his book, stating that psychoanalysis 'is shifting its emphasis from the concentrated study of the conditions which blunt and distort the individual ego to the study of the ego's roots in social organisation.' (op. cit., p. 13).

2. This is different from psychohistory as psychological studies of historical individuals; and also different from, although closer to, psychohistory as psychological analyses of socio-historical phenomena, of which Joel Kovel's *White Racism: A Psychohistory* is an example.

3. Neither Peter Sedgwick's critique of Laing, nor Juliet Mitchell's, address this aspect of Laing's work.

4. This was the 'Freud-Marx subgroup' of the Radical Science Journal Collective. The other regular members of the group were Karl Figlio, Les Levidow, Margot Waddell, and Bob Young. This Introduction, my chapter later in the book, and the project of the book, owe a great deal to them.

5. Elshtain's argument at this point may also apply to the positions taken by Kovel and myself in Chapters Five and Six; my own view is that there is more to the notion of 'normal psychopathology' than Elshtain allows for here.

References

Chodorow, N. (1978). *The Reproduction of Mothering*. U. of Calif. Press.

de Mause, L. ed. (1974). *The History of Childhood*. Souvenir Press.

Dinnerstein, D. (1976). *The Rocking of the Cradle, and the Ruling of the World*. Souvenir Press, 1978 (U.S. edition: *The Mermaid and the Minotaur*).

Elshtain, J.B. (1981). Against androgyny. *Telos* 47, 5–21.

Erikson, E. (1950). *Childhood and Society*. Penguin, 1965.

Fuller, P. (1980). *Art and Psychoanalysis*. Writers and Readers Publishing Cooperative.

Haugsgjerd, S. (1981). Report from Norway. In Ingleby, D. ed. *Critical Psychiatry*. Penguin.

Jacoby, R. (1975). *Social Amnesia*. Harvester, 1977.

Kovel, J. (1970). *White Racism: A Psychohistory*. Columbia University Press, 1984.

Kovel, J. (1976). *A Complete Guide to Therapy*. Harvester. (Penguin, 1978).

Laing, R. (1959). *The Divided Self*. Penguin, 1965.

Lasch, C. (1978). *The Culture of Narcissism*. Norton.

Mitchell, J. (1974). *Psychoanalysis and Feminism*. Penguin, 1975.

Rieff, P. (1966). *The Triumph of the Therapeutic*. Harper and Row, 1968.

Sedgwick, P. (1982). *PsychoPolitics*. Pluto.

Turkle, S. (1978). *Psychoanalytic Politics*. Basic Books.

Winnicott, D.W. (1965). *The Maturational Processes and the Facilitating Environment*. Hogarth.

FAMILY AND AUTHORITY

Christopher Lasch and Discussants

Although it is difficult to generalise about the various schools of thought on the Freudian left – followers of Marcuse, followers of Brown, Laingians, Lacanians, radical feminists, socialist feminists – they all share the central premise that the patriarchal family is the root of organised oppression. It is important to remember that this idea has a long history antedating Freud and has continued to develop independently of him. From the beginning, it had pronounced feminist and socialist overtones. Bachofen's study of mother-right, Lewis Henry Morgan's study of archaic kinship terminology and Engels' analysis of the connections between the family, private property and the state, all appeared to call into question the universality of monogamy and to trace its rise to the subjugation of women. The myth of matriarchal origins has remained attractive to feminists ever since, long after its abandonment by anthropologists. The idea that oppression originates in the family continues to find widespread acceptance on the left, even without the corollary of a matriarchal stage of social development allegedly antedating the patriarchal stage. In large part this is because it seems to explain the rise and persistence of the Faustian, acquisitive, aggressive, domineering character traits the left hopes to replace with peaceable, cooperative, and 'feminine' traits. Not only the radical left but the political culture of liberalism has been deeply coloured by a revolt against the discredited patriarchal authority of priests and poets and divinely anointed kings, and the critique of the family represents one of the most enduring ideological expressions of this revolt. Indeed, the imagery of revolutionary brotherhood, which has been bound up with modern state-building since the time of the French revolution, derives its emotional energy from the tension between the overthrow and reconstitution of patriarchal authority. Given the number of modern states that have originated in revolutions, it is not surprising that so many modern thinkers have associated the origin of civilisation itself with an act of rebellion against the father followed by the reimposition of his authority in new forms.

Freud's own theory of the primal horde incorporates much of this revolutionary imagery as well as the formal theories of nineteenth-century anthropologists. It is easy to see the attraction of this Freudian creation myth for the new left. It not only implicates the family in the origins of a repressive civilisation but it spells out for the first time the psychological linkages between them: linkages between political history and the family. The sons overthrow the father but internalise his authority and reimpose it on women and children. The original revolution thus becomes the prototype of failed revolutions ever since. The uprising of the rebellious sons momentarily breaks 'the chain of domination,' according to Marcuse in *Eros and Civilisation*, 'then the new freedom is again suppressed – this time by their own authority and action.' Once established, the 'rhythm of liberation and domination' repeats itself throughout history – as in the life and death of Jesus, which Marcuse interprets as a struggle against the patriarchal laws in the name of love, a struggle betrayed by Christ's disciples when they deify the sons beside the father and codify his teachings in oppressive new laws.

Dorothy Dinnerstein, like Marcuse, takes Freud's theory of the primal horde as a 'landmark account of the vacillation at the heart of rebellion', although she tries to extend it by arguing that the sons submit to the father not only because of their ambivalence but because 'patriarchy remains a [psychological] refuge' from the more terrifying domination of the mother. Juliet Mitchell likewise finds in *Moses and Monotheism* the 'story of the origins of patriarchy. The brothers identify with the father they have killed . . . The father thus becomes far more powerful in death than in life; it is in death that he institutes human history.' The theory of the primal horde appeals to the new left – even with the qualification that it is 'speculative' and 'symbolic' – because it links the social to the psychological in a particularly vivid way and seems to show how the Oedipus complex, and with it the whole apparatus of patriarchal domination, transmits itself from one generation to the next. The Freudian myth theory traces the Oedipus complex back to the dawn of history and helps to define the need for a cultural revolution that transcends a mere change in power or institutions and breaks the cycle of rebellion and submission.

The case against the patriarchal family does not of course rest exclusively or even primarily on the theory of the primal horde, but I stress this issue in the hope of clarifying some of the psychological assumptions behind the whole train of thought. As Norman O. Brown has pointed out, Freud's speculations about group psychology, both in his essay of that name and in *Moses and Monotheism*, rest on a model of mental conflict that Freud had already discarded in the more strictly psychological writings of his last phase, starting with *Beyond the Pleasure Principle* in 1920, or perhaps with *On Narcissism* in 1914. Freud's increasing awareness of a more deeply buried layer of mental life underlying the Oedipal stage, his revision of the instinct theory, and his new psychology of women pointed to conclusions incompatible with many of the generalisations he continued to advance in his sociological writings. For one thing, the new structural line of analysis suggested that sexual pleasure is not the only object of repression. For another, it suggested that the agency of repression is not simply 'reality'. Accordingly the outcome of the Oedipus complex – the theory of which Freud now made explicit for the first time – cannot be seen simply as the submission of the pleasure principle to a reality principle imposed on the child by the father. It is not just that parental commands and prohibitions, toilet-training practices, and threats of castration play a less important role in the child's development than Freud had previously thought. The entire conceptual scheme that opposes pleasure and reality, equating the former with the unconscious and the latter with conscious adherence to parental morality, gives way to a different model of the mind.

In many ways the most important feature of Freud's structural model is the theory of the superego, which reflects Freud's new understanding that the repressive agency is itself largely unconscious and that its demands go far beyond what is demanded by the reality-principle. Far from serving as the agency of reality, the superego derives at least some of its severity from aggressive energies in the id. The statement that it represents a 'pure culture of the death instinct', moreover, seems to imply an archaic origin of the superego and even to qualify the view that it represents the 'heir of the Oedipus complex'. The same discoveries that led Freud for the first time to give formal expression to the theory of the Oedipus complex seem to diminish the absolutely decisive and determining importance he assigned to it. At the very least they indicate that the Oedipus complex, in men as well as in women, has to be regarded as the culmination of a long series of earlier developments that help to determine its outcome. Instead of saying that the Oedipus complex bequeaths to the child a punitive superego based on the fear of castration, we might say that castration anxiety itself is merely a later form of separation anxiety; secondly, that the archaic and vindictive superego derives from the fear of retaliation by the mother; and thirdly, that if anything, the Oedipal experience tempers the punitive superego of infancy by adding to it a more impersonal principle of authority. That authority is 'more independent of its emotional origins', as Freud puts it, more inclined to appeal to universal ethical norms, and somewhat less likely, therefore, to associate itself with unconscious phantasies of persecution. We might speculate further that the Oedipal superego rests as much on the wish to make amends as on the fear of reprisals, though even here it is clear that feelings of gratitude – the most important emotional basis of what is called conscience – first arise in connection with the mother.

In any case, patriarchal domination has to be seen as a secondary formation. This seems to be the unmistakeable implication of Freud's later work and of much of the work subsequently produced by Kleinians, ego psychologists, and object-relations theorists, too quickly dismissed by the Freudian left as uncritical celebrants of the 'mature', integrated ego. It is not hard to understand why most writers on the left, with the exception of Brown and some of the psychoanalytic feminists, have shown so little interest in the implications of Freud's structural theory. Even Marcuse, who claims to take the later Freud as his starting point, makes little use of these ideas. The reason is clear: they undercut the idea that repression originates in the subjection of the pleasure principle to the patriarchal compulsion to work. Jacques Lacan is even more explicit in his championship of the early Freud and for something of the same reason: he can find no warrant in Freud's later works for the assumption that desire is inherently subversive and revolutionary and therefore has to be suppressed in the 'name of the father'. In the work of Lacan's followers – notably Deleuze and Guattari in their *Anti-Oedipus* – the Reichian theory of sexual revolution often re-emerges in all its crudity, dressed up with Gallic pretentiousness as a theory of 'schizoanalysis' that claims to go far beyond not only Freud but Lacan himself. Naturally Deleuze and Guattari see the Oedipal theory as Freud's greatest single mistake. Other writers on the left, correctly sensing that Freud's ideas are more important than his personal prejudices, have seen him as the first theorist of patriarchal psychodynamics, even as an unwitting critic of patriarchy. Deleuze and Guattari, on the other hand, unable to distinguish between theory and ideology, regressed to the vulgar stereotype of Freud as an apologist for patriarchal domination. Thus the platitudes of the old left, seemingly relegated once and for all to the bargain basement of social criticism, reappeared in chic salons as the latest Paris fashions.

There would be no point in discussing shopworn platitudes about sexual revolution in the same company with more sophisticated theories of cultural revolution if they did not share the central belief that mankind would be better off in a fatherless society. Even if patriarchal domination is viewed as a secondary formation, it remains the principal focus – the principal target – of the investigations undertaken by the Freudian left. The rise of Freudian feminism has fixed attention more firmly than ever on this issue. For feminists, the value of psychoanalysis lies precisely in the insight that male domination does not rest on brute force alone but has deeper psychological roots. If psychoanalysis shows that paternal despotism itself rests on an earlier despotism of the mother, this additional insight, in the opinion of the feminists, merely strengthens the case for abolishing the sexual division of labour that assigns early child care exclusively to women. Such is the argument advanced by Dorothy Dinnerstein in *The Mermaid and the Minotaur*,[2] a book conceived as an extension of Brown's *Life Against Death*, and, in somewhat different form, by Nancy Chodorow in *The Reproduction of Mothering*. Without quarrelling with the specific contention that men and women should cooperate more fully in the work of nurture, I should like to suggest that the same evidence by which Freudian feminists try to support it – namely the evidence that reveals the importance of the pre-Oedipal mother – undermines the more general contention that all forms of oppression lead back to the patriarchal family.

DISCUSSION
Patriarchy and Authority

BY: Could you outline your overall schema. I'm curious to know where you fetch up at the end of the series of lectures.
CL: I wish I could give you a clearer idea. The ground keeps shifting, the focus keeps blurring, I'm not at all sure what the best avenue is to pursue some of these ideas. My tentative scheme so far is to follow this with a couple or perhaps three lectures on authority: attempting to make use of Max Weber's distinctions between various types of authority – in particular charismatic, bureaucratic and patriarchal authority – and to argue that forms of discipline, particularly labour discipline, that seem to be most characteristic of our own industrial society (indeed which pervade our society) owe more to charismatic authority than to patriarchal antecedents: specifically that they owe more to military and monastic precedents than to the patriarchal family as such.

The argument that I'm essentially trying to make – and I'm indebted here not simply to Weber but more recently to Lewis Mumford – says that from the point of view of the general problem of authority, what's characteristic about industrial society is the universalisation and the extension into daily life and the realm of production of forms of discipline and authority that throughout most of history were confined to either military or monastic institutions. This is part of an argument not to defend patriarchy, nor to recommend a regression to it but to redeem what I think was useful in the patriarchal family, and in patriarchal religion, which must not be lost.

MM: Could you specify that?

CL: Maybe it will help to examine one variety of patriarchal authority in pre-industrial society – namely the early Protestant family, especially in its Calvinistic form, remembering the central role that Weber assigned to Calvinism in the growth of the Protestant work ethic.

In the lectures I'm attempting to show that in fact Calvinism, and Protestantism generally, wasn't particularly hospitable to the development of capitalism, nor to the aggressive, domineering attitude to the world of nature and human relations that it's associated with. In many ways its most valuable legacy, a stress on human limitations and the limits of human control, was antithetical to the industrial ethic and to the spirit of modern scientific enlightenment. Part of this analysis has to be understood as a critique of the Enlightenment which tries to build on the work of the Frankfurt School and to examine what it is about modern rationality that is so destructive.

Then there follow analyses of the nineteenth century: an attempt to isolate the particular configurations when the patriarchal family gave way to a new kind of family arrangement, and to argue that the distinctive patterns in nineteenth-century bourgeois family life, which are described best of all by Freud himself, were a result more of the collapse of patriarchal *discipline* than of patriarchy itself.

LL: Could we go back a moment to the early Protestant family? I'm not sure what you consider to be its redeeming virtues that we need to reappropriate. As I understand it, its resistance to the Enlightenment was based on a number of tendencies, in particular one counterposing the literal reading (or re-reading) of scripture to empirical investigation of reality, and another counterposing an ascetic work discipline to sensuous play. Now the connection between these tendencies and capitalism is a complicated one; I think that they did lay some of the preconditions for capitalism, at the same time as putting fetters on its development. If the early Protestant family did resist the scientific enlightenment, it was not on any kind of basis that I would want to appropriate. And the aspects of the Enlightenment that it opposed were not necessarily the quantifying aspects that we would most want to criticise.

CL: I certainly wouldn't want to argue that the play impulse in Protestantism was very highly developed. But on the other hand I don't think you're doing justice to its own critique of Enlightenment, which didn't rest on a scriptural literalism, or on the kind of anti-intellectualism which one associates today, or for that matter in the nineteenth century, with fundamentalism; but on an awareness of the psychological issues that I tried to deal with in this paper[1]: the danger of a Faustian conception of science that fosters the illusion of painless omnipotence. I think it's very suggestive, particularly in the light of the concerns of Freudian feminism with a model of psychic autonomy that stresses union rather than separation, that early Calvinist preachers had a surprisingly androgynous conception of God. Their sermons are full of maternal imagery and their notions of moral development and psychic autonomy, to use an anachronistic phrase in this context, are actually closer to what some modern feminists seem to be getting at than what followed.

I don't expect the argument to be convincing in this abstract and schematic form; it demands to be fleshed out with concrete examples. One book that I could recommend is by a fellow named Leverenz, *The Language of Puritan Feeling*. It is based on a study of American Puritan sermons, but much of it would apply to English Protestantism. Leverenz has recovered the feminine dimension of patriarchal religion. One last point: the most formidable defender of Calvinism in the eighteenth century was Jonathan Edwards, who was anything but an anti-intellectual. He was a man who would absorb Locke and who was making a rather hopeless attempt to reconcile Calvinism with the most advanced scientific thought of the day.

BY: One of the things that's common to what both our Freud-Marx subgroup[3] and you have been doing is a very precarious activity; the belief that on the one hand you can hold out a set of issues within Marxism or radicalism which are very problematic indeed, e.g. class, hierarchies, gender, race, collective work, splits, and that you can pursue these, and keep your nerve, by going further and further into very technical matters in psychoanalytic psychodynamics and metapsychology such as splitting, envy, sibling rivalry, Oedipal feelings, group psychology, work groups and basic assumption groups, the role of the Ego Ideal, projective identification. You have added a third dimension, which is to take on the terrain of cultural history in very general form, that is, the contours of epochs and their major institutions. Now we've been scared by just two of these and the third really does frighten me.

I want to go from that assertion to a theme which is common to all of these. I'm stimulated to do so by a paper by Mike Rustin ('A socialist consideration of Kleinian psychoanalysis' – Ed.). The theme is the attempt to locate in history, contemporary politics, and psychoanalytic metapsychology, the legitimate domain of the moral. It does seem to me that this unites the three aspects.

MM: When you argue that there really has been a decline in patriarchal control and domination, you talk about it strictly in terms of psychological development and change, and there's a tendency to minimise its material aspects. Yet two forms of material domination have continually reasserted themselves despite the seeming absence of psychological, emotional, or intellectual domination. Engels refers to them in terms of financial domination within the family, and physical violence. Unless the three are taken simultaneously (and this is the great lesson of feminist critics), we get a very uneven picture of patriarchy. Indeed we have periods in which it seems to fade into the background. It really lurks very strongly then, in a much more insidious way.

CL: Right. Well, I'm assuming that there's a good deal of conceptual clarification to be gained from dissociating the concept of patriarchy from male supremacy and a great deal of confusion resulting from the tendency to assimilate them to each other. It seems to me that what's really at stake here is a discussion about authority, and ultimately I think a discussion about politics, and the nature of power. This, incidentally, is astonishingly a kind of vacuum on the Left. So much attention has been devoted to the realm of production, and proportionately so little to politics and authority that it would help to be as clear as possible about what's meant by patriarchal authority.

Also, you mentioned violence. It is of course a cliché, but I still think a useful one, that people in power fall back on violence when their authority is no longer compelling, so that it seems to me that the current undisputed upsurge of violence in the relations between the sexes is precisely a reflection of the breakdown of a form of moral authority based on patriarchal models of the family.

LL: Violence as an act of desperation rather than as a successful reassertion of authority.

CL: Right.

MM: Yes, but what I'm saying is that, if you take the three elements together rather than separate them, you have a very different picture of what the pattern of the relationship is [psychological, economic and physical domination]. I don't see any way in which you can concentrate on patriarchal control in a cultural or ideological sense without seeing the three elements in relation to one another.

CL: No, it's not sufficient, but it's simply an attempt to delineate the area of concern and to identify the problem of authority as the central issue.

BY: Do you mean legitimate authority or authority in general?

CL: I think authority implies legitimacy.

BY: Authoritarian*ism* doesn't imply legitimacy, it implies arbitrariness.

MW: You're right to make the distinction. I think they're different words with very different meanings.

CL: Again, two words that are often assimilated, in the discourse of the Left in particular.

MM: But am I correct that the implication of what you're saying is that we should simply arrange things so that there is no longer the need for assertion through violence? As far as I'm concerned that doesn't solve the problem; it just redistributes it, in a form that's not quite as objectionable. I see your focus is about the redistribution of authority in three different forms. I would like the attack to be a more fundamental one.

CL: Let me just make one last comment to your question. I do assume, as I tried to make clear in the paper, that it was a distinct conceptual advance on the part of feminism to turn to psychoanalysis, because they recognised that male domination cannot be explained simply in terms of pure force or anything like it, and it seems to me that an argument that stressed the latter would be a conceptual regression.

Gender and Narcissism

MW: I took you to be saying not what Maureen just characterised, but that if we interpret Freud along the lines you were suggesting, particularly putting a lot of stress on the later Freud (and as someone with a Kleinian background I wanted to know why you put comparatively little stress in detail on Kleinian and object-relational thought), then we'd begin to get a sense of the recalcitrance of an oppressive notion of patriarchy. We would understand why, in a situation that's politically and socially and culturally changing so fast (and I'd want to take the new technologies into account here) the internal mechanisms remain so intact, and what it might be like to think of what an alternative would be. Now that's where I get pretty depressed, I must say, given that in practising clinically I find the problem of what comes up in the consulting room in relation to my politics so continuously problematic. For example, people's primitive reactions are not just intensifications of their stated politics: they often contradict them quite deeply, and ambivalences also make political rhetoric seem uselessly simplistic.

CL: Well what would an alternative look like in theory first of all?

MW: I can see the beginnings of a theoretical advance in terms of understanding the significance of very primitive experiences of oral and anal aggression and the 'archaic mother' of the sort that Janine Chasseguet-Smirgel describes. A lot of so-called patriarchal attitudes would then emerge as being crudely defensive against much more primitive impulses and splits. Now in the thinking of our group we've got somewhere in the understanding of a possible relationship between for example the most primitive aspects of psychological development, e.g., splitting, basic assumption groups – which are hardly talked about in social and political contexts – and the much wider political splits and group processes. But we're only at the very beginning. Having a two-year-old around whose gender identity and roles are very conventional in spite of our beliefs and efforts doesn't encourage me at all in terms of what we feel is possible as alternatives in child-rearing. I mean, we've all read our Dinnerstein and our Chodorow and so on, and it seems to me that the solutions they offer at the ends of their books, which are good and weak in different ways, are very paltry, given the scope of their analyses.

BY: Given the return of the repressed in our own practice.

MW: Yes, exactly.

BR: I think that highlights quite a deep confusion which I suspect I have. The confusion is about the relations between three of the key notions here: patriarchy, narcissism, and feminisation. In some of the feminist critiques of the narcissism debate, there seems to be just a simple opposition between patriarchy and narcissism, and the idea that it's the latter we ought to opt for. Whereas I tend to think that the clinical concept of narcissism cuts across the notions of patriarchy, masculinity and femininity. (See below, pp. 130–136.)

As I understand it, although one can see how the decline of the father has played a very important part in creating the conditions for the emergence of the narcissist as the 'person of our times', that's not the sole and sufficient cause of it. The conditions that produce the narcissistic individual are more pervasive conditions of social relations. They're not only, and perhaps not even ultimately, to do with specific gender arrangements of parenting.

I'm also anxious to relate Dinnerstein's work to the critique of narcissism in culture. I wasn't sure whether you were incorporating Dinnerstein and Chodorow into the old Left Freudian critique of patriarchy. Whereas it seems to me that Dinnerstein especially has a great deal to offer which is actually quite different from the sorts of things that Juliet Mitchell and other people are offering. On the other hand Dinnerstein doesn't actually talk about narcissism. I want to try and bring what she says about the infantile roots of gender into some relationship with the idea of narcissism as a clinical and cultural condition.

CL: Well, her book was written before narcissism became an issue at all, so it doesn't speak to it; but attempts have been made to assimilate her work into a critique of patriarchal authority which in some way or another upholds narcissism as an alternative, or at least would stress the positive aspects of narcissism in character development.[4]

Responsibility and Morality

LL: Some of your critics appreciate your critique of the possessive individualism of the so-called 'liberation movements' of the 1960s, then increasingly commercialised through the seventies, but they also criticise you for counterposing to that 'narcissism' certain traditional family values which I would think need to be overcome rather than reappropriated.

CL: Well, let me ask you what you mean when you say that 'those aspects of family life are to be overcome'. What is it specifically that needs to be overcome?

BY: I don't think that's an entirely serious question, because we'd all agree about the idea of the family as mediator of authoritarian ideologies, as a training ground for social deference, etc. The problem is, the attack on the family that was mounted in the late sixties and early seventies in the form of communes, collective households, multiple relationships, group child-rearing, simply didn't touch those things, because it was so superficial.

LL: Not exactly. It did touch those things, but at a superficial level – as formal structures and rules about sharing tasks, for example, but not as something embedded in people's psyches.

BY: It was reduced to moralism.

LL: Yes. You (Lasch) criticise the 1960s experiments as lacking any sense of responsibility. But you resort to counterposing traditional values of the family, rather than challenge what they mean by responsibility, standards, morality.

CL: Yes. One thing that disturbs me very much about this debate is that questions of the family all the time seem to be on the point of flying off into total abstraction. This is partly because, as was suggested before, there seems to be such a disparity between these very sweeping and indeed probing theories like Dinnerstein's and the institutional recommendations which are not only disappointingly insignificant at times but in any case seemingly very remote from any practical reality.

Take an old tradition of the Left which has been shared by

people of widely different views, now a very old-fashioned position. An early formulation would be Bertrand Russell's *Marriage and Morals*. This just assumes, like H.G. Wells' writing on the subject, that the problem is very simple: the State assumes the functions of the father. That tradition is by no means dead; I think it's been resuscitated in more sophisticated form, and yet there seem to be far more important and interesting political issues at this time.

The U.S. and Britain Compared

MM: Quite frankly, if I were a man in the present situation I'd find it difficult to write in a way which criticised feminism and advocated any form of the reassertion of the family.
CL: I'm constantly being told that I've exaggerated the uniformity of opinion among feminists; that I have characterised feminism as a monolith whereas actually there are many different feminist positions on everything, including the family; and that indeed these issues are very much open for discussion. But what you say reinforces my sense that they're not open at all, and that there is an effort among feminists to make sure that they aren't. In America, the question of whether one is basically for or against the nuclear family is one that very much defines whether one considers oneself a feminist, and certainly whether one deserves to speak as one.
BY: I think, to be fair, that's less true in this country than it may be in America. I mean that the kinds of American feminism that I have a feeling are behind your reply such as radical feminism and other highly unconventional life styles are less apparent here, certainly in circles in which we move which have lowered their expectations. They are less utopian about living arrangements and about forms of organisation of work.
CL: Well, I would certainly like to assume that feminists are as undogmatic about this issue as others. I still insist that I'm addressing issues that feminists themselves have raised, and that I'm sympathetic to feminism though I'm not very much inclined to posture and make a great point of it, because I think that many such protestations are quite shallow and insincere. And I consider that this is not at all incompatible with a position on the family that rests, as I said before, on an attempt to disentangle the notions of patriarchy and male supremacy; and to examine male supremacy today much more in the light of the dissolution of patriarchal authority than its persistence.
LL: I think in part you misunderstand what was behind the question. As I understand it, to the extent that you criticise feminism, it's secondary to, or one of many examples of, the way you criticise

the culture of narcissism, a cultural tendency which manifests itself to some extent in every movement of liberation. So *The Culture of Narcissism* may appear as a criticism of feminism, but it is not a criticism of feminism as such. Rather it asks whether the 'narcissistic' tendencies of feminism in any sense represent something worth calling women's liberation – or human liberation of any sort, for that matter.

MR: I think there's quite a considerable problem of cultural disjunction. When I was reading *The Culture of Narcissism* I found myself really not recognising the object at all. And I partly thought, well is it a problem of method, all this cultural criticism? There's a lot that can be said about that, but I don't actually think that's the issue at all. I think the issue is that there is an object, which is represented and felt to be widely evident by some readers, but I can find very little in my experience that corresponds to it. I think you oscillate in the book between a deep pessimism about what you experience and feel around you, and a reversion to what do seem to be rather conservative ideas as possible antidotes or props against this creeping kind of familial dissolution.

BY: Do you mean conservative, or nostalgic, Mike? I detect in Christopher Lasch's book on narcissism a note of nostalgia but not conservatism.

MR: Well, I would think family, and authority, and puritanism – God help us . . . no, I shouldn't say God help us, because I do think that the point about limitations which you made early on is a valid one – are an unlikely place for radicals to look for sustenance.

Popular ideas of personal and sexual liberation *are* I think much more general and pervasive in the United States than here, where the structures of personality, family, and being-where-you-are-in-your-own-limitations are much less eroded. Here, there isn't a problem about people having half-absorbed psychoanalytic or personal growth concepts which they then misuse. My picture of what you're describing is a state of affairs like the films of Woody Allen where everyone is armed with insights or a vocabulary to describe their interaction with everybody else, but using the insights *as* an armament.

I don't think that corresponds to one's experience in England, even in relatively intellectual circles. There isn't too much phony liberation around to be worth attacking, you know. It's not exactly an everyday part of everyone's experience, to have been through a bogus cultural liberation and overthrow of the social world.

But anyway my main point is how far the object of the narcissistic personality, and all the phenomena and symptoms that you describe, are actually registered by people as the predominant features of their social and cultural world.

CL: I think once again you're confusing the epiphenomena of narcissism with the culture of narcissism. What's really at stake here seems to me to be a radical shift in the way that culture is transmitted and internalised. Your analysis – that the structures of authority and family are all too intact in Britain – would make it very difficult to explain the emergence of the youth culture among working-class young people. Insofar as I know anything about this, this also applies to the breakdown, even within the last generation, of traditions of working-class culture transmitted from parents to children, perhaps particularly from fathers to sons. It might also make it difficult to explain some of the political or quasi- or proto-political forms that that disaffection has taken, which are I think alarming. I don't know how you explain all that on the assumption that familial authority is still intact.

I deny altogether that this is an American phenomenon. I think that again what's at issue is a very radical transformation of culture which results in a form of personality that, to put it crudely, is dominated by very early and archaic psychic mechanisms. It's only by equating narcissism with Woody Allen that you're arriving at your view.

To demand the restoration of patriarchal or familial authority would be idiotic. Regardless of its political implications there's no hope of resuscitating those patterns. Let me put it as simply as I can. It seems to me that the problem is how to reconstruct a moral universe, which also means a realm of public discourse, so as to recapture a notion which has been discredited by its association with liberalism and more generally an exploitive system of social relations; and that is the notion that authority can rest on a rational basis, that authority does not equal authoritarianism.

It seems to me that the restoration of political authority, which I guess is what ultimately interests me, is possible *only* in the context of the most radical changes. The collapse of authority which strikes me as a pervasive phenomenon is ultimately to be attributed to the corruption of and the appeal to valid traditions on the part of a social system which is anything but valid, whose illegitimacy is now widely recognised. If this is conservative, if it's nostalgic, so be it – I'm not interested in those labels.

MR: We could be disagreeing about how to evaluate changes we might broadly agree about. One argument is that the symptomatology that now predominates reveals such a catastrophic loss of structure that the restoration of some structure becomes imperative. Another is that this symptomatology is not an excessive cost in that the loosening of authority and the greater space for the development of feeling which have been opened up also allow other kinds of development. This is not the extreme one sees in crazy kids, but development which for lots of people was not available under the old structures. That is, the levels of symptom, their unmanageability and the problem that they cause for individuals doesn't fill me with a greal deal of pessimism. Your book very powerfully evokes innumerable images which are really intended to make people realise that the situation is absolutely awful. Yet the American political environment is one thing and ours is another; ours is not deficient in a certain kind of authority, even a moral authority. People are for instance much less disaffiliated than is the case in the States. Measured by voting patterns, 70 per cent of the people vote here, and 45 per cent in the States. I would identify that with the fact that the prevailing values and laws of the American social structure are more individualist, competitive, and hedonistic to start with than they are or were here on account of class and the continually structuring effects of class. This turns out from the point of view of authority to have certain benefits. It does hold structures together, whatever else it does.

CL: Yes, at the same time I want to continue to do justice to the feeling, or the very accurate perception, that these are not unambiguously negative developments; and that the loosening up of emotional life and sexuality is very important and cannot ever be taken for granted, especially in this country. I agree with you there. But I cut off if you tell me that Mrs. Thatcher represents a tenable principle of authority; or that the level of political alienation in this country is significantly lower; I'm just sceptical.

Furthermore, much of my analysis after all derives from – shamelessly plagiarises – continental theory, especially German social theory, and God knows Germany is a country with a much stronger tradition of oppressive authoritarianism than anything that can be found in the United States. Yet it was in Germany, *not* the United States, that the breakdown of earlier forms of authority was first noticed, with the concomitant of a rootless, narcissistic type of personality.

Notes

1. The first part of this chapter is an extract from a paper read by Christopher Lasch to a seminar organised by the Radical Science Journal Collective in February 1981. The paper was also the first in the series of lectures delivered by Lasch as Freud Professor at University College, London, in Spring 1981. The full text subsequently appeared in *New Left Review* 129, pp. 23–34, with the title 'Freud and the New Left: the theory of cultural revolution'. The extract is followed here by edited excerpts from the transcript of

the discussion which followed the paper at the RSJ seminar. The participants were LL – Les Levidow (member of the *Radical Science Journal* Collective = RSJ; writer, agitator, editor); MM – Maureen McNeil (RSJ; Lecturer in Cultural Studies, Birmingham University); BR – Barry Richards (RSJ; cf. Notes on Contributors); MR – Mike Rustin (see Notes on Contributors); MW – Margot Waddell (RSJ; psychotherapist); BY – Bob Young (RSJ; writer, broadcaster, editor).

2. British edition entitled *The Rocking of the Cradle, and the Ruling of the World*. See 'Introduction' to this book, and the chapter by Elshtain.

3. A reading group within the RSJ Collective. See Note 4, 'Introduction'.

4. The chapter in this book by Jean Bethke Elshtain takes up, in a critique of Dinnerstein and Chodorow, a number of the questions raised in these last few contributions.

References

Brown, Norman O. (1959). *Life Against Death*. Sphere pb, 1968.

Chasseguet-Smirgel, J. (1976). Some thoughts on the ego-ideal. *Psychoanalytic Quart.* 45, 345–373.

Chodorow, N. (1978). *The Reproduction of Mothering*. University of California Press.

Deleuze, G. & Guattari, F. (1977). *Anti-Oedipus: Capitalism and Schizophrenia*.

Dinnerstein, D. (1976). *The Rocking of the Cradle, and the Ruling of the World*. Souvenir Press, 1978.

Freud, S. (1914). On narcissism: an introduction. *Standard Edition* Vol. 14, 73–102.

Freud, S. (1920). Beyond the pleasure principle. *Standard Edition* Vol. 18, 7–64.

Freud, S. (1921). *Group Psychology and the Analysis of the Ego. Standard Edition* Vol. 18, 69–143.

Freud, S. (1939). *Moses and Monotheism. Standard Edition* Vol. 23, 7–137

Lasch, C. (1978). *The Culture of Narcissism*. Norton.

Leverenz, D. (1980). *The Language of Puritan Feeling*. Rutgers University Press.

Marcuse, H. (1955). *Eros and Civilisation*. Beacon Press.

Mitchell, J. (1974). *Psychoanalysis and Feminism*. Allen Lane.

Rustin, M. (1982). A socialist consideration of Kleinian psychoanalysis. *New Left Review* 131, 71–96.

CULTURAL FORMS AND PSYCHOANALYSIS: SOME PROBLEMS

Peter Barham

The arrival of socialism has certainly been much delayed and, as we must now accept, we have not always known where to look for explanations of the delay. Historically, conceptions of the socialist project have, as it were, provided a window through which from within the confines of our present circumstances, we could look for indications of how our collective life might be recast. Messages from other parts have from time to time been passed through the window and there was, for a period, the expectation that we had only to wait patiently for the arrangements not only of the immediate room in which we stood but of the whole house of capitalism, through from the basement to the attic, to transform themselves.

But events have shown many of these messages to have been distorted and only those possessed of a peculiarly quaint form of superstition can these days muster claims to belief in the 'cunning of Reason in history' (Hegel). The prospects for a socialist project do not therefore vanish but consideration of how people as they are might become something other than what they now are must be set about rather differently. Quite contrary to the assumptions of classical canon there does not exist (and, more strongly, in principle there could not exist) a science of Marxism onto which we can clamber to get out from under the predicaments of liberal-individualist existence. The window, if that was what it was, has provided at best only a very patchy illumination of our situation, and a better understanding of what is at issue is likely to be got from turning our gaze back into the room and to an inspection of the constraints and possibilities of life that are to be found there. The cultural dimension of human life is neither secondary nor epiphenomenal but in crucial respects determining, and progress is therefore more likely to come from a rigorous examination of how the forms of liberal-individualist culture sustain their hold, and of what is most intimately involved in seeking to reach from one form of the human project to another.

That, at any rate, is one way of putting the case for the current interest in the study of cultural forms and in the development of a theory of cultural materialism.[1] It also provides a background against which the attraction of psychoanalysis in certain versions for socialist thinkers needs to be understood. For what psychoanalysis does is to draw us back from the window deep into the insides of the room and thus to promise insight into what sustains and subverts different kinds of human projects. But from the fact that misgivings about classical Marxism are well-grounded it does not follow that psychoanalysis is the right place to look for alternative sources of understanding. Psychoanalytic theory has, after all, been no more immune to what Alasdair MacIntyre once nicely termed 'epistemological self-righteousness' than has socialist theory. No more than Marxism can it offer a secure scientific structure onto which to clamber. It keeps common company alongside other theories and ideologies as an instance of what is fought out and argued for from within our cultural circumstances.

What therefore can psychoanalysis offer to the reconstruction of the socialist project? How far has psychoanalysis been able to get to grips with its own cultural origins and locations, to see itself both as a protagonist in a field of power relations and as a potential instrument of understanding of that field? We can make these questions more specific by setting them in the context of a history of cultural forms. Raymond Williams has given us just such a history in his analysis, in an extended body of writing, of the history of dramatic forms.[2] Dramatic forms are to be understood not as codifications fashioned within a specialised realm of the aesthetic, so much as exemplifications of characteristic forms – or the crisis of those forms – of social relationships in a given period, and of the way in which these are lived, understood and projected as standards of comparison and judgement. Through these we can come to identify and analyse the perplexities of human action that informed, and continue to inform, the general history of a society. For our purposes perhaps the most central issue concerns the crisis of social relationships that finds expression through the crisis and breakdown of naturalism and in the variations – subjective expressionism, social expressionism, etc. – that have followed upon that breakdown.

Naturalism in this context refers to the working out of the relationship between the 'individual' and the 'environment' that emerged in the mid- and late-nineteenth-century drama: the attempt to understand human affairs as strictly natural, determined by human nature and environment rather than any supernatural or transcendent force. The pivotal contrast here is between 'traditional' ways of feeling, thinking and representing that depict people as suffering a process determined by forces beyond the space of the stage; and experiments – as in Brecht – in producing an action, in rendering people as makers of history within the constraints of their situations. We can study the successive development of these forms but equally in a given social moment different forms may be simultaneously available. And the significant questions for psychoanalysis become: how far are the dramatic possibilities of psychoanalysis caught within the crisis of naturalist and post-naturalist dramatic forms? To what extent is psychoanalysis capable of grasping problems of human action as historical problems?

In what follows I shall put these questions to the practice of the Tavistock Institute of Human Relations and the Tavistock Clinic, one of the most formidable bodies of psychoanalytic praxis to have emerged in this country in the past forty years. The tradition, perhaps best characterised by its early post-war designation as *Operation Phoenix*,[3] is of particular interest because from the outset preoccupations about the social role, and even mission, of psychoanalysis have been well to the fore. The tradition has its immediate institutional origin in the reworking of psychological experiments undertaken under military conditions into a moral programme of post-war reconstruction, adapted to new and emerging 'civil needs'. 'The large positive part which military experience has played in the post-war reorganisation of the Tavistock Clinic', writes Henry Dicks, the official historian of the Tavistock, 'has been commemorated by naming this process *Operation Phoenix*.'[4] What we find in the Tavistock is a range of analytic practices, some definitively 'therapeutic', some more geared towards what is termed 'professional development'; but it is perhaps in the preoccupation with 'groups' and with the refinement of methods for the exploration of 'group phenomena' that we find best exemplified the form that defines the range. In post-war documents the 'group' is put forward as a crucial site for the Tavistock mission. A new method has been developed and we now have

> a form of group therapy which is also an occupational therapy; but the occupation deemed to be therapeutic is the study by the group itself of the tensions within it. So far it seems clear that in this procedure real problems of both individual and group are made manifest and the group shows signs, according to the capacity of the individuals composing it, of mastering an approach to the problems of human relationships which stands them in good stead in everyday life and sets them on the road to a progressive

> liquidation of their neurotic disabilities after they have left doctors' care.[5]

And the account continues:

> Such a development indicates that a creative evolutionary process may soon be offered to the community as an alternative to apathy on the one hand or revolutionary discontent on the other. The individual for his part is offered the possibility of development rather than "neurasthenia or psychoneurosis" . . . The method opens up many new fields of enquiry into the relation of domestic or nursery culture to later political and economic behaviour on a large scale. It provides a possible link between intimate personality study and political attitudes and group dynamics. It ties up childhood patterns with later political and social projections, applicable to any group or institutionalised behaviour.[6]

The most notable theorist of the new method, the legacy of whose thinking has informed the shape and character of this whole formation, was W.R. Bion, DSO, Kleinian psychoanalyst, tank-commander in the First World War, army psychiatrist in the Second. The excitement around the method is readily evident in the war-time account given by Bion and the analyst John Rickman of an experiment in military rehabilitation:

> There was a subtle but unmistakable sense that the officers and men alike were engaged on a worthwhile and important task, even though the men had not yet grasped quite fully the nature of the task on which they were engaged. The atmosphere was not unlike that seen in the unit of an army under the command of a general in whom they have confidence, even though they cannot know his plans.[7]

It is difficult to exaggerate the excitement among these practitioners in the immediate post-war period. 'For many psychiatrists,' wrote J.R. Rees, himself a notable protagonist in the Tavistock tradition, 'war has meant leaving the almost cloistered seclusion and static efficiency of the mental hospital and getting out into the field'; war provided a challenge that '[brought] us out of "our tents", our hospitals, laboratories and consulting-rooms'.[8] The major preoccupation of psychiatry in the war was with 'morale-building, as exemplified in man-management problems between officers and other ranks'. As Rees puts it, 'This war has been different from other wars . . . The enthusiasm and sense of easy conviction have been less marked in this war than they were in the last war . . . New techniques have had to be devised for educating and orientating men and women to the war.'[9]*

The concern with morale disclosed itself both in the search for methods to bring about new forms of co-operation between 'the officers' and 'the men', and in work on problems of leadership and officer selection. The basic idea underlying Bion's 'leaderless group' principle, Rees writes, is 'that when a group of candidates are presented with a problem that they have to solve as a group, i.e., no leader is appointed by the testing officer nor is any help given, then a situation arises that *reproduces the fundamental conflict between the individual and the society*'.[10]

The confidence of these writers took, of course, from the expanded role that they now found themselves playing but also, and just as importantly, from the belief that they had now discovered a method that could penetrate to the heart of the malaise in human relationships and turn it in a healthier direction. Bion and his colleagues believed that the sorts of dramatic actions generated within the frame of the method were to be viewed as expressions of essential and permanent truths about human relationships, as manifestations of a universal problematic of 'the group'.

Psychoanalytic psychiatry, it would seem, had now come into its own as a powerful social force. No longer were these practitioners the beleaguered products of a bourgeoisie past its ascendancy, lost between the claims of labour and capital and with only a minor and precarious contribution to make to the operation of the public good. We can perhaps detect in these descriptions the seeds of the attempted post-war alliance between 'the organised working-class and professional middle-class progressives' which Gareth Stedman Jones has described: the pursuit by the professional middle-classes of a 'civilizing mission' that drew heavily upon 'assumptions from pre-1914 liberal imperialism' and that in the immediate post-war years was to produce the 'last and most glorious flowering of late Victorian philanthropy'.[11] Rees' tone exemplifies Stedman Jones' point. 'We must come out into the open', he proposed, 'and attack the social and national problems of our day.'[12]

The Tavistock practitioners could look forward eagerly to the post-war period secure in the belief that the consulting-rooms and other institutional spaces to which they would return would not be the ones that they had left and could, in contrast to their pre-war experience, be made instruments of a wider social purpose. Bion

* The issue of a possible endorsement of patriotism, militarism, or psychological manipulation of the civilian population on the part of psychiatry or psychoanalytic psychiatry is not dealt with in this chapter. [Ed.]

has provided a vivid account in *Experiences in Groups* of how he put his new method to work under post-war conditions. The dramatic conventions of the method were then as they are now: a room, sparsely furnished and with a bare floor, a circle of up to twelve actors ('members') with the task of examining the group's 'own behaviour as it occurs'; and a 'consultant' whose job it was to aid the group in its inquiry. The possibilities and limitations of the form come through early on in Bion's account. The key theme in the opening phase of the dramatic action that Bion describes is frustrated expectation: the members of the group come expecting and desiring one kind of event, one kind of relationship with the 'expert' on groups, to find another. Confronted by Bion's silence they fall now into desultory conversation, now into silence; Bion is made uneasily aware that he is 'expected to do something'; he confides as much to the group to discover that his confidence 'is not very well received':

> Indeed there is some indignation that I should express such feelings without seeming to appreciate that the group is entitled to expect something from me. I do not dispute this, but content myself with pointing out that clearly the group cannot be getting from me what they feel they are entitled to expect. I wonder what these expectations are and what has aroused them . . . The friendliness of the group, though sorely tested, enables them to give me some information. Most members have been told that I would "take" the group; some say that I have a reputation for knowing a lot about groups; some feel that I ought to explain what we are going to do; some thought it was to be a kind of seminar, or perhaps a lecture. When I draw attention to the fact that these ideas seem to me to be based on hearsay, there seems to be a feeling that I am attempting to deny my eminence as a "taker" of groups.[13]

And so the action develops into a sequence of interpretations in which Bion both abdicates and intrudes, 'exposing ever more mercilessly the wish of the group to idealise him despite his abandonment of them'.[14]

The contrast between the conditions of war and of peace is remarkable enough: for an experiment that is directly embedded within a purposeful national action we find substituted a meeting in a room in a clinic; instead of 'the men', in the traditional military style of subordination, we now have 'members', men and women, and most of them from the professional middle class. From military action to action within a closed room; from action across the frontiers of class and rank to action internal to the preoccupations of a class: this is the extension of reach that Operation Phoenix promised. But that is all one way of putting it, for the wider and encompassing social process is in another sense drawn back into the room: 'the method . . . ties up childhood patterns with later political and social projection, applicable to any group or institutionalized behaviour'.[15] What we can discern is actually a critical ambiguity in the meaning and significance of the room, of the reality that is generated on this site. From within the dominant tradition comes the claim ('any group . . .') that the action, and thus the method that both stimulates and interprets the action, possesses a universal significance. The group is seen as a site on which are exposed the fundamental dilemmas of the human project, as a nursery within which the primitive roots of human functioning are laid bare and new possibilities are fostered. But claims of this sort are only workable in so far as those to whom they are addressed can both believe in and profit from them and do not find themselves fatally undermined or bewildered. They presuppose for their effect, that is, a shared confidence between 'consultants'/'officers' and 'men'/'members' as to their respective social roles and as to the meaningfulness and viability of the 'mission' in which they are jointly engaged. In so far as consensus is lacking and the members come to experience themselves as drawn into a form of passivity and bewilderment, to feel that they are in some sense victims of a process that they cannot fully fathom, then the viability of these co-operative undertakings is put in question. So by implication is the credibility of their exponents' claims to expertise. Instead of room as the site of social reconstruction, we have room as displaced from the site of the real action, from the significant social determinants; instead of room as laboratory of human regeneration and development, room as trap and isolation.

The question is then whether the form can allow and provide for exploration of this area of ambiguity and difficulty. It is evident enough from *Experiences in Groups* that like 'the men' in Bion and Rickman's military experiment the men and women in Bion's Tavistock group had 'not yet grasped quite fully the nature of the task on which they were engaged'; and evident also that Bion's own ideas as to what adequate comprehension amounts to did not include *historical* understanding. The renowned 'basic assumption groups' were generated, exposed and defined within institutional conditions of frustrated expectation.

A 'basic assumption' is, according to Bion, a group state of mind in which primitive and sometimes quite psychotic modes of experience prevail. The Tavistock group situation he describes was constructed to elicit these modes, for instance by frustrating the group's need and expectation that Bion should be its 'leader'. However *all* human groups were seen as potentially vulnerable to the influence of 'basic assumption' processes. Such therefore is the pressure of the universalist claim – the individualist picture of people as like onions which, once their outer, culturally-relative skins are peeled off, are 'much the same in all times and places'[16] – that an inquiry within the dramatic action into the particularity of the conditions in which states of mind and forms of response and relation are engendered must always issue in the reincorporation back into the received terms of the ideology.

What comes through in Bion are, in part, the idiosyncrasies of a particular style, so we may be tempted to displace the problems of a form onto the excesses of a given practitioner or of a particular brand of theorising *within* the form. But we have to see that beyond questions about local variations the real problem resides in the form itself, the whole conception of an investigative, experimental drama geared around a group reflecting upon itself, upon its own behaviour. It is perhaps less in the details of his procedure and theory that Bion has proved paradigmatic for subsequent generations than in terms of his expression of the shaping impulse – the organising principle – of this experimental project as a whole.

The ambiguity of the whole form can be shown through the conflicts and confusions of meaning that are engendered toward the person of the consultant, around whom there is a necessary and inevitable tension. This is because what the form throws up is the idea of something that is then persistently displaced and disrupted. What it holds out is, so to say, the promise of a realist novel, with all its established modes of orientation. What it then offers is *Finnegans Wake*, with its dislocation of semantic bearings. The designation 'consultant' is itself ambiguous as between (i.) a joke or a taunt, the elicitation of an expectation that is then frustrated, and (ii.) the affirmation of an available and enacted expertise. (In *Roget's Thesaurus* 'consultant' appears under the heading for 'remedy', and 'consultation' under the heading for 'advice', thus 'advise with, lay heads-, consult-, together'.) The consultant serves, through his inactivity, to displace and disrupt commonsense assumptions and expectations about his expertise. Yet, at the same time, the action of the form and the cultural power that attach to it affirm his power. He is both joke figure and expert; both powerful and inadequate; both the presence that conjures the lure of an absence and the embodiment in the present of an authority that is thoroughly inadequate in the face of prevailing circumstances; sometimes marginal or redundant to the course of an action, sometimes an involved drama critic or disgruntled participating audience, and sometimes the lead actor about whom the members of the group form a supporting cast.

The relationship between the consultant and the group creates its own possibilities for exploration, but its limitation lies in the specialisation of the action of a form into an interaction between individuals; and, in a related sense, of an historical action into a psychological one, the action of a 'group process'. The pressure that is engendered leads to a conception of the occasion and its dramatic conventions as a neutral space from which the intrusions of 'the social' have been temporarily removed: an 'illusory' space in which the psychological condition of a group process can then, without impediment, be explored and in which the significant determinants are psychological rather than social. But the licence to explore – the illusion of a 'free' exchange – is of course licence to explore within an institutional definition, a distinct set of parameters. It is then difficult to trace back the immediate and felt difficulties with the consultant (the difficulties of an interaction) to the form that has brought this particular scheme of relations (between 'consultant' and 'members') into play in the first place; in fact to investigate the peculiarity, the 'strangeness' of the whole occasion, its origins and adequacy as an investigative mode within the complication of a certain world. Hence there occurs a kind of neutralisation of the ground on which the significant questions are asked, and hence, ultimately, also both of the questions and the possible answers.

Within the most powerful embodiments of the naturalist tradition, argues Raymond Williams, we find 'the literal staging of the radical question: how do we, how can we, how should we live in this specifically tangible place and way of life?'[17] And it is against the force and particularity of these questions that we can see what has been displaced in the dramatic action of the group reflecting upon itself. What has been displaced into a self-consciously ambiguous condition is precisely the specificity of place: this room, in this institution, in an identifiable history of relations. And as a consequence the problem of the room, of the room as an 'actively shaping environment',[18] a set that can both define us and trap us, cannot be brought into focus.

We can understand some of this better by locating it more directly against the background of the history of dramatic forms. The living-rooms of naturalist drama, Williams has suggested, were 'in the fullest sense *living* rooms: places made to live in in certain ways: environments which both reflected and influenced their possibilities of life'. The 'site of decisive action' within this form 'was the private family room: a room, however, that was predominantly shown as a trap: the centre of significant immediate relationships, but with larger determining forces operating beyond it, to be looked at from the window or to arrive as messages which would reshape their lives'. And we can see that the form expresses a contradiction in bourgeois relationships: 'that the centre of values was the individual and the family, but that the mode of production which sustained them – the world they went out into and returned from – was in a quite different social range, much wider, more complex and more arbitrary'.[19]

We find in the Tavistock tradition that we have been discussing an extension, beyond the living-room and its drama of largely known intimates, into a more public but still intense setting. It is an extension into what is best characterised as a waiting-room, but still in an important sense a living-room because it is here that – within a significant form of cultural experience – life is predominantly lived: a waiting-room that is at once a point of repose, even of refuge and retreat, from that arbitrary and troubling world and also a point of proximity to, and thus of displacement from, a desired centre. The cultural power of psychoanalysis resides partly in the promise that it holds out and reinforces of the rediscovery of a lost 'centre'. And this sense of proximity to, but displacement from, a desired centre may then be worked out in a number of ways: for example, in a wondering about, and sometimes an active exploration of, the dimensions of the Tavistock institution – rooms, corridors, lavatories etc. – and other available forms of penetration into the life of the institution; or in a search for a group – a form of solidarity – that cannot be found.

There are, in all this, identifiable continuities with the preoccupations and responses of naturalism at its height, but there are also other developments that have to be conceived from within the crisis of naturalism itself – of increasingly isolated 'individuals' ranged against an abstracted 'society'. We can perhaps begin to see how a tradition of experiment that began with the affirmation of a resolution to the crisis of naturalism finds itself ineluctably drawn down into that crisis. That is, at different moments in its relatively brief history it has come to reproduce some of the critical dramatic forms that Western culture has generated over the past hundred years, in effect to reproduce on its own stage the history of a dramatic crisis, of a crisis in social relationships. In late Chekov, Williams writes,

> at the crisis of high naturalism, the social group which could grasp its own world was dissolving. Indeed the originality of Chekov was that he found new kinds of action and language to express just such a dissolution: a shared breakdown and loss of meaning. His determining form is then that of the "negative group". The

> people are all still there and trying to communicate, but have actually lost touch with each other and with their world: a loss realized in their dramatic language, which is that of people speaking at or past rather than to or with each other.[20]

Taken a stage further, in the post-naturalist dramatic form of subjective expressionism, this central inability to communicate becomes the substance of a dramatic action: '. . . people still assemble or are assembled, meet or collide. A given collectivity is in this way taken for granted. But it is a collectivity that is only negatively marked. A common condition is suspected, intimated, glanced at but never grasped.'[21]

And that, certainly, is one not uncharacteristic outcome within the Tavistock tradition:

> – Will we ever reach a point when we can get rid of Dr. Barham?
> – No, that we can't do – he's our anchor.
> – How could we get rid of him anyway?
> (silence)
> – If only everyone would say something, then perhaps we could get somewhere.
> – No, there's not much conversation, is there? But then I don't much like what there is.
> – I'm bothered about that empty chair.
> – Empty chair? You took over the room when you came in.
> – If only we could bring out the energy in the group.
> – Well, we're passengers on this ship, what can we do?
> – Do you think Miss Y will come back?
> – Oh, she'll come back, she'll swim back.
> – There are people here who know about this kind of thing. Why won't they tell us?
> – Have you learnt anything? I don't think I've learnt anything. I just feel violated by what some of the other people have been saying.
> (silence)
> – I'm beginning to feel really pissed off.
> – I'm all at sea (said very painfully).

It would seem that some thirty years later these men and women had still 'not yet grasped quite fully the nature of the task on which they were engaged'. This is the breakdown of the co-operation between officers and men, of the possibilities of new kinds of alliance across social groups and classes, that had been envisaged by immediate post-war theorists. An assessment of that breakdown is pursued in an illuminating discussion by Gustafson and Cooper, two

American practitioners working directly within this tradition.

Gustafson and Cooper start from the concept of the 'holding environment' in its application to the treatment situation: that is, the provision, as in the image of an infant held securely by its mother, of an adequate or 'good enough' environment in which 'reality is not over-intrusive', 'fantasy is allowed its own sway', and the 'patient feels held by the understanding of the analyst of matters the patient cannot hold in his own mind'. They are vexed by what they perceive to be the failure of the 'holding environment' in the group setting. In the early days, we learn, participation in these group experiments was 'counted on and needed no theory of its own'. The group 'space' could be thought of as 'the kind of preserve from reality that is possible in the psychoanalytic consulting room'.[22] ('The analyst', Winnicott wrote, 'does not wish to take sides in the persecutory systems even when these appear in the form of real shared situations, local, political etc. Naturally, if there is a war or an earthquake or if the king dies, the analyst is not unaware.'[23]) But, alas, these days are no more and the 'holding environment', and thus the 'collaborative' relationship between consultant and group, is now seen to break down in two ways: through 'personal' or 'depth-psychological' disruptions from within, and through 'sociological' intrusions from without.

Thus, for example, there is a tendency for the group to become organised 'around having either an internal or external enemy . . . There is the feeling that to work with the consultant is to collaborate with the enemy; consultant comments are used begrudgingly and there is a continuous underlying feeling that one must be on guard against vulnerability to withdrawal by or assault from leadership.' In psychological terms the life of the group becomes dominated by 'scarcity' problems – 'scarcity of attention, honor, love or whatever is wanted' – and the members preoccupied by primitive anxieties that concern either the fear of others' total indifference or the fear of their retaliation.

Furthermore, today 'racial and class antagonisms remain literal in the study group. The boundary between street or bureaucratic life and the possibility for allowing illusions to unfold in a protected space is lost.' The group occasion is, in addition, vulnerable to exploitation by capitalist market values and tendencies and 'can become reduced . . . to an opportunity not for learning, but for impressing and allying oneself with other important people'. Groups sometimes become 'completely immobilized by such preoccupations, as if each member were a kind of common stock and the process that of a stock exchange in which values rose and fell'.[24]

The question that concerns the writers is how to restore the 'possibility of collaboration in depth in a study group', to get beyond the fears of indifference and of retaliation from others – beyond the 'depressive' and 'paranoid' positions, in Melanie Klein's idiom – into 'illusion and learning', into play, 'a new kind of beginning'. The sort of approach adopted by Bion, they argue, serves only to exacerbate the conditions of scarcity and the eruption of primitive anxieties within the life of the group, and they propose in its stead an approach that takes more from Michael Balint's concerns with the provision of conditions of safety. 'We discover through Balint', they write, 'the cardinal importance of being there when needed (not abandoning), but not being intrusive and prescriptive.' Thus they argue that the 'material' of the group should be used not only in its meaning as resistance, to expose 'the infantile side of group behaviour', but also 'as an expression of difficulty in experiencing one's strength, skills and competence, taking responsibility for these experiences, and functioning in a collaborative way in the face of strong irrational desires and needs'. We need, that is, to recognise that 'members not only resist collaboration but may also *make prominent* what their difficulties are in collaborating in order that the difficulties may be clearly grasped and overcome.'[25]

The discussion is important for what it discloses of the invocation of a different strand of theorising within the object relations tradition of psychoanalysis in response to a perceived set of pressures within the form. We can, readily enough, see the preoccupation with the 'holding environment' as an address to the problem of the form in the contemporary social world: the problem of holding onto certain ways of seeing, a certain order of relations, against insistent and agitating pressures from other directions. But to say this is to set the 'holding environment' within a cultural discourse, to see it as a cultural product, and thus to view the crisis of the form as, also, a crisis of the relations within which it is conceived and variously held and jeopardised. This is not how Gustafson and Cooper view the matter. For what happens in their account is that the crisis in relations is projected as being external to the form – as arriving from without through those literal antagonisms of race and class and through the exploitation of the form by the values of the market; or as arising from within through shortcomings in the style and approach of the consultant. I do not mean to suggest that the kind of reorientation that they propose – from Bion to Balint – is not, within the limits of the form, of value; but what then occurs is that problems of 'security', 'safety', 'collaboration', all of them deeply problems of subjectivity within an historical process, are referred to a psychological condition to be secured or adjusted by a concomitant psychological method. Members may very well '*make prominent* what their difficulties are in collaborating in order that the difficulties may be clearly grasped and overcome', but to take these seriously – to enquire into the sources of this problematic of 'collaboration' – would take us beyond the form.

Paulo Freire, the writers remind us, distinguished between the Director Culture and the Culture of Silence, and they compare their own practices with Freire's educational-political experiments. The 'problem solving technique used by Freire', they assert, 'completely avoids the formulation by the leader, because of the endemic tendency of the participants to then become lost in using the leader's terms.'[26] But this is to sunder Freire's method from its context of origin and application, and to collapse the political complexities of the form into the formulations of the leader, into adjustments of technique, to ignore what – quite beyond the terms of individual leaders – is articulated through the form itself.

Raymond Williams writes of the 'fundamental tension' of high naturalism and its 'intense awareness of powerful and relatively unseen forces which were pulling the form – and within the form every kind of observation and interpretation – in apparently opposite directions. On the one hand there was an awareness of the processes of the deepest kinds of individual consciousness' and 'at the same time there was an at least equal awareness of the most general social processes – historical moments, the condition of a particular people, economic pressures, the condition of the family and of marriage, the general complex of institutions and beliefs'. High naturalism selected as its form a

> kind of middle ground where all those extended processes could be shown as interacting . . . Yet what was shown was never a neutral interaction, but in a number of ways the crisis of such interaction: a crisis which was most often evident in the very failure to articulate (in their own terms but also in relating and interacting terms) the full process which lay beyond the "middle ground" of the form.[27]

The mission of this analytic tradition was, as we have seen, to lay claim to some version of a 'middle ground', to establish a point of meeting and interconnection between social groups and classes, between the 'psychological' and the 'social', between the terms of an older order and the emergence of a new one. This has been, in a number of respects, a powerful and compelling tradition of work, but the hold on the 'middle ground' is now lost, if ever it was temporarily established. The difficulty is now to recognise in the interaction a crisis that is both the crisis of a form and of a professional and social formation. The informing conception of a group reflecting upon itself is perhaps, in any case, cast within the tension and ambiguity of a 'middle ground' between the discourse of strangers trying to communicate in unpropitious social conditions and a definite social mission, an instrument in a new kind of social co-operation. The crisis of the interaction is evident in psychoanalysis more generally in the preoccupation that we now find with the relationship to the 'setting'. Thus André Green distinguishes between a classical analysis 'where the silent setting, as though absent, becomes forgotten'; and a new situation in which 'the setting makes its presence felt' and where 'something is happening that acts against the setting'.[28]

But then a kind of ground has continued to be held and what we in fact find is a deep reluctance within this formation to grasp the crisis of its theory and activity, and the possibilities that arise within it, in these larger terms; to recognising itself as a cultural product in its affinity with the history of bourgeois dramatic forms that have been produced within the dimensions of a dying order. Better to sustain the form on its own terms, for all the limitations on what can be achieved than to proceed beyond it; and for the reason that to proceed beyond the form with its insistent commitment to the authoritative delineation of 'human relations' would be to displace a professional formation from its own confident settlement, from its sense of itself as a defining centre.

But this is not to say that new accommodations have not been made. The Tavistock tradition was in its early years deeply committed to, and interwoven with, the Welfare State. The Welfare State was indeed seen as providing the institutional mechanism through which the forms of co-operation and man-management that had been developed during the war could be carried over into peacetime conditions. Now, from a contemporary spokesman for this same tradition, we learn that

> There is a wish, sometimes quite explicit and not so unconscious, that the State through its agencies will look after each individual. The governments of advanced industrial societies pride themselves on their ability to provide welfare services. Increasingly, however, it is expected that the State will always be able to find the resources to meet these demands. Such a primitive dependency arises when groups or institutions find it difficult to face the realities of their situation . . . This is an outcome, or at least one effect, of . . . the "I want" philosophy of society . . . The "I want" is related to the feeling of envy that others may also want and get. And so institutions are developed in society to ensure that there is an equitable distribution of resources thus further reinforcing dependency upon the State and its agencies.[29]

My discussion should not be taken to imply that psychoanalytic theories have not succeeded in formulating important properties of human functioning, of what any embodiment of 'social being' must necessarily contend with; nor should it be taken as lending support to the view that we can project some future condition in which such tendencies and difficulties will be done away with. But what, perhaps, we must persist in questioning is the specialisation of psychoanalysis understanding into autonomous bodies of theory and practice that are then sundered from the historical process within which they originate and continue to be active. We ask a social theory to investigate 'not just social institutions and practices, but also the beliefs agents have about their society – to investigate not just "social reality" in the narrowest sense, but also the "social knowledge" which is part of that reality'. A social theory is 'a theory *about* (among other things) agents' beliefs about their society' and 'it is *itself* such a belief'. Thus for a social theory to be a properly critical social theory it must process a 'reflective cognitive structure' that enables it to give an account of its own 'context of origin and context of application'. The task of a critical theory is to bring to the agents' 'awareness unconscious determinants of their own consciousness and behaviour' in pointing out to them 'that their own coercive social institutions are "determining" them' and thus to make 'the subjects in society aware of their own *origin*' by showing them 'under what conditions, in what "context" . . . they came to hold their basic world-picture, that is, how they came into being as social subjects'.[30] And it follows that a critical theory must, as an essential component of this task, be capable of elucidating its own origins and that of the social institutions in which its own activity is constructed. It should now be plain that psychoanalysis as represented by the tradition of the work discussed here is not, nor could it be without a drastic revision of its epistemology, *that* kind of theory.

Notes

1. See, e.g. Raymond Williams, *Culture*.
2. See, e.g. Raymond Williams, *Modern Tragedy*.
3. I was myself a practitioner within this tradition over a number of years and in the discussion that follows I draw upon notes, internal memoranda, etc., pertaining to the group activities of the Tavistock Institute and Clinic over the years 1975–80.
4. Henry Dicks, *Fifty Years of the Tavistock Clinic*, p. 138.
5. Ibid., p. 145.
6. Ibid.
7. W.R. Bion & J. Rickman, 'Intra-group tensions in therapy', in: W.R. Bion, *Experiences in Groups*, p. 21.

8. J.R. Rees, *The Shaping of Psychiatry by War*, pp. 21, 51.
9. Ibid., p. 16.
10. Ibid., p. 69.
11. G.S. Jones, 'Marching into history?', p. 12.
12. Rees, op. cit., p. 133.
13. Bion, op. cit., p. 30.
14. J. Gustafson & L. Cooper, 'Collaboration in small groups', p. 162.
15. Dicks, op. cit., p. 145.
16. S. Lukes, *Individualism*, p. 151.
17. Williams, *Culture*, p. 170.
18. Williams, *Drama in a Dramatised Society*, p. 19.
19. Williams, *Culture*, pp. 169, 171.
20. Ibid., p. 175.
21. Williams, *Modern Tragedy*, p. 214.
22. Gustafson & Cooper, op. cit., p. 159.
23. D.W. Winnicott, 'Metapsychological and clinical agents of regression within the psychoanalytical set-up', in: *Collected Papers: Through Paediatrics to Psychoanalysis*, p. 285.
24. Gustafson & Cooper, op. cit., p. 157, pp. 160–62.
25. Ibid., pp. 164–5.
26. Ibid., p. 165.
27. Williams, *Culture*, pp. 176–7.
28. A. Green, 'The analyst, symbolization and absence in the analytic setting', p. 10.
29. W.G. Lawrence, in: Lawrence ed. *Exploring Individual and Organizational Boundaries*, pp. 236–7.
30. R. Geuss, *The Idea of a Critical Theory*, pp. 56, 70.

References

Bion, W.R. (1961). *Experiences in Groups*. Tavistock.
Dicks, H. (1970). *Fifty Years of the Tavistock Clinic*. Routledge.
Geuss, R. (1981). *The Idea of a Critical Theory*. Cambridge University Press.
Green, A. (1975). The analyst, symbolization and absence in the analytic setting. *Int. J. Psycho-Anal*. 56, 1–22.
Gustafson, J. & Cooper, L. (1978). Collaboration in small groups: theory and technique for the study of small-group processes. *Human Relations* 31, 155–71.
Jones, G.S. (1982). Marching into history? *New Socialist*. Jan./Feb. 1982, 10–15.
Lawrence, W.G. ed. (1979). *Exploring Individual and Organizational Boundaries*. Wiley.
Lukes, S. (1973). *Individualism*. Blackwell.
Rees, J.R. (1945). *The Shaping of Psychiatry by War*. Norton.
Williams, R. (1975). *Drama in a Dramatised Society*. Cambridge.
Williams, R. (1979). *Modern Tragedy*. Verso.
Williams, R. (1981). *Culture*. Fontana.
Winnicott, D.W. (1958). *Collected Papers: Through Paediatrics to Psychoanalysis*. Tavistock.

SYMMETRY AND SOPORIFICS: A CRITIQUE OF FEMINIST ACCOUNTS OF GENDER DEVELOPMENT

Jean Bethke Elshtain

Would you like to live in the 'symmetrical' society? If this is a question you've not previously put to yourself perhaps it's time you did. A symmetrical social world is one the most important feminist theorists of gender development propose to put in place of the 'asymmetrical' world we now inhabit, one they condemn as being systematically deranged. This derangement, on their view, flows in a direct line from child-rearing practices, usually called 'socialization', to political, economic and social structures on a broader scale. That is, the thinkers I shall take up assert that their arguments are *politically* compelling because they have demonstrated in theory a tight *causal* nexus between familial arrangements and public outcomes. Why our gender arrangements are so badly botched and how they can be transformed radically to attain a world of gender symmetry is a matter I shall explore with a sceptical eye.

But before I turn explicitly to this new variant on a fairly traditional concern – socialization – a few words on socialization theory itself are in order. The question socialization theory seeks to answer is simply put: how is it that persons and their social contexts may be said to be related to one another? Alas, it is not so simply answered. But socialization theory, which first came into use in mainstream political discourse in the 1950s, proposed to answer it. Most practitioners of political socialization have been rather unabashed celebrants of the status quo. The most systematic, and powerful, version of socialization theory may be found in the functionalist approach to social explanation. For the functionalist all elements in a social system are linked together in a way that promotes, if things are going smoothly, equilibrium: all units neatly tied together in a relationship of interdependence. On this account, the family gets linked 'functionally' to the total order as both family structure and function are largely determined by the 'needs' of the 'macro-order'.

Socialization, then, is the way in which infant 'recruits' become full-fledged participants in a tautly structured social system. The theory tends towards a determinist explanation that strips individuals of agency and can treat 'failures' in socialization only as instances of 'deviance' (not protest!) What feminist accounts feature is a questioning of *why* socialization has gone forward in ways they find oppressive to women. But the problem here, and it is one I shall take up below, is whether one can finally construct an alternative account of the individual/social relation if one occupies much of the same conceptual terrain as the standard socialization-functionalist models. Although classic functionalist doctrine masked the question of power there was an implicit assumption that in a hierarchical, well-ordered social world an importunate entity – the overall system or society – pulls other institutions along without the rude incursion of outright coercion or the use of force. *If* one were to make the presumptions about power lodged in classical functionalist theory explicit it would look very much like standard 'top-down' presumptions with those on 'top' having more power than those 'down' below.

It is important to situate current feminist debates within this – and other – broader intellectual and doctrinal currents for it helps us to make sense of the project and the aim of 'symmetry', which is very much the notion of a reordered social system in a *new*, but good, condition of equilibrium. The ideal symmetrical world is construed as a social universe in which the sexes have identical, or nearly so, commitments to, involvements with, and interest in child-rearing, often called reproduction, and careers (often called production). This 'symmetry' holds across the board, even into the world of sexual fantasy, at least for the Total Symmetrist. It is my conviction that symmetry emerges as a soporific, one that aims to blur or eliminate gender-based differences but would do little to eradicate gender-based injustice.

I shall lead into my subject by noting an important distinction, one taken for granted as the backdrop to the explanatory frameworks I shall explicate and criticize, between biological sex and social gender. Though one cannot altogether sever biological maleness and femaleness from the social creation and meaning of norms of masculinity and femininity and the distinctive parts men and women play in the human story, the accounts I shall take up propose a very sharp fissure between the two. A brief caveat also seems necessary when one takes up these highly charged matters. Here is mine: I think it is vital and important to develop a social theory that gives us rich and robust pictures of how people live, that moves us closer to understanding the kinds of lives that various social structures and diverse societies support. And I certainly favour both the loosening up of rigid and destructive sex roles that lock people into positions and practices for which they may not be well suited, as well as the elimination of gender-based, structural injustice. The problem, then, with the theories I shall take up is that they fail, in the first instance, to provide the 'rich and robust picture' I note as desirable. There are no recognizably *human* lives of either adults or children engaged in complex social relations in these accounts. They fail, as well, to provide a *coherent* notion of how we are to move towards a more sexually egalitarian society.

This essay is divided into four parts. First, I shall make some preliminary comments on psychoanalytic theory and what it offers to social theory construed as an *interpretive* enterprise. Second, I shall submit the three most widely discussed and disseminated feminist accounts of gender to a critique that moves on a number of levels, theoretical and political. Given the daunting problems of methodology and theory articulation posed by *any* appropriation of psychoanalysis for social explanation, and given the explicit political aims of feminist gender theorists, theoretical *and* political arguments are invited and required. Third, I shall propose an alternative in this sense: I shall indicate what an alternative account must account for, or take account of, that seems to me to offer a more coherent theory and a more plausible, and democratic, politics. Finally, I shall conclude by drawing the gender debate into a series of brief reflections on that crisis of contemporary culture Christopher Lasch has called one of narcissism.

I thought of calling this essay 'The Case of the Missing Child'. Were a search for this missing person conducted in the pages of the most important feminist treatments of gender identity and development, the case would go unsolved. For what is conspicuously absent in these texts is a recognizable human being of *any* sort, including the youthful, the very being whose development each claims to explain. It may seem unreasonably contentious of me to suggest that children are not really present in texts that specifically treat childhood development. I hope my quarrel here becomes clearer as the argument develops. But let me just indicate that there are specific and important features of children that get bleached out of the accounts I take up. To be sure, there are voracious infants (in Dinnerstein) and developing children snarled in a number of asymmetrical, gender-linked, familial knots (in Chodorow) but their respective contributions to the perspectives I shall explore nowhere captures the sense of children as *beings* or the being of the child, in part because children are not treated as agentic, reflective, capable of thinking and acting their ways in and out of complex situations, and so on. Why is this a problem? To answer, one must take up the nature of social explanation itself. For example: for social scientists devoted to positivist analyses and abstract formal models far removed from their subject matter, the missing child poses no particular problem, for *no* human subject has ever intruded upon the tidy order of their schema or undone the rigour of their correlations. Nor, for that matter, does the missing child figure centrally within most Marxist debates which are couched on the level of modes of production, structures, and the State, and grounded in universal, aggregate abstractions like 'class'. To be sure, all sorts of people can be theoretically subsumed within the conceptual space occupied by a term like 'class' or 'the State' but they are, none of them, particular or distinctive, nor can they be: a systematic theory of the sort Freud criticized as a *Weltanschauung*, 'an intellectual construction which solves all the problems of our existence uniformly on the basis of one overriding hypothesis, which, accordingly, leaves no question unanswered and in which everything that interests us finds its place',[1] washes out the particular in favour of making vast claims and a broad sweep.

I shall be clearer in a moment about how it is I think psychoanalysis can be appropriated by social theorists without making it the centre-piece in a tautly drawn and rigid circle of certainty of the sort positivist explanation and the quest for law-likeness lead to. My objection is not to 'abstract' theory, for every theory, whose coin of the realm is and must be conceptual, is abstract. Instead I am arguing against *abstracted* theory, against concepts far removed from what it is they purport to explain. (Those who wish to pursue this epistemological debate can turn to many important and influential critiques of positivist social science, and these critiques hold whether the thinker in question comes with the label 'radical' or 'mainstream' or 'conservative'.)[2]

Psychoanalytic theory, as developed over forty years by Freud, is not, and cannot claim to be, a predictive science. That is, it cannot be reasonably deployed to construct a set of presumed universalisms, as feminist gender theories do, along the lines of 'If x, then ineluctably y . . .' Such arguments are not only culture-bound, they are culture-blind, for the extraordinary complexities and diversities of human cultures, of intersubjectively shared, hence public, symbols, meanings and ideas, as well as individual creativity, variations, and consciousness, get fused together and then overassimilated to explanatory frameworks that presume to explain everything from one basic 'something'. Why this won't do is what I hope to show.

The case of the missing child, then, *should* pose a dilemma for the thinker indebted to psychoanalysis and if it does not there is,

I shall argue, slippage in the version of psychoanalytic theory being taken up. For one might suppose that the theorist who turns to psychoanalysis would be interested in grinding her analyses fine, in bringing things down to the most concrete and basic levels, to cultural realms inhabited by human beings, not by statistics. One can reasonably hold to this hope, for psychoanalytically based accounts are about how we get to the beings we are, males and females alike. As conceived by Freud, psychoanalysis is preeminently a theory of the psychodynamic self, the discontented citizen of civilization, the night traveller who wakes in wonder or in terror, the rational irrationalist, the romantic hero or heroine, the vulnerable child, the builder, the destroyer, the giver, the taker, the authoritarian, the anarchist, attempting to carve out a liveable life, in history, between the intractable pole of necessity and the ephemeral dream of possibility.

My initial objections, my concern with whether the accounts I shall take up proffer a plausible picture of what they purport to explain, speaks to important theoretical debates that are linked, in turn, to political questions. There *are* approaches to social theory that require the analyst to construe her subjects, including children, as importantly self-defining, expressive, and active agents, not as mere social 'products'. A rich notion of the subject is featured in various interpretive or hermeneutical studies of human life and culture. For the interpretive theorist, and it is an interpretive account with a 'critical edge' that I shall propose below, the essential task of theory is to probe meanings, individual and social.

A second, not unreasonable expectation to hold as one plunges into texts that acknowledge Freud as their honourable godfather if not their infallible patriarch, is that the authors would show evidence of knowledge of debates about Freud's method. Freud's remains *the* psychoanalytic theory; all later revisions and recantations have to position themselves with or against, for better or for worse. At this point it is worth recalling that Freud's devotion to a scientific world-view did not blind him to the somewhat rueful recognition that his peculiar science could not be contained within a language which failed to make essential reference to the human being as meaningful. Given this recognition, he could not, and did not, claim that he had promulgated a set of laws with the power to predict. Instead, what one could do with such resonant theoretical concepts and constructs as projection, displacement, regression, repression, identification, the Oedipus complex, and so on, was, on one level, to forge an explanation having the form of a *post-hoc* reconstruction of a particular individual's psychic history which, if the account was detailed and 'thick' enough, might have broader applicability to an understanding and explanation of human psychic life in more general terms. This reconstruction could not be a venture of the positivist-historiographical sort. Freud made no claim that he had got things *wie es eigentlich gewesen* (as they really were). Instead, the psychoanalytic dialogue, grounded in a powerful theory, aimed at the active *construction* of an explanation that made sense to the analyst – the better interpretation being one that could account for more details than some alternative – and made sense to the subject as offering a rock to stand on, a foundation from which he or she could move into a less tormented future.[3]

Freud's persistently fresh case histories retain their vitality because, in seeking to explain, he never explained away by abstracting his explanation from the intrapsychic world of his subject. Before others, particularly cultural anthropologists and social historians, embraced the notion, Freud had mastered the art of 'thick description', the commitment to present human contexts as tangled webs of meaning, both open and hidden. If done well, the theorist's explanation should take the reader or critic 'into the heart of that of which it is the interpretation'[4] – in Freud's case the densely populated world of the human mind. Despite Freud's occasionally reductive statements and hopes, his method and his own account of that method locate psychoanalysis firmly as one of the most powerful of the 'human sciences', the *Geisteswissenschaften*. For within psychoanalytic theory, language (linguistic expressions), action, and non-linguistic experiential expressions all become grist for the theoretical mill, but not in isolation from one another *nor* from a powerful dialogue of a certain kind, the psychoanalytic setting. Unlike those who would model human sciences after a mechanistic account of nineteenth-century natural science, psychoanalytic theory, if it is to remain true to its most potent expressions and possibilities, cannot take the form of prediction or post-diction. Instead, the psychoanalytic thinker must rely on the *coherence* of interpretive accounts, on the inner links between minute details and higher level abstractions.[5]

Following through on this interpretive imperative, if what is being understood is the gender development and identity of human beings, a coherent interpretation should help us to 'get inside' the worlds in and through which such development and identity emerges – the inner world of children and the social world, first and foremost, of families. We must be able to see that world from the 'inside out'. It is particularly important for an analyst of radical sensibility to avoid replicating in her account the manner in which many academic psychologists and sociologists devoted to so-called 'scientific' analyses have constituted the human subject, child and adult, as an 'object'. This object bears only a thin relation to real, active human subjects though it is frequently confused with the 'real thing'. This guarantees a particular sort of tendentiousness as social explanation and the concrete arrangements and experiences of the social world, including, centrally, human subjects who are born, grow up, work, love, and finally die, pass one another by.

Often these exercises are relatively harmless, fading into that obscurity reserved for those who persist in repeating things that were not worth saying once. But occasionally matters are not so benign. For when world-changers, like their status quo counterparts, set about conflating human subjects and social life with their 'scientistic' theory or ideology, and then one day discover that the real world is recalcitrant, its human subjects frustratingly intractable, they may wind up embracing a politics that aims to bring reality into conformity with their abstract system. This may require 'reconstructing' real persons into the sorts of 'objects' their discourse has constituted in the first place, thus inviting a manipulative or coercive political strategy.

The minimal point for now is this: theoretical commitments secrete political imperatives; theoretical frameworks have consequences as to the social arrangements they either call into question or call for, they either move to undermine or aim to sustain.[6] Our understanding of human beings and their social worlds will vary dramatically depending on whether we view those beings and that world through the lens of abstracted categories and formal models which aim to give us the Big Picture, to excavate some underlying causal context of which social participants are said to be unaware, or whether we embrace a mode of theoretical reflection that places human self-understanding and self-definition into the heart of theory construction. To do the latter yields both a different theory *and* a different politics. First, it makes the interpretive theorist's life complex; she cannot set about making vast proclamations about the world and the folks who inhabit it without making a serious effort to explore and to enter empathically into their contexts and meanings. Second, her theoretical commitments exude a certain humility as she confronts the inexhaustible richness of *a single* human life. If she is to be consistent, to ensure coherence as between her approach to social theory and her political stance, she must embrace a strategy of social change which incorporates as essential the assent of human beings to the changes being made. In what such 'assent' consists is a controversial and arguable point; I am not calling for a vote, say, as to whether or not to end laws requiring segregation of the races. Rather, what I have in mind is a public debate of a certain sort which must precede, and be a concomitant of, social changes that will affect human beings, their children, and their communities. I am positioning myself against the notion of a social engineering elite or a vanguard *imposing* changes 'for the good of' others when those others have had no opportunity to participate in the process of change, even to take up an oppositional stance.

One implication of all this is that a radical agenda that fails to garner the reflective adherence of the people in whose behalf its dream of change is being dreamt is an agenda that either will fail of realization or whose realization must be coerced and manipulated. There is a moral distance separating interpretive thinkers, whose method, as I sketch it, commits them to radically democratic political change, from defenders of an increasingly undemocratic status quo and, as well, from tough-minded revolutionaries who will remake society at whatever human cost and who dismiss opposition to their plans as so much 'false consciousness'.

Bear in mind, briefly, the claims thus far lodged. I have claimed that the most widely disseminated feminist accounts of gender development fail to give us a recognizable picture of the human child in her social world, in part because these analyses do not construe the child as an importantly self-defining human subject. I shall extend and defend this claim below. Second, I have insisted that theoretical commitments gear political options and proposals. What is required next, as I explore specific accounts, is an appraisal that traverses the terrain between theoretical argument – are the arguments coherent or unconvincing and why? – and political ends – does the politics flow logically from the theoretical conclusions (for good or ill) or has the author gerrymandered the discussion in order to focus attention only on the most favourable possible outcomes of her agenda for change? and so on.[7] If feminist gender arguments are to be compelling as theory *and* politics there must be a concretely specific connection between the particular nature of 'private' arrangements and public outcomes, both by way of explanation as to what is wrong and by way of prescription for what must be changed. This is a requirement gender theory forces upon the critic, for gender theorists insist that they have explained where the problem lies; seen what must be done to put things right; and foreseen what the effects of transformation along the lines they demand must be.

There are three central texts involved: Juliet Mitchell, *Psychoanalysis and Feminism*; Dorothy Dinnerstein, *The Mermaid and the Minotaur*; and Nancy Chodorow, *The Reproduction of Mothering*. Each of these texts involves a different appropriation of psychoanalysis for purposes of feminist social thought, though each winds up with basically the same thesis as to what is wrong and what must be done to achieve a gender revolution. For each locates the ultimate, underlying causal context for human malaise in what is called the 'universal fact' that it is women who mother. This thesis cannot, finally, bear the explanatory weight placed upon it.

I turn first to Mitchell's account, one which suffers from an excessive abstractedness that is far removed from Freud's own method.[8] Like those structuralist thinkers to whom she is indebted, for Mitchell, structures, laws and ideological formations are the agents of history. Persons are construed as vehicles for the ongoing operation and transmission of structures and laws. For one of the points of structuralism is the elimination, or what is called the decentering, of the subject. Questions involving intentions, purposes, understandings, meanings are set aside as irrelevant. According to the structuralists one can seal off social explanation from any fieldwork data or inferences concerning human beings and one can, therefore, engage in what might be called disembodied social theory. Mitchell's persons emerge as objectified entities subject to universal laws. Psychoanalysis, in turn, becomes the way we acquire the laws of human society *within* the unconscious mind and how these laws, which underlie and underwrite patriarchy, function within each of us unawares. Within Mitchell's frame, women are prevented from constituting themselves historically as subjects; her analysis squeezes out any room for subjects to reflect their situations.

Psychoanalysis is set up, by Mitchell, as scientific laws operating in the sphere of reproduction, a sphere construed as an analogue of the sphere of production for which we also have scientific explanatory laws. The human beings who emerge with such complexity in Freud's case studies are stripped by Mitchell to the bare bones, to objects acquiring laws as unaware, passive reactors. Despite Freud's repeated warnings that unconscious mental processes should not be reified and made thing-like or lawlike, Mitchell writes of the Unconscious as the object of psychoanalytic science. When Freud deployed the language of 'laws' he referred to probabilities and tendencies to be found in human mental life, e.g., the pervasiveness of mental conflict. He denied, as I noted above, that psychoanalysis could be a predictive science. Freud's complex subject gives way to an ahistorical woman inculcated into the human order under the workings of the inexorable laws of patriarchy. Although Mitchell's woman is present at the initiation ceremonies, she is an un-self-aware initiate and her unreflectiveness continues into adult life. The Law of the Father she carries about is held in the Unconscious which operates with no regard for the human subject it inhabits; it is more a machine in the ghost than the ghost in the machine.

Culture is treated as an unspecified whole. Beneath all the 'apparent' variations in economy, ecology, history, religion, politics, art and language an adamantine deep structure, universal and formal, operates. But if the 'law of the father' can be deployed to explain the life of the Zuni, the life of the female professional, and the life of the Queen of England, what, ultimately, has been explained? Mitchell's evidence that women, and all others, fall under the universal edict of patriarchal laws is simply definitional. It goes like this: as members of the human order women *by definition* must operate under the laws of patriarchy for patriarchy is *culture itself*. Mitchell states: 'This symbolic law of order defines society and determines the fate of every small human animal born into it.'[9] Part of this law and order is the dictum that it is women who mother. Freud's stress on psychic bisexuality and the child's identification with both parents (hence two genders) fades into the background.

Mitchell's way out of this structuralist iron cage is a move to Levi-Strauss's claim that women have been universal objects of exchange. This, strangely, becomes a ray of hope. It turns out that the law of patriarchy, including the incest taboo, operates to maintain a situation in which women are construed as universal exchange objects in *all* cultures and it is patriarchy that 'describes' this so-called universal culture. Evidence as to diverse ways of life is by-passed or brought into line with a series of purely abstract claims which Eleanor Burke Leacock calls 'unwarranted teleology' belied by actual anthropological and historical evidence.[10]

By setting psychoanalysis up as a series of ahistorical, universal categories, Mitchell's only way out is to challenge the Law of the Father. This leads to her most implausible move and claim, namely, that the incest taboo, though essential to precapitalist social formation, is 'irrelevant' under capitalist economies which do not turn on women exchange. The contemporary 'ban on incest', in Mitchell's terms, is stressed 'so loudly' because we no longer, strategically, require it. Political change demands doing away with the incest taboo, the Oedipus complex, and hence's women's gender construction as a process of feminization.

If the incest taboo is but an artifact of the exchange of women capitalist society had made redundant, it seems our best bet lies in undoing the tangled skein of patriarchal law lodged in the taboo itself – in upending our current familial relations. But given Mitchell's previous tie-up of the incest taboo and the Law of the Father with human culture itself, it is difficult to imagine what will supersede it. A primal horde? A self-limiting polymorphously perverse paradise? Or will we choose to behave 'as if' such a taboo still exists in order to prevent the sexual exploitation of children by adults on whom they are dependent? These questions go unanswered. Instead, Mitchell speaks vaguely of a cultural revolution to usher new structures into being. 'It is', she concludes, 'a question of overthrowing patriarchy,' but this *desideratum*, within the frame of her own analysis, has about as much chance of success as overthrowing the law of gravity.[11] I believe there is much more flexibility in our situation. But to demonstrate this requires a more fluid, less rigid, appropriation of Freud. I will turn next to an account that sees psychoanalysis, hence gender development, through a different theoretical lens though the ultimate conclusions are very like Mitchell's and this is, at best, problematic.

Dorothy Dinnerstein's *The Mermaid and the Minotaur* provides a startling alternative to Mitchell's rationalistic, formal account. Her work should be located within the wider project of cultural, left-wing Freudianism of whom Norman O. Brown and Herbert Marcuse are the best-known representatives. Dinnerstein begins her discussion with what she calls the 'normal psychopathology' of the human race, a starting point that I shall question below. Dinnerstein's descriptive language of our current conditions (which, of course, yields evaluative conclusions) is extreme. Characteristic descriptive terms include 'intolerable', 'diseased', 'malignant', 'maiming', 'pathological' and 'poisoned', and, at one point, motherhood is termed 'monstrous, atavistic'.[12] Dinnerstein's argument is grounded in the Kleinian concept of 'splitting' as a basic process in human mental life, one that, for Dinnerstein, is importantly 'getoverable'.[13] Dinnerstein places the greatest explanatory weight on the oral stage and the pre-verbal level of development. It is always difficult to attempt to take theoretical account of what happens before human beings become language-users. My quarrel with Dinnerstein is not that she has made this attempt, or even that she has made this the centrepiece of her argument, but that she creates what, in philosophic terms, is called a 'privileged' epistemological position, having a foundational imperative that overrides all that follows. For pre-verbal development, she insists, under terms of female-mothering, leads inexorably to a vast array of specific evils that flow from the splitting that such mothering trails in its wake.

Dinnerstein's argument runs along these lines: (1) the 'normal' condition of the human species is psycho-pathological – maladaptive and life-threatening; (2) this malaise has its roots in our intolerable gender arrangements; (3) what is intolerable about these arrangements, what makes them maiming and oppressive to everyone, is that they are 'asymmetrical' leading to specific, paranoid and other defences around gender; (4) the central marker of this asymmetry is the fact that 'for virtually every living person it is a woman' who provides the first and most important 'contact with humanity and with nature'. All of this leads to the conclusion that female monopoly of child care, given all Dinnerstein packs into it, makes the human race mad. Indeed, she foresees the end of civilization, and soon, if something isn't done to 'break the female monopoly over early child care'.[14]

I shall linger, for a moment, over two of Dinnerstein's key presumptions. To the extent that these presumptions can be seriously challenged or questioned her overall analysis and the high-pitched claims that go with it are at least partially eroded. First, the notion of 'normal' psychopathology. Every critical social theorist posits some characterization of a transformed human condition as a contrast model of what things might be or become if certain changes are made. For example, Marx's conception of 'alienation' comprises both a condemnation of the distortion of humanity that emerges under conditions of exploitation and oppression but holds forth the promise of a more complete, even transcendent human possibility once those conditions have been eliminated. The problem with Dinnerstein's argument along these lines is its utopian absolutism. Her language blurs important distinctions. If, for example, we are all 'normally' deranged what are we to make of those unfortunate souls who cannot function at all in the world, victims of persistent and destructive delusions or fixations of one sort or another – are they simply more 'normal' than the rest of us? This easily gets silly. Or, if it is the case that we are all in the grips of a shared, universal psychopathology, how is it possible for anyone to attain the merest intimation of what a normal, non-psychopathological human condition might be? If we have always been crazy, perhaps that *is* the human condition.

Dinnerstein pulls something of a sleight-of-hand here. Her premise of 'normal' psychopathology is parasitic upon some absolute but tacit standard, one thus far not approached by any known human society anywhere at anytime, of what robust psychic health for the human species would look like. Where does this standard come from if all we have ever known is psychopathological? Marx's vision of the non-alienated future made explicit contact with his assessment of life in non-capitalist historic eras and societies. But Dinnerstein doesn't give a defence of why it is we should find her utopian promise plausible as an alternative to what we have got. Surely these questions are central ones. What a social theorist must be about, if she is not to lapse into abstract evocations, is to attempt to sort out those features of the human condition that cannot be changed, we being the kind of beings we are and none other, and those miseries attributable directly to exploitative social forms. Evading these considerations, Dinnerstein launches her programme for world change from a therapeutic perspective which ushers in the dictum that the sick must be made well and this, in turn, requires doctors to prescribe the medicine. What we get, then, is a people-changing enterprise, always a high risk undertaking, particularly for those said not to know their own minds who are to be changed along lines dictated by those who have figured things out. My criticisms here are not narrowly rationalist ones that yield excessive caution, but flow instead from a recognition best called dialectic. A new world will always be parasitic upon an old one; we can never simply leap-frog into another era by gerrymandering gender arrangements or anything else.

A second presumption Dinnerstein privileges is that splitting, occurring most importantly in the pre-verbal stage of development, is the key to the psychopathology of our gender arrangements. One dimension of this privileged starting point is the insistence that the oral stage and preverbality set a powerful *causal* context for all that follows. The effect of this portion of her argument is to undermine any account of language as that which makes human beings vitally and irrepressibly self-defining and self-creating. By putting so much weight on the stage when we do not use language, Dinnerstein, ironically, could be thought to reduce the import and use of language by construing meaning as a putative correspondence between words and states of affairs. Dinnerstein, surely, would not share this view; however, by eviscerating the possibility that human beings, through language, can 'talk' their way into and out of alternative ways of being by changing their self-descriptions, she joins hands unwittingly with narrow rationalists who also underplay or ignore humans as speaking subjects.

A second dimension Dinnerstein privileges is the notion of splitting itself. I cannot here enter into a full-fledged theoretical debate drawing on the vast, but contradictory, clinical and analytical evidence in this area. But what seems to be going on in *The Mermaid and the Minotaur* is a strong notion of splitting involving not only *mechanism* but *meaning* and *content*, one that has causal consequence for individual subjects and for *all* of human life and history. Given the position splitting occupies in her scheme of things, Dinnerstein would have strengthened her case had she spent a bit more time defending her notion against alternative possibilities. Another and related problem is the fact that Dinnerstein, in an unmediated way, links splitting along gender lines to the totality of arrangements in the social and political world. This tight construal is not persuasive. I shall get to this point below, but, first, a few words on splitting. A first, crude notion of splitting was held by Janet and characterized by Freud, in 'An Autobiographical Study.' Freud writes: 'According to Janet's view a hysterical woman was a wretched creature who, on account of constitutional weakness, was unable to hold her mental acts together, and it was for this reason that she fell victim to a splitting of her mind and to a restriction of the field of her consciousness.'[15] Though Freud's views grew richer and more complex with the emergence of the structural theory of mind, the concept was not as central to his theory as to that of later thinkers, including Melanie Klein. The problems, and richness, of the thesis go hand-in-hand, for splitting is used to refer to a host of manifest behaviours or activities 'whose nature evokes hypotheses concerning either an underlying rent in the process of awareness or alternatively the simultaneous experience of contradictory, mutually exclusive events within awareness.'[16] Some thinkers construe splitting in essentially negative or defensive terms, stressing the vicissitudes of internalization. Others argue that splitting may be a non-defensive dimension of the way in which the infant mind *must* work simply to organize itself and to participate in experience.[17] The upshot of this latter view is that splitting *can* take on defensive purposes, but that the mechanism has limited theoretical cogency within the frame of an analysis of pathological mechanisms of defence.

I cannot sort out these debates here. But it is important to note, once again, that splitting is granted such heavy theoretical weight for Dinnerstein that psychopathology emerges as an *ordinary*, not an extraordinary phenomenon.[18] The relation between 'infantile normative' and 'adult pathological' splitting is problematic, but for Dinnerstein there is a smooth conduit between the two. She seems unaware of the leap she is making from pre-verbal development to the entire structure of complex social systems. Another irony: given her dramatic leap she winds up fusing two incompatible phenomena, a Hobbesian characterization of what *is* with a romantic view of what *is-to-be*. At least Hobbes was consistent. Given his depiction of a dire human condition, he opts for a coherent, if unacceptable, conclusion: absolutist control to prevent the abuses that flow from the human condition itself.[19] But Dinnerstein does not bridge the gap between her despair, even contempt, for how we now are with her utopian picture of what we will or can be if . . .

Let me explain. Dinnerstein observes correctly that '. . . the private and public sides of our sexual arrangement are not separable, and neither one is secondary to the other.'[20] She goes on to insist that *every* aspect of these arrangements is traceable to 'a single childhood condition'. But does this latter claim follow coherently? She states that both our private and public arrangements 'will melt away when that condition is abolished', that condition, remember, being the fact that it is women who mother and destructive splitting which follows. To explore this contention, one must take the measure of the malaise Dinnerstein locates in gender based distinctions in the first place. She presumes a world in which psychological imperatives, instilled from female mothering, flow upward and outward resulting in women who depend 'lopsidedly on love for emotional fulfillment because they are barred from absorbing activity in the public domain' and men who depend 'lopsidedly on participation in the public domain because they are stymied by love'.[21] This outcome is inexorable, 'woven into the pattern of complementarity between male and female personality that emerges from female-dominated early childhood'.[22] Male privilege and female oppression (the 'universal exploitation of women') are caused by asymmetry. Why? Because female power in the preverbal stage is so overpowering for male and female infants, but with different results for each, that mother-raised humans will never be able to see 'female authority as wholly legitimate'.[23]

One curious aspect in this account is the way in which Dinnerstein constitutes the infant as a powerfully sensual being with tumultuous feelings but omits the fact that this infant has a complexly functioning mind and becomes, rather early on, a sophisticated language user who, through these aspects of language and mind, is complicatedly self-defining. What follows is a corrective to Dinnerstein's construal of humans as not only *in part* but as *nearly completely* 'infantile'. Children are inventive language users, despite the fact that adults bent on making them sensible and rational creatures who think about the world 'realistically', aim to shrivel that expressivist spark down to manageable proportions. There is little sense in Dinnerstein that children, or adults for that matter, have minds which can be put to purposes not ultimately or finally or 'really' reducible to infantile drives, desires or wishes. For Dinnerstein we remain infants. In her discourse adults emerge as wilful, capricious, frequently devious, hugely voracious, alarmingly untrustworthy, narrowly self-seeking and clingingly dependent. There is, of course, a partial truth in all this but it is a truth Dinnerstein takes for the whole. I know a child lurks in each one of us, threatening to erupt, disrupt, or fall apart. But that is not all we are. To reduce male activity to the defensive and destructive history-making of naughty boys and female activity to the play-acting of maternal menials or coy sex kittens (with some possible redeeming social features) is to sink into one-dimensionality.

Let me elaborate. Dinnerstein's characterization of the public world is abstract and denunciatory. She does not distinguish between the many kinds of activities that fall within what we usually consider the public domain; nor does she indicate which of these activities may be properly seen as 'political' and which are something else. In other words, she has no *political* sense of the public world. For a political theorist, of whom I am one, this is a serious shortcoming. There are other problems. Dinnerstein describes the public world as both history-making and 'nature-assaulting'; indeed for her history-making is coterminous with assaults against nature, against the female. Women, embodying nature, have been excluded from history-making but have also refrained from nature-killing. Men, in murdering nature, are in the first and last instance also getting back at their mothers. All-in-all, it seems a rather good thing Dinnerstein's women have been exempted from the thoroughly nasty business of history-making. (Though, finally, they are complicit.)

Before I continue with my reservations and disagreements, let me note that I accept it as given that much current male and female self-definition is defensive in relation to one another (whether this is best explored through the prism of 'splitting' is another issue); that human beings, at least some of the time, *over*-define themselves as 'real men' or 'true women' defensively, given their internalized images of the opposite sex. To the extent that this is the case, we must aim to enhance our capacities to secure our male-female identities in ways that are less limiting. But this is not Dinnerstein's project. She accepts no limits on human 'freedom' once the thorny matter of gender asymmetry is ironed out. Hers are a set of maximal claims that begin by locating men *in* history destructively, and women *in* a rigid dichotomy between nature and culture.

In an important essay, 'Natural facts: a historical perspective on science and sexuality,' L. J. Jordanova traces the antecedents of a presumed nature/culture split to the rationalizing discourse of eighteenth-century science.[24] In documenting the way in which the categories of 'nature' and 'culture', emerged Jordanova challenges feminist accounts that assume these categories.

The nature/culture split entered feminist discourse with Simone de Beauvoir's *The Second Sex*. De Beauvoir located men squarely in the realm of Transcendence as Being-for-themselves and women in the bog of Immanence as Beings-in-themselves. De Beauvoir's model offered an unambiguous linkage from nature/culture, woman/man, to oppressed/oppressor. It made 'women . . . the bearers of ignorance and men of knowledge', rather a baffling notion to set as the basis of feminist discourse.[25] In de Beauvoir's argument, men and men alone are declared the agents and bearers of culture; women, the flip side of the coin, outside civilization, in nature, are inessential to culture though they are a necessary condition for the reproduction of human life, a process de Beauvoir does not find one of the tasks of culture.

Although Dinnerstein's use of the dichotomy is not so severe in its devaluation of women's traditional spheres as de Beauvoir's, she repeats the notion that women are oppressed and victimized because they are located in 'nature'. This is a serious distortion. Anthropologists and social historians have shown that there are 'no simple scales on which men and women can be ranged.'[26] Moreover, Dinnerstein's diminishes women, historically and presently, by presuming that they would have given their consent, albeit tacit, to a social situation which was one of unrelenting debasement or infantilisation. We know of no human society based on such debasement which has enjoyed a continuing existence. The upshot is: rather than countering the categorical rigidities that have plagued our understanding of past and present social life, Dinnerstein retains several of them. Jordanova makes a telling point against this hardening of the categories when she states that 'one of the problems with the current promiscuous use of the nature/culture dichotomy in relation to gender is that it has taken the claims of Western science at face value, and so lapsed into a biologism which it is the responsibility of the social sciences, including history and anthropology, to combat.'[27]

Given the fact that she carves up the social universe along the lines of a nature/culture dichotomy, Dinnerstein proposes, as *the* solution to all our ills, a break in the female monopoly of early child care. Only this will defuse female linkage with nature and female oppression by culture. She calls for men and women to 'mother' in identical ways and to participate in the public world in full parity. Were this done, our public and private arrangements would be transformed in one fell swoop. Children would no longer grow up maimed and maladaptive; nature would no longer be assaulted; history would no longer be destructive. To attain this end two sorts of pre-conditions are required. The first is psychological (just described) and the second, not political but *technological*. This technological condition is characterized as 'the practical possibility of making parenthood genuinely optional, the concrete feasibility of adult work life flexible enough so that men and women can take equal part in both domestic and public life' – something, she insists, that is 'already available', just as the restructuring of child-rearing, if we really want it, is ready-to-hand.

On the road to sex-equality something curious has happened: important considerations involving the structure of our political and economic life are drawn in *ad hoc* and reduced to 'technological' factors. In this way Dinnerstein reflects rather than challenges a dimension of the current public world she deplores – the tendency to reduce vital human issues to technical problems amenable to technological resolution at the hands of social engineers. Surely the public conditions she requires for her solution to asymmetrical disorders are profoundly and inescapably political. But she has no way to handle these issues because she has neither a political analysis of the present, nor a political vision of the future.

Because Dinnerstein evades how it is, politically, we shall get to the world of gender symmetry save through willing it (given that the 'technological' prerequisites for its implementation currently exist), her prophecy encounters no points of friction. One *political* precondition that stands in her way is the self-identity of women themselves, one still tied for most to primary responsibility for care of the young. This cannot be attributed wholly to the defensive aspects of femininity flowing from centuries of enforced domesticity, not even within Dinnerstein's analysis. I refer back to her insistence that women have certain qualities not given over to nature-killing *because* of their roles in the arrangements Dinnerstein wishes to overturn. Women, identifying with Mother (Nature) have no need to plunder and rape her. What Dinnerstein foresees, in her post-gender-revolution society, is a world in which all the present plunder, exploitation and nature-assaulting of men will have melted away, and all the loving, concern and caring now almost exclusively female traits (in her view) will remain, shared by men and women.

Is this convincing? If the gender revolution will radically alter men, turning them away from destruction and towards nurturance, why will it not also alter women, turning them way from nurturance and towards destructive history-making? Women, it seems, stay as 'sweet as they are' even as they gain full public power. In the process they will not take on the bad male qualities previously denied to them. Human nastiness evaporates on Dinnerstein's road to the future. It doesn't suffice to say Dinnerstein looks forward to integrating the now split parts of her goal, rather than simply abolishing the unsavoury stuff. For what needs to be integrated, but cannot, argues Dinnerstein, given that we are all mother-reared and split, are current gender rigidities.

Finally, what seeps through Dinnerstein's pages is what Michel Foucault might call a form of evangelical sexual liberationism that fuses the promise of destroying old repressions, fulfilling immediate desires, and ushering in future happiness. I do not find this palatable medicine in an era confronting Reaganomics and Thatcherism, the rising danger of a nuclear confrontation, additional confirmation (as if this were required) of the repressive nature of state socialist regimes, and, in America at least, the growing forces of right-wing reaction. These dangers and dilemmas require the concerted political efforts of men and women who share a humane vision *now*, not generations away once the symmetrical world is attained. And it *is* possible for men and women to work together, politically, as citizens rather than to regress, incessantly, as Dinnerstein's men and women do, into an infantile *pas de deux*, mamas and babies waltzing into the apocalypse. Her vision is fantastic and has all the appeal of other apocalyptic prophecies, for at base each promises, once and for all, an end to it all since everyone, deep down, knows that the revolution the prophet requires to forestall the end she foresees is impossible to attain in practice.

I shall move, now, to a very different framework, and hence account of gender development, from Dinnerstein's in Nancy Chodorow's book, *The Reproduction of Mothering*. Chodorow owes as much to functionalist sociology as she does to psychoanalysis. She draws heavily upon a theory or model of the relationship between the family and society developed in the functionalist sociology of Talcott Parsons in two essays written in 1942 and 1943.[28] Her implicit acceptance of this model precludes taking up the self-understanding of social participants, or seeing social worlds as webs of meaning. Her model presupposes a stable congruity or 'fit' between the modern industrialized economy and the nuclear family, a tie-up challenged by the new family history. Family functions are given. Male and female roles are predetermined and 'asymmetrical', a term deployed by Parsons. These roles revolve around the division between what Parsons called the instrumental, adaptive father and the nurturant, expressive mother. Parsons saw the division as necessary to the ends of maintaining the equilibrium of society. The family, in his functionalist terms, was one substructural buttress in a pattern of systems maintenance; in other words, the family is construed instrumentally. Functionalists hold to a unilinear theory of history which, in the words of Lawrence Stone, 'ignores the ups and downs of social and intellectual change, the lack of uniformity of the direction of the trends, and the failures of the various trends to synchronize in the way they ought if the paradigm is to fit. Above all, by sweeping broadly across the vast spectrum of highly distinctive national cultures, status groups and classes, these theories reduce the enormous diversity of social experience to a uniformity which has never existed in real life.'[29] Chodorow shares these aspects of the functionalist paradigm. Now this sort of perspective exudes a political stance that stresses stasis; Chodorow, however, beginning from the same premises, wishes to bring about revolution. I shall explore whether this can convincingly be done or not given her own analysis of the situation.

Human subjects are constituted by Chodorow's discourse as objectified role-players, turned out as over-socialized beings stuck in a rigid 'sex-gender system and sexual asymmetry.'[30] Sex itself, Chodorow argues, sexual desires and fantasies, including the progressive 'libidinization' of various zones, as well as final gender identity, are *wholly* 'social products'. There is little depth psychology in this scheme of things. Instead, there is a sociological construct, a product of social factors, that gets construed as exhausting the 'psychological'. The human subject as a desiring, fantasizing, self-defining agent is lost. Children are human clay awaiting their moulding into 'gendered members of society'.[31] By stripping human beings of any self-sustaining, autonomous capacities for fantasy, by evacuating them of sexual drives as in any way bodily and given, by ignoring consciousness and language, Chodorow eliminates children and adults as beings who may 'dwell in possibility', to use Emily Dickinson's blithe turn of phrase, beings who are sentient and imaginative, capable of reflection, of symbol-making, of identifying with beings outside the asymmetrical knots into which she ties up the family and, from there, the broader social world.[32]

Chodorow's account, like Dinnerstein's, involves a few central premises. The lock-step ordering goes like this: (1) the normal pattern of human gender development leads to the construction and reproduction of male dominance; (2) our gender arrangements are blatantly asymmetrical, hence systematically disordered; (3) this derangement generates male dominance and female subordination because psychologists 'have demonstrated unequivocally that *the very fact* of being mothered by a woman generates in men conflicts over masculinity, a psychology of male dominance, and a need to be superior to women',[33] pointing to the conclusion: it is women's mothering which guarantees continuing male dominance and female subordination: the cradle-rocking hand strikes again! Her conclusion suggests a counter-factual, namely, that men not mothered by women exclusively experience no need to be superior to women and are not warped by a psychology of male dominance. Whether this is so or not is a matter for exploration on many levels; but there is compelling anthropological evidence to suggest that *the* male psychology Chodorow finds inevitably caused by female mothering is not as universal as she claims. Indeed, many men in our own societies, mothered by women, have no apparent need to bully over women nor to dominate them.

To the riposte that, although such men do not engage in bullying or domineering *action* vis à vis women they may still harbour vestiges of a fantasy world in which they subdue women, my response would follow along these lines: it is not the business of feminist politics to expunge fantasy. To hope to create a world in which male fantasies have been sanitized of any content that might contain brutalizing images, however fleetingly, is to embrace a moralistic politics that easily turns repressive. There is a vast difference between a fantasy and a brutal rape. What society can and must do is *punish the action, not move to eradicate the fantasy.* Otherwise we require moralistic thought-control.

Back to Chodorow's sex-gender system, then. In her terms, it is set up as 'a fundamental determining and constituting element' of society; it is 'socially constructed, subject to historical change and development, and organized in such a way that it is systematically reproduced', though there is, in fact, no sense of historic movement or change in her analysis.[34] Given this tautly drawn system, Chodorow cannot take account of human beings as reflective and active; instead, they are reactive, shaped by external forces, primarily by the 'object relations' of family life. Most puzzling, in a psychoanalytically oriented account, is the disappearance of embodiment. In her understandable determination to construct a social analysis, Chodorow excises the body-subject. Zones become libidinized only – and this is quite extraordinary for it turns children into precocious Benthamites – because the child recognizes, calculatingly, that this will help to attain personal contact. If what one is explaining is gender identity, it is a rather serious omission to disconnect the body. Shrinking embodiment down to 'variables' termed 'biological', Chodorow's arguments constitute human beings in, and through, a series of prefixed social predicates.

Though Chodorow explicitly discounts biology as important in any deep way to her account in her book, she later acknowledged that 'biological variables' are something feminists must be open to, for we are, after all 'embodied creatures' and there is 'certainly some biological basis, or influence . . .' etc. But biological 'variables' are precisely what I am not concerned with, for their incorporation only leads to tedious social sciency notions of 'interaction' and 'multiple causality'. To call the body-subject a 'variable' is baffling indeed, for the fact that we are never-not-our-bodies and never in the world save as body-subjects seems a rather more basic and ungetoverable reality than to strip our bodies down to size as but one 'variable', among others. Variables don't grow up, grow ill, make love, grow old, and die. This paring the body down to size is not radical at all; it is typical of academic social science and a throwback to plain, old-fashioned dualism.[35]

There is more. Children in *The Reproduction of Mothering* identify not so much with recognizably real, particular mothers or fathers but with role players, again making her indebtedness to functionalism clear. Following as she does Parsons' vectors of gender-specific, socially induced identifications is unconvincing, in part because one gets no sense of *families* in social settings, no thick description of the social worlds of intimate human life, nor the complex inner worlds of infant life. Her system appears to squeeze out the central importance of the *quality of mothering and parenting* to the development of the human person. Yet psychoanalytic evidence is clear on this score: what is of vital importance is the *quality* of care the child receives.[36]

Chodorow's system has very little elasticity. Freud, on the other hand, was aware of variations in human possibility, including resolutions to prototypical crises. He recognized that children, like that cunning fellow, little Hans, could conjure up fantastic resolutions to important conflicts, not reducible to some standard formula. Chodorow often makes stronger claims for the explanatory power and application of her model than Freud did for his as social explanation. Yet, in the breach, she cannot account for the many human lives that diverge in interesting ways from her static functionalist construction of the sex-gender system.

Here it is worth pondering Chodorow's determination to unravel heterosexual knots and smooth out gender asymmetries. By asymmetry she, and Dinnerstein, mean men and women playing different parts in the social world and having predominant interest in, even effective control over, different activities on the basis of gender identity. This would not seem to be an evil *simpliciter* unless these differences were *invariably* the basis for destructive inequalities or distinctions *always* invidiously drawn to favour one group, to downgrade the other. But by defining 'asymmetry' as male dominance, female oppression, Chodorow construes social reality in a way that downgrades women's contributions and magnifies those of men. That is, she winds up sharing the 'devaluation of domesticity which is the hallmark of the very sexist society she deplores'.[37] Rather than challenging the terms of male dominant society on the basis of its respective valuation of men and women's worlds, Chodorow attacks gender differences themselves, seeing them as the root of social evil. It follows that the radically de-gendered society becomes a prerequisite for social 'equality'. Indeed, the de-gendered society becomes by definition, in her frame, one of equality.

Conflating differences with domination, Chodorow has little choice but to embrace the feminist future as a picture of a social world in which human beings are rendered as sexually homogeneous as possible. Denying possibilities for reciprocal interdependency as one plausible outcome of gender differences viewed as complementaries, and as making possible fructifying mutualities at variance with destructive sexual divisions or cleavages, Chodorow embraces the symmetrical future. This leads one critic, Zelda Bronstein, to argue that Chodorow's equation of difference with domination and her call for a non-oppositional social world in which 'all good ends are reconcilable', places her squarely within the tradition of mainstream liberal ideology.[38]

In her determination to make things symmetrical, Chodorow does not consider the possibility that her argument might lead to the elimination of differences but would do little to eradicate social injustice. Her call for 'more collective child-rearing situations', for example, as demonstrably preferable to what we have in Western societies, is instructive in this regard. She claims, without citing compelling evidence, that more 'collective' methods reduce, or eliminate, the fruits of our gender arrangements – 'individualism . . . competitiveness'. Her terms of description are crucial. Another observer, looking at the same picture as Chodorow, might speak of our concerns with 'being an individual', with 'moral autonomy', as one aspect of our child-rearing arrangements. We would then respond very differently. None of us lauds individualism, which, rightly, has a bad name, but all save those blind to concerns with human freedom and responsibility want children to grow up to be individuals with a sense of moral responsibility, beings who can be held accountable for their deeds. Chodorow points *only* to the possibly good outcomes of collective child rearing, finding no irritants in the image, though there are such, even as she overdraws the bad results of our childrearing. She is insouciant to the potential dangers of flattening out the social world, of erecting a single standard for organizing and evaluating human life.

There is important, and growing, anthropological evidence about male and female power and authority in societies different from our own which call the symmetry imperative into question. One obsever, Peggy Reeves Sanday, analysing over 150 societies for which detailed ethnographies were available, concludes that the only symmetry of which we know anything – by which she means a rough parity of power between males and females – is grounded in sex differences, not the blurring of those differences. Sanday's study is particularly interesting because she began with the presumption that women were universally subordinated, men dominant.[39] To her initial consternation, Sanday found that the evidence pointed to something very different. Not only was it *not* the case that men were the universal culture-creating, dominant sex, women the nature-struck subordinate sex, but there were many societies in which women wielded, or had wielded, great authority and power.

In such societies, it was women as bearers of children and nurturers of plant life who occupied central positions in the realm of social authority.

Gender identity leading to the two sexes predominating in different spheres of social life, tied, in turn, to powerful, organizing, symbolic principles, lay at the basis of those societies featuring rough integration between the sexes, as well as those societies that were genuinely separate but equal. In such societies the power to give life – woman's power – was as highly valued as the power to take it away – male power (yet paradoxically also male weakness, as the male warrior is expendable, making men the expendable sex). Conceptual distinctions demarcating femaleness from maleness, Sanday argues, are universally evident and, moreover, are necessary if human beings are to create cultural forms, are to order their worlds in some coherent way.[40]

Finding peculiar as feminist argumentation though understandable as Western bias the view that male dominance is universal, Sanday says this flows from our tendency to equate dominance with official public leadership. Karen Sacks adds that to view male and female authority in societies like the Iroquois, where women wielded great power, as *unequal* rather than *different* reflects a 'state bias in Western anthropological interpretation of prestate politics.'[41] When one looks at societies within their own terms, Sanday concludes that female economic and political power or authority flow as a right due the female sex where one finds a 'magico-religious association between maternity and fertility of the soil' linking women 'with social continuity and social good'. In certain West African dual-sex systems, for example, the power and invincibility of womanhood emerges with startling force. 'Whether the male chief is big or small', said the woman of a West African solidarity group, 'what matters is that he was given birth by a woman.'[42] Dozens of societies, it appears, were worlds in which sex differences signalled parity and complementary balance, with neither sex wholly dominant over the other, but with each dominant in particular areas of social life.

Examples of other male-female arrangements unpacked by Sanday feature ways that *formal* male authority is balanced, or undermined, by *actual* female power. This gender balance-of-power is maintained by culturally sanctioned strategems, including myths of male dominance though males do not actually dominate. In peasant societies, for example, the appearance of male dominance provides an umbrella beneath which women exercise actual power over key sectors of community life, areas where men are not allowed to interfere. (This was certainly my experience growing up on a farm in rural Colorado, in the American West.) In this world of complex asymmetry, power and authority between the sexes is balanced.

Sanday concludes that arguments calling for sexual symmetry, understood as a world in which males and females have decisions over the same activities and exercise power in identical ways over the same things, makes little sense. No society has ever existed in which the sexes gave equal energy to exactly the same activities and decisions, nor does such a society seem plausible, even desirable. This vision of symmetry conflates equality with sameness and it strikes a responsive chord, Sanday insists, only if 'one has no knowledge of the many societies which attach supernatural importance to the creation of life.'[43]

The nature/culture split on which the thesis of male dominance/ female subordination is based does not stand up to historical and anthropological investigation. There are many societies in which women are the central civilizing influence and men are associated with decivilizing force. Sanday's study suggests that secular male dominance is more likely to occur in societies in which an imbalance has congealed between male and female-linked activities. The way to combat such destructive cleavage is *not*, it appears, to call for a total fusing of male and female activities and spheres such that no vital distinctions remain – impossible in any case – but to expand the actual and symbolic importance and vitality of female-linked activities and systems of meaning for, to repeat Sanday's findings, the only symmetry of which we have real evidence has not arisen on the basis of gender blurring, but has been grounded in sex differences. This suggests a very different feminist task from that of the symmetrist. The implications are vast, troubling and complex and I cannot spell them out here. But I do wish to turn to one piece of powerful, contemporary evidence that calls symmetrical presumptions into question.

The work of Diana Grossman Kahn challenges the Chodorow image of parents cloning same-sex children to live in an unchanging world.[44] According to Kahn, Chodorow's argument washes out the complexities of cross-sex identifications. In a series of studies, involving over 100 college women, juniors and seniors, with whom she conducted open-ended interviews that went on for many hours, Kahn found that daughters were not 'locked into' some automatically second-rate model if their mothers were 'traditional wives and mothers'. Indeed, such mothers were described, with few exceptions, as strong, active, loving and supportive. Most important, for feminist considerations, were the roles of fathers as mentors to daughters. The research literature on what are called 'achieving women', including feminists, both nineteenth-century and contemporary activists, shows the encouragement of fathers to be particularly important,

Kahn found that fathers made their own 'unique contribution' to the development of their daughters. Only two of her subjects reported fathers who clearly downgraded their capacities compared with those of their brothers. Kahn concludes, after evaluating the *quality* of actual individual lives and experiences, that mothers and fathers played importantly complementary (not identical or symmetrical) roles. Kahn also challenges the notion that men, by definition, are deficient in their capacities for intimacy. This formulation, she argues, emerges as one-sided and polemical because it makes intimacy, by definition, that of which women are capable – even as it condemns the situation that ostensibly makes the woman superior in intimacy.

Clearly, the ball is now in my court. Given my disagreement with accounts of 'sex-gender systems' and calls for symmetry, I must move to articulate some coherent alternative. Perhaps it is worth putting the following questions. What is the point of social explanation? Is it to figure out what is really going on, to probe meaning, to satisfy our curiosity? Is it to determine how to organize the social world in order to help ease its burdens for those men and women who inhabit it and who try, often against daunting odds to be decent, loving parents towards their children? Or is our end point the implementation of a vision of social change as preordained by a theoretical elite with a blueprint for reordering society? If reform of family life, or gender arrangements, emerges as importantly decent in itself, that is one thing. But if radical change in human intimate life is deemed necessary in order to attain other ends, to remake the world in conformity with some overarching *Weltanschauung*, that is quite another. In this latter instance, theoretical explanation becomes a power play in a cultural struggle and must be eyed, queasily, as such. For those who propose to undo the way we now do things at the most basic level sometimes aim to 'reconstruct' the human subject. We are well to be wary, for 'reconstruction' (meaning, by definition, that we are now 'unreconstructed') all too easily translates into a politics of coercion, buttressed by the notion that the majority of human beings are hapless 'products' of social condition who do not know their own minds, their 'true' interests, or their 'real' needs, a sorry state from which the reconstructors have somehow escaped.

In setting down the markers of an alternative, I must be brief. What I shall provide is not a full-blown alternative account, impossible in a short essay, but those imperatives I believe such an account must take account of, or account for. First, a compelling alternative must recognize the singular importance of construing the human subject, child and adult, as self-defining. This need not mean that one ignores the developmentally early. But to the extent that feminist social explanation and ideology eliminates the self-understandings of social participants, and such explanation and ideology gains acceptance and adherence, feminists, paradoxically, promote a set of presumptions that have historically been arrayed against female selfhood. Nobody is well served when human beings are shrunk down to the status of objects of analysis or deprived of consciousness, language and agency.

A second feature of an alternative account, tied to the first, would be to frame that account, in part, from what might be called the standpoint of the child, featuring the child as a body-subject, seeing his or her world as a complex web of social relations and meanings alive with competing possibilities. Getting inside the child's world means construing child development and the emergence of gender identity as a dynamic discourse, the history of the 'I' ('das Ich'), framed with reference to what I am not. This dialectic of human development involves complex negations and affirmations. The child is no passive recipient of this process but the active constructor of various possibilities.

The child's inner discourse of the I/not-I is powerfully structured within the ordering dialogue of child and mother. Louise J. Kaplan has traced the child's dialogue of 'oneness and separateness', the coming-towards and pushing-aways that are the punctuation points of a process that, in Kaplan's words, 'insures our humanity'.[45] The evidence of what happens when things go wrong, when children suffer the diseases of non-attachment and neglect, is proof of the child's needs for constancy in the form of specific, adult others. The child does not become a language defining 'I' until around thirty months of age, yet well before that she has been interpreting the meanings of space and time, exploring what Kaplan calls the 'choreography' of mother and child, carrying on an active dialogue involving mutual excitement, games and responses. Kaplan demonstrates that the babe in arms is no passive bit of human clay but 'an artist', helping 'to create the world which holds him',[46] with a repertoire of 'grunts, sighs, coos, postures, droopy-eyed looks, alert looks, finger grabs, head turnings and mouthings and a set of cries and fretting sounds that give a mother some idea of how she should hold him and interpret the world to him.'[47]

The baby is the educator of her own body. She experiments with what it can do. She tests what it cannot. She assays how it all fits together. She locates it in the world.[48] This self-motivation, if all goes well, grows more and more powerful. The child's capacities for translating bodily imperatives into mental activity; her growing emotional complexity; her burgeoning capacity to comprehend and create meaning – all paint a picture of a being with agency, not an indeterminate piece of stuff awaiting moulding by the organized forces of society. Another important point, lost in most gender accounts, is the fact that adults-as-parents are not unchanged by the discourse of childhood. Each child, a being unique and like no other, calls forth a variety of responses from her parents. Every child–parent dialogue is distinctive and, in subdued or more dramatic ways, may transform *all* participants.

Just a few other bits of evidence on the child as subject: Rosalind Gould has detailed the ways in which 'fantasy activities have a vital place in the child's development, in expanding horizons of thoughts and feelings, and as a potential means of achieving some internal distance from affective dilemmas.'[49] Gould shows that the child's 'internal well-springs and external world experiences intermingle or oscillate in various ways in fantasy expressions, to the enrichment of both sources of knowledge.'[50] Myra Bluebond-Langner, in her account of dying children, documents the two-way nature of a process (socialization) often seen as unilinear, flowing from adult shapers to infant shapes. Not so, argues Bluebond-Langner, for such models fail to grasp 'the shifting, unfolding, creative aspects of all human behavior', thereby failing to really *see* children and their world.[51] Her months spent with terminally ill children provide poignant evidence that children are wilful, purposeful beings who possess selves, who interpret their own actions, incorporating their self-interpretations and their perceptions of interpretations of others as a way to obtain a view of themselves, others, and objects in the world, who initiate action so as to affect the views others have of them and they have of themselves, who are capable of initiating action to affect the behaviour of others towards them, and who attach meaning to themselves, others, and objects, moving from one social world to another and acting appropriately in each.[52]

Finally, in an account at once playful and powerful, Gareth B. Matthews, a philosopher, assays the child as a philosopher. It turns out that 'for many young members of the human race, philosophical thinking – including, on occasion, subtle and ingenious reasoning – is as natural as making music and playing games, and quite as much a part of being human.'[53] Matthews makes the case for the sophistication of young minds. More provocatively, he argues that adults, in their treatment of 'childish' questions, should refuse to play the therapist. Instead, parents and teachers should accept a child's inquiries on the level on which they are couched, rather than scouring every utterance for hints at repressed content. He writes, 'Even when one suspects that the comment or question carries considerable emotional freight, addressing the question, rather than treating it *simply* as an emotional symptom, may be part of showing proper respect for the child as a full-fledged human being.'[54] His argument here is not that dramatic symptoms should be ignored but that children's expressions of strong views, or children's questions, should not be reductively treated as necessarily symptomatic, thereby abstracting from the child's serious intellectual concerns and development.

A critic might reply at this juncture that he was persuaded by the evidence that children are active agents within a richer social world than the one conveyed in sex-gender system accounts. But, he might then continue, your alternative thus far seems to turn solely on the self-definitional moment of social theory. That is, he might go on, you have made the case for the child as an importantly self-creating subject. But this, in itself, offers no *explanation* of how it is that gender uniformities do emerge, or why it is biological males wind up as men and biological females become women. A child may understand many things but the stages of her own psycho-sexual development, in some compelling theoretical form, are not amongst them. We cannot turn exclusively to the child for this, so how do you propose to *explain* social gender identity?

I would begin like this. We can assert certain things with certainty in advance of any particular, concrete investigation of gender development in specific families and cultural systems. We can, for example, assert that such development will involve the complex emergence of a body-subject within a social matrix. We also know that the human infant comes biologically 'prepared' for all sorts of things: there is something like an inner developmental clock that, all other things being equal, will come into play at roughly similar times for human infants. I refer here to nervous system and motor development and the like. We know that babies are self-motivatedly embodied from the start and act in and upon their worlds on the bases of powerful imperatives which (if possible) translate, very quickly, into complex social feelings, emotions, needs, demands and desires. We know that young children are extraordinarily preoccupied with their own bodies, though what they can or are allowed to do with those bodies varies from culture to culture. We know that it is impossible to rush this age-specific (over a range) developmental picture; a child before a certain age doesn't use language, not because her parents haven't taught her but because she literally *cannot* given the early structure of mouth and tongue, cognitive capacities, etc. There are biological capacities and limits, then, when one is dealing with human infants and children. That it seems, somehow, 'non-progressive' to note this fact or even to attempt a non-reductive account of human embodiment, is a peculiarity of current discourse which seems to find unacceptable control in every constraint; the heavy hand of oppression in every limitation; exploitation in every necessity.

An alternative account would also begin with another presumption, one supported by extant anthropological theory and evidence, that the division of humanity, on the conceptual and symbolic level, into two distinct sexes is an essential aspect of human identity and cultural life. Males and females, of course, are beings who share in the most basic general characteristics; yet they differ along recognizable and distinctive lines. To introduce the sex distinction, and to recognize its importance along the whole range of cultural meaning, is not to surreptitiously smuggle in a sex-gender system geared against women. Feminist arguments for gender symmetry are problematic in part because they aim to downplay or render uninteresting one of the most important distinctions of all.

To agree that the sex distinction is ineliminable and important, does not mean one must acquiesce in received notions of the 'masculine' and the 'feminine'. Clearly not. To demonstrate that bodily identity is a feature of personal identity, meaning that such identity will also be a sexed identity, one needs a dynamic, developmental account of the human subject. I have traced out such an account elsewhere; one which owes much to Freud's theory of human development as dynamically embodied *and* social, for we are inherently body-subjects.[55] The human body registers itself through a complex inner-outer dialectic in which the human infant makes internal representations to herself of her own body.[56] From her first moments, the infant experiences her body as a source of pleasure and unpleasure that goes beyond the mere registering of sensation. Embodiment implicates her in the active construction of her inner world, in part through the 'taking in' of the body's surfaces as part of 'external' reality. The human infant does not have the cognitive nor the neurological structure or organization necessary to demarcate tidily inner and outer, internal and external. What the infant does it to incorporate with eyes, ears, mouth and touch a world complicatedly inner/outer. Slowly, the I is built up, in part through complex representations of the child's body, in part through inner representations of the bodies of others (objects) with whom the child is implicated in exquisitely social relations from the start.

Our corporeality bears powerful imperatives for how we come to know and to be. A child can neither negate physically nor transcend conceptually the manner in which his or her body 'registers itself' within the successive stages of psycho-sexual maturation. The body evokes and mediates ways of knowing. Our most original, primitive experiences with the world cannot be understood save as an embodied engagement with the world. At the beginning a child has no sense of belonging to one gender or another, though male and female bodies from the beginning will surely register themselves somewhat differently. But when the child begins her early 'sexual researches', certainly by the time the child is five or six, she will have distinguished two central types of embodied beings; though she may remain uncertain as to the full meaning of this distinction she knows it is important. To live in a sexed social world is not, necessarily, to inhabit one in which differential evaluations, to the detriment of the female, are placed on gender identity.

This much is clear: gender identity is a central feature on the child's formation of a 'self'. Children locate themselves in their worlds on the basis of gender. This not only makes human sense, it is inescapable. All human beings and cultures differentiate form from non-form and provide the conceptual orderings minimally necessary if that culture is to have any coherent sense of anything whatever. Children live out a deep sense of urgency in and through their bodies: Is mine whole? Is it strong? Will it grow? Am I the 'right' kind of what it is I am? Plans to 'transcend' or eliminate the importance of gender run directly counter to every culture's world of shared meanings, for gender is precisely what children try to figure out, to work on, and to work through in all cultures, though, of course, the difficulty of the task and the outcomes of such figurings turn dramatically on the social frame within which the child's creation of a gendered self is set.

What would a world in which gender didn't figure centrally, and sex distinctions were downplayed or ignored, look like? It is difficult even to get a handle on such a world, for to be male or female is not just a patina *on* human existence, it is the mode *in* and *through* which life is lived. A de-gendered world would have to be one in which the repression of infantile sexuality was deep and pervasive in order to forestall moves by children to experiment and play with their own bodies, for only in this way could one prevent the child's inner representations of body surfaces from forming. Children would be barraged with the insistence that sex differences did not matter, were of little interest, were inessential in determining their future identities and existences. This would be a cruel deception. It would also hamper that development of self grounded in the child's emerging linguistic ability to differentiate objects, things, events, and experiences along lines of what is more or less important, what is central or peripheral, and so on. For a child such distinctions will also include 'my body'/'other bodies', 'male bodies'/'female bodies', 'my family'/'other families', etc.

The claim that bodily identity is necessarily a gendered identity, as one feature of personal identity, neither presupposes nor entails social and political inequality between the sexes. The sex-linked distinctions used to justify sexual inequality are not necessarily thus linked. Although sex distinctions in some societies, including our own, have served as justifications for sex inequality, they need not thus serve; moreover, as I argued above, the burden of anthropological evidence suggests that sex distinctions historically have formed the basis for systems of parity of power and authority between men and women. Indeed, the insistence that sexual 'symmetry' is the *only* foundation on which to build sex equality *displaces* a political focus upon structures of social, economic and political equality, lodged importantly in class and race, in favour of advancing rhetorical claims about the transformation of human personalities and gender identities.

A few modest conclusions suggest themselves. The first is that we would all be better off, and come closer to creating a world to our heart's desirings, if we accepted out bodies in better grace and recognized that a sexual *difference* need not be an affront, an outrage, a narcissistic injury, a blow to female self-esteem forced on women by a male-dominant world; that, at present, these voices have found a resonant echo among other reformers and radicals signifies something important. It means, first of all, that there is some important partial truth to this construal, that the world has been set up in such a way that large numbers of females could come to see themselves through such a lens. It means, as well, that many feminist thinkers have implicitly embraced a vision of the human person that flows from, rather than standing in opposition to, cultural definitions of human beings indebted to utilitarian and market images. As those images have shifted from one revolving around the self as a being who must limit present pleasure to guarantee future 'goods' (the world of the Protestant ethic and the middle-class producer), to one encouraging a grandiose view of an aggrandizing, consuming self, radicals have often gone along. Committed to modes of analysis based on the notion that what was, and remains, 'bad' is overly harsh repression of natural drives in the interest of capital accumulation, radicals continue to speak, and to write, as if the unchained self, free to pursue his or her own ends in untrammelled ways, is a radical notion. In fact, the entire thrust of consumer society is to unleash grandiose ambition and to encourage unlimited self-gratification. The ideal consumer is a being not essentially connected to any other being, nor to a specific sense of place, to rootedness in family, community, or tradition. Such a being is more readily shunted about according to market imperatives. What we are suffering from at present, perhaps most dramatically in American society, is a surfeit of the politics of the grandiose self. Feminist analyses which fail to counter this image may wind up serving, in the warning of Julia Kristeva, as part and parcel of capitalism's needs to rationalize.

Missing, then, and needed is a vision of politics, a theory of the political community, an ideal of the critical citizen as one who shares in the deliberate efforts of human beings to order and direct their collective affairs. But needed as well is some alternative vision of family life that can account for the ways in which it has constrained us as well as the ways in which it is required to make us human. If we continue to locate the family as *the* first and foremost breeding ground of sexist privilege we will be unable to see the ways in which women, historically, have been empowered by their appropriation of the private sphere as a social identity *in* the world.

Our situation is ambivalent and we must acknowledge that ambivalence so that we do not make common sense, unwittingly at times, perhaps knowingly at others, with the social engineers and public policy technocrats whose ultimate end is the complete rationalization of all areas of human existence so that 'society' as a whole can function more smoothly. It is quite possible for pro-family platitudes and technocratic politics to co-exist.

The left, then, faces a bind. We would also strengthen the capacities of human beings to live out long-term ties and commitments to one another, and such relations are based upon, and infused with, values counter to those that prevail on the market or in the instrumentally rationalist world view. Bronstein claims that marriage and the family, or familial-like bonds, are 'the last institutional intermediary which still stands as a buffer between increasingly impotent individuals and the organized forces of domination'.[57] I would put the matter less defensively but I agree that we must find some way to engage the problem of the family without, at the same time, impugning the *ideal* of these social relations. With all the problems and abuses that we have become conscious of (child and spouse abuse, most importantly wife battering) we sometimes forget that for the vast majority of individuals the family involves a struggle to hold onto meaning and purpose in a social world in which other public and private instititutions have been drained of much of their previous legitimacy and normative force. If we further the disintegrative processes we simultaneously distance ourselves from our putative constituencies; on the other hand, we cannot forego the questioning and critique exemplified by the feminist gender theorists I have, in turn, challenged. Perhaps one of our best hopes remains this process of debate and disputation so that we do not follow – in this matter of gender development and relations – previous generations of social thinkers who embraced too readily models that quickly rigidified into conceptual tombs.

Notes

1. Sigmund Freud, 'The Question of a *Weltanschauung*.'
2. Two of the important critiques include Charles Taylor, 'Interpretation and the sciences of man,' and 'Neutrality in political science.'
3. Sigmund Freud, 'Construction in analysis.'
4. Clifford Geertz, *The Interpretation of Cultures*, p. 18.
5. See Marie Jahoda, *Freud and the Dilemmas of Psychology*, and Jean Bethke Elshtain, *Public Man, Private Woman. Women in Social and Political Thought*.
6. I have drawn on an unpublished essay by Charles Taylor, 'Social theory as practice.'
7. It may be possible that good arguments do not necessarily make for good politics, nor that bad arguments necessarily make for bad politics. Most of the time, however, one's assessment of a thinker's arguments and her politics must be of a piece because the thinker herself has forged such a tight link between the two that they cannot be separated. Even if such a link hasn't been forged, I am persuaded this separation cannot, finally, be made in any tidy way.
8. Juliet Mitchell, *Psychoanalysis and Feminism*, passim. Other structuralist renderings include those of Louise Althusser, Jacques Lacan, Claude Levi-Strauss.
9. Ibid., p. 391.
10. Eleanor Burke Leacock, 'The changing family and Levi-Strauss, or whatever happened to fathers.'
11. Mitchell, *Psychoanalysis and Feminism*, p. 416.
12. Dorothy Dinnerstein, *The Mermaid and the Minotaur*. Dinnerstein's appropriation of Freud, of psychoanalytic theory in general, is highly selective. For example, Freud's metapsychological papers, case studies, major theoretical renderings are all ignored. Only *Civilization and Its Discontents* and *The Future of an Illusion* are mentioned.
13. Ibid., p. 33.
14. Ibid.
15. Sigmund Freud, 'An autobiographical study.'
16. Jeffrey Lustman, 'On splitting.'
17. Ibid., p. 122.
18. Ibid., p. 130. 'It may be that splitting, by permitting oscillating expression of polar clusters of mental content, provides the requisite psychic 'stimulation' through which sustained boundary phenomena initially emerge.'
19. See the discussion of Hobbes in Elshtain, *Public Man, Private Woman*.
20. Dinnerstein, *Mermaid and the Minotaur*, p. 159.
21. Ibid., p. 70.
22. Ibid., p. 210.
23. Ibid., p. 179. In this Dinnerstein is importantly wrong, as I argue below.
24. L.J. Jordanova, 'Natural facts: a historical perspective on science and sexuality.'
25. Ibid., p. 43.
26. Ibid., p. 65.
27. Ibid., p. 67.

28. Talcott Parsons, 'Age and sex in the social structure of the United States,' (1942) in *Essays in Sociological Theory*; and Talcott Parsons, 'The kinship system of the contemporary United States,' (1943) in above.

29. Lawrence Stone, *The Family, Sex and Marriage in England 1500-1800*, p. 416.

30. Nancy Chodorow, *The Reproduction of Mothering. Psychoanalysis and the Sociology of Gender*, p. 9.

31. Ibid., p. 39.

32. Here, for example, is a bit of first-hand empirical evidence Chodorow's functionalist account would have difficulty with. In a recent conversation with three female graduate students I had taught in a political theory seminar at Yale University, I mentioned that when I was a teenager in the rural American West, I loved movies but could go only occasionally because the nearest theatre was 12 miles from our home. But I never got over the impact of certain films, particularly seeing Marlon Brando in 'On the Waterfront' when I was around ten years of age. Overwhelmed by Brando's sexual power, gripped by the tantalizing threat he posed, I, in the parlance of that more innocent time, 'got a crush' on Marlon. But it was not so simple, for I both desired Brando and longed to be Brando. This was not the first, and would not be the last time that I saw myself as, and in, the male character I admired: I, too, could write like Hemingway; I could be as powerful as Brando. I felt constrained in no way whatever by the fact that these were males and I was a female, therefore doomed to identify overwhelmingly with 'Mommy' and to constrain myself thereby. To my astonishment, my graduate students told similar rates. They, too, were puzzled at feminist accounts that tidied up the world of identification with 'objects' by simplistically rigidifying the complexity of cross-sexed identifications.

33. Chodorow, *Reproduction of Mothering*, p. 291. (Emphasis added.)

34. Ibid., p. 8. Chodorow draws uncritically on Gayle Rubin's essay, 'The traffic in women: notes on the "political economy" of sex,' borrowing Rubin's claim, one seriously contested by most anthropologists, including feminists, that women's relegation to domesticity makes them 'less social, less cultural, as well as less powerful than men.' Rubin adopts the notion that women, everywhere, have been 'goods' to exchange and that the sex/gender system was set up to facilitate such exchange. Given that we no longer require this exchange, we can do away with the organization of sex/gender. Within her functionalist rendering, a conclusion emerges, namely, 'eradicating gender hierarchy (or gender itself)'; the dream she finds most compelling is a 'genderless (though not sexless) society, in which one's sexual anatomy *is irrelevant to who one is* . . . ' (204) (Emphasis added.)

35. See Judith Lorber, Rose Laub Coser, Alice S. Rossi and Nancy Chodorow, 'On the reproduction of mothering: a methodological debate', and Jean Bethke Elshtain, 'Against androgyny'.

36. The much-maligned Bowlby remains compelling in his stress on quality of care, though we could, surely, counter the notion that this much be an exclusively female activity. See John Bowlby *Child Care and the Growth of Love*, p. 13, where Bowlby states that the 'quality of parental care is what is of vital importance.'

37. Zelda Bronstein, 'Psychoanalysis without the father,' p. 200.

38. Ibid., p. 207.

39. Peggy Reeves Sanday, *Male Power and Female Dominance*, passim.

40. See Mary Douglas, *Purity and Danger*, passim.

41. Sanday, *Male Power and Female Dominance*, p. 133.

42. Ibid., p. 155.

43. Ibid., p. 176.

44. Diana Grossman Kahn, 'Fathers as mentors to daughters.' Also her 'Daughters comment on the lesson of their mothers' lives.'

45. Louise J. Kaplan, *Oneness and Separateness. From Infant to Individual*, p. 27. Another important consideration, omitted from feminist gender theorists, is the thought and practice of mothering, or, better, the ways of thinking and acting tied to, or flowing from, engaging in mothering practices, in which mothers engage. Mothers' concerns for their children the *meaning* of mothering to mother-subjects themselves, in all its complexity and conflict, must be taken up with cogent empathy and theoretical clarity.

46. Kaplan, *Oneness and Separateness*, p. 51.

47. Ibid., p. 95.

48. One powerfully compelling feminist complaint has been that female children were restricted in early experimentation with their bodies, in 'doing' things physical.

49. Rosalind Gould, *Child Studies Through Fantasy. Cognitive-Affective Patterns in Development*, p. 273.

50. Ibid., p. 274.

51. Myra Bluebond-Langner, *The Private Worlds of Dying Children*, p. 5.

52. Ibid., p. 121.

53. Gareth B. Matthews, *Philosophy and the Young Child*, p. 36.

54. Ibid., p. 86.

55. See Jean Bethke Elshtain, 'Against androgyny.' I would also take account of the work of the philosophers Richard Wollheim, Bernard Williams, and Merleau-Ponty on identity.

56. Sigmund Freud, 'The ego and the id.' Cf. Richard Wollheim, 'The mind and the mind's image of itself,' p. 53.

57. Bronstein, 'Psychoanalysis without the father,' p. 207.

References

Bluebond-Langner, M. (1978). *The Private Worlds of Dying Children*. Princeton University Press.

Bowlby, J. (1965). *Child Care and the Growth of Love*. Penguin Books.

Bronstein, Z. (1980). Psychoanalysis without the father. *Humanities in Society* Vol. 3, No. 3, 199–212.

Chodorow, N. (1978). *The Reproduction of Mothering. Psychoanalysis and the Sociology of Gender*. University of California Press.

Dinnerstein, D. (1977). *The Mermaid and the Minotaur*. Harper.

Douglas, M. (1966). *Purity and Danger*. Routledge and Kegan Paul.

Elshtain, J.B. (1981). Against androgyny. *Telos* 47, 5–22.

Elshtain, J.B. (1981). *Public Man, Private Woman. Women in Social and Political Thought*. Princeton University Press.

Freud, S. (1923). The ego and the id. *Standard Edition* Vol. 19, 12–59.

Freud, S. (1925). An autobiographical study. *Standard Edition* Vol. 20, 7–70.

Freud, S. (1933). *New Introductory Lectures on Psycho-Analysis. Standard Edition* Vol. 22, 5–182.

Freud, S. (1937). Constructions in analysis. *Standard Edition* Vol. 23, 235–270.

Geertz, C. (1973). *The Interpretation of Cultures*. Basic Books.

Gould, R. (1972). *Child Studies Through Fantasy. Cognitive-Affective Patterns in Development*. Quadrangle Books.

Jahoda, M. (1977). *Freud and the Dilemmas of Psychology*. Hogarth Press.

Jordanova, J.L. (1980). Natural facts: a historical perspective on science and sexuality. In C.P. MacCormack and M. Strathern, eds., *Nature, Culture and Gender*. Cambridge University Press.

Kahn, D.G. (1980). Daughters comment on the lesson of their mothers lives. Radcliffe Institute Working Paper, unpublished.

Kahn, D.G. (1981). Fathers as mentors to daughters. Radcliffe Institute Working Paper, unpublished.

Kaplan, J. (1978). *Oneness and Separateness. From Infant to Individual.* Simon and Schuster.

Leacock, E.B. (1977). The changing family and Levi-Strauss, or whatever happened to fathers. *Social Research* 44, 235–289.

Lorber, J., Coser, R.L., Rossi, A.S., and Chodorow, N. (1981). On the reproduction of mothering: a methodological debate. *Signs* 6, 482–515.

Lustman, J. (1977). On splitting. *The Psychoanalytic Study of the Child* 32, 119–145.

Matthews, G.B. (1980). *Philosophy and the Young Child*. Harvard University Press.

Parsons, T. (1964). *Essays in Sociological Theory*. Free Press.

Rubin, G. (1975). The traffic in women: notes on the 'political economy' of sex. In R.R. Reiter, ed., *Toward an Anthropology of Women*. Monthly Review Press.

Sanday, P.R. (1981). *Male Power and Female Dominance*. Cambridge University Press.

Stone, L. (1979). *The Family, Sex and Marriage In England 1500-1800*. Harper Colophon.

Taylor, C. (1967). Neutrality in political science. In P. Laslett and W.G. Runciman, eds., *Philosophy, Politics and Society*, Blackwell.

Taylor, C. (1971). Interpretation and the sciences of man. *Review of Metaphysics* 26, 4–51.

DEPRESSED WOMEN: OUTPOSTS OF EMPIRE AND CASTLES OF SKIN

Sue Holland and Ray Holland

When capitalism was in its infancy the psychological damage inflicted on its labourers was overshadowed by the sheer physical brutality of the workplace. Now that capitalism has passed into its higher and conceivably last stage – imperialism – psychological damage becomes more visible and psychic processes are increasingly recognised as, actually or potentially, processes of domination. One element of this domination can be seen to arise directly from the higher stage of capitalism: racism. For, as Lenin said,

> Monopolies, oligarchy, the striving for domination instead of striving for liberty, the exploitation of an increasing number of small or weak nations by a handful of the richest or most powerful nations – all these have given birth to those distinctive characteristics of imperialism which compel us to define it as parasitic or decaying capitalism.[1]

Exploitation needs justification. Without falling into the Weberian trap of attributing too much importance to ideas, it is possible to read *The Protestant Ethic and the Spirit of Capitalism*[2] as portraying a relationship in which certain religious ideas facilitated the emergence of capitalism, at the same time posing problems for its moral justification. Such justification was found, however, in the notion of primitive, uncivilised and therefore unsaved people whose exploitation could be disguised as a civilising and progressive influence.

Colonialism may not be the only source of racism but it is a powerful one. When the victims of colonialism now meet their fellow oppressed and even their oppressors there is a danger that racist dynamics will become interwoven with interpersonal and intrapsychic dynamics, fuelling and disguising each other in complex interplay.

For many of us it is difficult to conceive of God as black, so fully are we socialised into the fantasy of white supremacy. If we do manage to make that leap it is near certain that we fall at the next psychic hurdle – to conceive of him as a woman. Put together these two powerful forces – racism and the oppression of women – and the mixture is explosive. It may explain the phenomenon, in certain places within a mother country into which various colonial groups have been admitted, when considered economically desirable or politically unavoidable, of personal relationships mobilising a range of sociopsychological forces beyond the understanding of the participants. In these relationships, hatred and aggression may quickly turn into self-hatred and self-damage because the participants do not know who the real enemy is. History is not on their side and neither is God.

The study that follows is based on cases encountered in a psychotherapeutic project which has strict boundaries in two senses. Firstly, the project is located in a small, geographically distinct area of London and accepts referrals only from within that area. Secondly, it is confined to cases of depression in women. Such a focus is partly chosen and partly dictated: chosen, because depressed women in inner city areas carry problems resulting from an interplay of psychic misery and external pressures; dictated, because these days only clearly defined projects of help and prevention find access to funds.

The challenge of relating personal misery to its environment, history and political context is clearly evident in the choice of problem and in the strategy adopted for dealing with it. The aim is to give full weight both to the personal aspects of depression in the light of psychoanalytic theory and to the contextual factors by means of sociopolitical analysis.

Before entering the clinical material, which loses richness and force when stated with all its necessary but tedious qualifications, we acknowledge our limitations. The cases encountered have passed through a series of self-selected and institutionally imposed filters which may have rendered them atypical. Our intuitive claims about their wider significance of course await further research. A second problem arises from the nature of our subject matter: it is that any reference to the consequences of being black, white, a woman or a man may touch on the stereotypes which underly racism and sexism. We cannot avoid these consequences, since they are the very stuff of which many of the following interactions are made. To refer to such consequences is neither to condone nor accept them as natural, inherent qualities of race and gender differences.

The most dangerous pitfall awaiting psychoanalytic accounts of human distress, however, is that the delving into fundamental processes of early life can be misread as an effort to reduce socio-psychological problems to biological problems, with all the mystifying and oppressive consequences of such a strategy. Peter Fuller[3] has met similar problems in seeking to account for aesthetic judgements which are not reducible totally to the categories of a bourgeois ideology but derive from more basic childhood experiences of fusion and separation.

We have not yet learned to construct theories or texts that are fully insulated against perverse reading. Foolproof texts are as yet not available since nothing is proof against a perfect fool. All we can do is mention these typical misreadings and then get on with the job of describing certain themes which have emerged in a project which knows its limitations yet has something new to report.

Depression and Relationships

Our study is concerned with depressed women and their 'significant' others – husbands, lovers, children, parents etc. Depression, most psychoanalytic theories would claim, springs from feelings about others who are important, indeed vital, to our survival. Awareness that the parent is separate from the self – and can therefore abandon – is the first step towards sociability and concern for others, but also the terrors of separation anxiety and depression. It is also the point at which the earlier and more primitive defence of 'splitting' is replaced by 'repression' in the classical sense.[4]

Object relations theory names this stage of development of self the 'depressive position', a crucial situation which must be experienced in order to 'grow up'; which in social terms means to be civilised. From the mental health point of view, can the 'clinically depressed' person then be considered *over*-civilised? Depressed women do seem overly concerned to be approved of and accepted by a 'significant' or 'dominant' other. That 'significant' person's sudden exit or betrayal may precipitate a suicide attempt, oblivious to the pulls of children or friends. Perhaps a better way of describing their situation is to say that they are oversocialised into the too-dependent role of woman in modern society and that therefore depression is a likely consequence of the normally occurring losses which make up a typical life cycle.

Research into the 'social origins' of depression by Brown and Harris[5] suggests that one key factor which makes women vulnerable to depression is the lack of an intimate and confiding relationship with a male sexual partner. This factor – along with the other 'vulnerability' factors of losing a mother before the age of 11, having three or more children under 14 years at home, and lacking paid employment – is more likely to be found in a working class population. So is it that the woman is not able to select 'intimate and confiding' partners? Is it that something about her inhibits her partner from being intimate and confiding? Or is it that working class males are not socialised to express themselves in such a manner?

These possibilities do not exclude each other. Many depressed working class women complain that their sexual partners cannot 'talk' to them: they tend not to use the more middle class expression, 'communicate', but the meaning is the same. The women are often expansively verbal themselves and have a huge need for social contact and reassurance through words. They are frequently seen by their men as being 'all mouth'; domestic arguments may terminate in the man's battering the woman simply because physical force is a mode in which the man can 'win' the argument. Many of the women can recall a childhood in which father's physical abuse or injury of mother was experienced as an aspect of their sexual intercourse. They could derive from this no image of a tender and expressive *spouse-confidante* on which to model their present adult longing. Some do recall their mothers as 'good', yet betraying and forsaking them in favour of father's demands. So where does this ideal image of an understanding, confiding parent-spouse spring from? It could perhaps come from their longing for the attentive, child-reflecting mother who was otherwise distracted. Their experience of their parents' lack of a tender love strengthens them in their determination to find the loving *confidante* of their conscious ideal, but their *actual* choice of partners often sabotages this goal.

Fairbairn's concept of the Central Ego-Ideal Object alliance describes this self-sabotage in terms of psychic structure. The Ideal Object and the Central Ego comprise good ('accepted') representations which remain in consciousness after the bad ('rejected') part-objects and their affiliated bad part-self-representations are relegated to the unconscious.[6] The trouble with rejected part-objects and part-self-representations is that, although relegated to the unconscious, they continue to find expression in the behaviour and experience of the adult. One of the rejected part-self-representations, the experience created by 'rejecting others', persists in the unconscious as an 'internal saboteur' attacking and undermining libidinal choices. The other rejected part-self-representation is the Libidinal Ego, created by attachment to exciting others who in the nature of the caretaker-child relationship cannot satisfy the child's libidinal needs. The Libidinal Ego adds unrealistic intensity to the conscious ideal of a *spouse-confidante*, only to bring into play the aggressive forces of the internal saboteur, and producing an overdemanding attitude which at the same time is doomed to defeat in its unrealistic aims. The result is neither a balance nor cancelling out of conflicting forces, but an intense dynamic generating extremes of behaviour, mood and psychosomatic disturbance.

Splitting and Race

Fairbairn's account of 'rejected' and 'accepted' part-objects and their part-self-representations is a powerful model for describing the depression of some white and black women, and their sexual relationships with black men from certain colonial cultures. 'More than one, less than two' is an expression from the Kama Sutra which conveys the enraptured merging of ego-selves in sexual union. It could also be a more cynical description of the working class white woman's relationship to her black co-habitee and father of her children. The woman is not self-sufficiently and independently single, as are many of her black sisters, but nor does she feel confident that she is in a mutually dependent partnership with the man. The relationship is constantly on trial, comparison being made in the minds of each partner with imagined white husbands/lovers and black/wives/mistresses – 'my people', 'your people'. Each hides from the other the secret of having been rejected by or rejecting their own people. Past family relationships and national and cultural histories have propelled them towards each other, at the same time putting down the roots of a terrible repulsion. Sexual desire, stimulated by the 'forbidden' strangeness of the other, is sabotaged by the absence of affection and tenderness for the other's people: the fact of their own deep racism. The classical Freudian hysterical split between sexual desire and tender love is expressed in the meeting of two national histories, in which the humiliation and guilt of white domination outside is assuaged by black domination in the bedroom. At the same time, the woman's guilty desire for a lost white father who was both exciting and hateful (because rejecting) can find its object in the disguise of a black face, a black lover. Exciting and rejecting at the same time, the original object of this contradictory love has long since been buried, walled up within the psyche, but yet appears in the disguised form of her lover.

The children of these white/black unions, in the beauty of childhood, are poignant symbols of a wished-for social harmony between the parents. Yet the psychological struggle is continuous and intensifies as parents wait to see the 'choice' the children will make in response to the inevitable question 'Who am I?' Of course, there *is* no real choice, as the children are already labelled 'half-caste', a term at worst humiliating and at best meaningless. They are pushed toward the only tolerable and self-respecting stance – that of identification with their black fathers. They adopt Afro hairstyles or dreadlocks, speak in *patois* and move easily among black friends.

The white women who raised them, usually single-handedly and with what they now see as little thanks, are bereft, with a deep feeling of rejection and anger. Mrs X, an Irishwoman in her mid-40s, speaks of her black lover and her young-adult children: "When they are all in the sitting room playing their Boom Boom music, I feel I can't go in because I'm the wrong colour!" The women now feel separated and distant from their children, which may re-awaken their first, terrible experiences of rejection in childhood, to which they responded with the rebellious rejection of mother. Loss upon loss. They cannot now return to their 'own people'; they have burnt their boats. Miss Y, an Irishwoman in her mid-50s who has brought up four sons by black lovers who left her long ago, went 'home' to Ireland recently on a holiday. She had hoped to re-unite with her ageing father and her brothers and sisters. She received a cold welcome and returned abruptly. She believes they disapproved of her black children and the fact that she never married. She disapproves also but cannot admit this to herself. The fear of future loneliness is terrible for these women, and is compounded by the belief that 'Black men don't want you once you can't have children or can't work for your living.' The situation and the feelings are intolerable, and the women's escape is into depression. (Mrs X is kept on repeat prescriptions of the tranquilliser Ativan by her GP as he does not see her depression. Miss Y was admitted to hospital and given a course of electro-convulsive therapy.)

It is too painful for these women to acknowledge consciously their realisation at some level that they have made a sexual and parental union with the incarnation, in disguised form, of the exciting and rejecting parental figure of their childhood whom they renounced in disgust. Their consoling daydream is that they are looking for, or awaiting, the kindly caring man of their conscious fantasies. This ego-ideal is patched together from the bearable fragments of their childhood experience plus a rag-bag of other real and imagined experiences, some stimulated by the mass media, some by the religious teaching of their culture.

Miss Z complains that her black lover and father of her youngest child doesn't sit around together with her five children 'like a real family'. She longs for the kind of family life depicted in the Ovaltine advertisements on television. For many years she has been depressed, but in a 'hidden' way, and people know her as a very jolly person. Following her recent sterilisation, however, her depression broke through the surface. Miss Z's family of childhood split up when she was 7 and her mother ran off with a younger man. Her father raised her and her brother, and was furious when she became pregnant by a West Indian at the age of 16 (he was strongly anti-black). She and her father grudgingly forgave each other on his deathbed but she cannot forgive her now old and dying mother and is repulsed by the woman's cringing pleas for affection and reconciliation. Yet her own disgust and hostility appal her, and she is overwhelmed by floods of tears when she speaks of her mother. Miss Z is warm and loving to her children, and a pillar of strength and humour to her friends and neighbours who come with all their problems, which serves to distract her from her sadness. With her black lover, as with her mother, she finds it difficult to express tender and dependent feelings, preferring to adopt a brisk and jokey style. When hurt and angered by him she arms herself with racist epithets, but protests with militant fury against any racist innuendo from outsiders.

Women Amongst Women

White women whose lovers and fathers of their children are black display strong comradeship and interest in each other which they often use in sisterly ganging-up against their menfolk. They commiserate with each other on the trials and degradation of their lot as black men's women. Indeed they often try to extend their sisterly feeling to black women. (This is not always reciprocated by the black women, however, who show a lofty pity for them rather than the competitive disapproval which the white women expected.) The black single woman and parent, in her militant independence from the father(s) of her children, is often an object of admiration and envy for the white single parent who is frequently berated by her black lover for being weak and stupid in comparison to strong and clever black women. For these black women have a long cultural history which has tempered and strengthened their independence from men. Migration from the West Indies has given them opportunities to be independent from men which they did not have back home, such as Supplementary Benefit and day nurseries. In addition, generations of colonial enslavement and neo-colonial 'under-development' have taught them to adapt to the absence of fathers and husbands. This they have in common with their white Irish sisters. Also like them, the real well-spring of their depression, when it comes, is not their dislocation from their men (though this is the form it takes), but rather the seemingly infinite distance that separates them psychologically from their mothers, who left them in the care of grandparents while they migrated in search of jobs. The reunions which followed, months or years later, were not the loving homecomings so fondly imagined but rather the meetings of strangers preoccupied by grief for lost grandparents or distracted by new sexual liaisons and financial burdens. Bitterness and resentment were all that could be found to bridge the yawning distance of lost love.

Miss A, a West Indian woman, recalls how she was brought over to England to rejoin her mother when she was a teenager. She did not remember her mother and felt only hatred for her: her mother would beat her because she would not show her affection. She was taken into care in a children's home. Some women with this sort of history feel an aching rage for their mothers which haunts them when they face their own daughters, making them dread that the same rage will spring up in their daughters' hearts against *them*. They swear to themselves that their daughters' upbringing will be different. They struggle to give their daughters a motherly love, the inner blue-print for which they have constructed partly from their imagination and partly from true memories of their grandmothers' care of them.

Their children are black and will not reject them as not-black, but ironically they themselves, in hating their mothers, are expressing the self-hatred of black women. White women in general are seen as more kind, more likeable, not as 'angry'. Deference to white superiority is internalised in a dependency which assumes that white people will be more kind and helpful than their own. This dynamic is adopted as a conscious attitude which may confuse and undermine their children's self-assurance, a dynamic reinforced by the white schools' cultural dominance.

Conscientisation

The Barbadian novelist George Lamming finds an exemplar of this kind of self-hatred in the psychology of the black overseer.

> Occasionally the landlord would accuse the overseers of conniving, of slackening on the job, and the overseers who never risked defending themselves gave vent to their feelings on the villagers who they thought were envious and jealous and mean. Low-down nigger people was a special phrase the overseers had coined. The villagers were low-down nigger people since they couldn't bear to see one of their kind get along without feeling envy and hate. This had created a tense relationship between the overseer and the ordinary villager. Each represented for the other an image of the enemy . . . Like children under the threat of hell fire they

> accepted instinctively that the others, meaning the white, were superior, yet there was always the fear of realizing that it might be true. This world of the other's imagined perfection hung a dead weight over their energy.[7]

But what Lamming does not convey is how the experience of maternal separation can *intensify* the self-hatred which he has located in the divisive exploitation of the black by white colonial ownership and control. The political and economic fact of migration to Britain has created separations between mothers and children which go on to become the psychological root of self-hatred, and rejection of their black mothers, and, consequently, self-hatred of themselves as mothers. They cannot forgive their mothers and cannot forgive themselves.

Depression is one expression of this hatred. The black woman's disowning of her mother's love and her self-love, which has come about through maternal separation, is the intra-psychic expression of that familiar technique of 'divide and rule' which colonised people have been subject to for generations of British domination. When that technique is resisted by colonised people in favour of collective identity and solidarity, the result is nationalist struggle and liberation. But when such divisive splits are not consciously rejected but psychically internalised, the consequence is self-hatred. Sexual and child-rearing partnerships between colonised peoples – blacks and whites, men and women – illustrate fear of and revenge against parental abandonment, the struggle for domination over the other, sexual desire sabotaged by disgust; and the punishing, persecuting religious and racialist mythology which always lies waiting close to the surface.

There is now clearly a question of mental health at risk. Individualistic psychotherapy focuses not on the global struggles between imperialism and subjected peoples, but on the microcosm of marriage and the family within which those global forces are transformed as intra- and inter-psychic relations. Enemies *internalised* can be fought by the method of self-struggle which is mapped out, though only partially, by Fairbairnian object-relations theory and therapy. On the other hand, a comprehensive therapy must include not only a recalling of repressed, 'rejected' part-objects and part-self-representations, but *also* 'conscientisation' (as Paolo Freire[8] calls it) concerning people's own historical roots through which, for instance, a mother's failing and rejection can be understood in its political and economic context. Here, paradoxically, the religious orientation of Rastafarians restores pride in black identity but reasserts male superiority and domination.

The Irishwoman's desolation at finding herself stranded, between a past she has forfeited and her black children's rejection of her identity, must lead her to seek a somewhat similar path out of her depression. Psychodynamically she must bring into consciousness the desolate rejection she felt at the hands of a preoccupied mother, and the confusing sexual excitement and hatred for a father which drove her into the arms of a 'forbidden' black stranger. In addition, conscientisation will inform her of the religious, political and economic forces which served to keep her parents trapped in a cage of sexual repression, uncurbed procreation, and self-destructive alcoholism, from which she took precipitous flight. Her own deep racism, instigated by her white culture, must be acknowledged as the very fuel which gave sexual excitement to her liaison with her black partner, but which at the same time inhibits the mutual expression of tenderness and caring which she so desires.

References

1. Lenin, V.I. (1970). *Imperialism, the Highest Stage of Capitalism*. Foreign Languages Press, Biejing.

2. Weber, M. (1930). *The Protestant Ethic and the Spirit of Capitalism*. Allen & Unwin.

3. Fuller, P. (1980). *Art and Psychoanalysis*. Writers and Readers.

4. Rinsley, D.B. (1979). Fairbairn's object-relations theory: a reconsideration in terms of newer knowledge. *Bulletin of the Menninger Clinic* 43, 489–514.

5. Brown, G. and Harris, T. (1978). *Social Origins of Depression*. Tavistock.

6. Fairbairn, W.R.D. (1952). *Psychoanalytic Studies of the Personality*. Routledge & Kegan Paul.

7. Lamming, G. (1970). *In the Castle of My Skin*. Longman.

8. Freire, P. (1970). *Cultural Action for Freedom*. Penguin, 1972.

RATIONALISATION AND THE FAMILY

Joel Kovel

In Kafka's *Trial*, K. succeeds in proving to the Priest that the Doorkeeper who keeps the man from approaching the Law is no more than a simpleton. The Priest, however, objects. No one has the right to pass judgement on the Doorkeeper, for he serves the Law; to doubt his dignity is to doubt the Law itself. K. fights back:

> "I don't agree with that point of view . . . for if one accepts it, one must accept as true everything the Doorkeeper says. But you yourself have sufficiently proved how impossible it is to do that." "No," said the Priest, "it is not necessary to accept everything as true, one must only accept it as necessary." "A melancholy conclusion," said K. "It turns lying into a universal principle."[1]

True enough . . . and melancholy enough. Kafka is describing the predicament of those trapped by rationalized, lucid madness – the world of modern administration. To the extent that his vision is true, i.e., to the degree that the administrative mode is totalized, people living in this mode are as insects caught in the web of a spider to whose power they cannot help but aspire. This is not an encouraging picture, nor is it the picture of man Marx had in mind. Yet, it contains a deep human truth, one which may tell us something about the failure of the left and of the radical consciousness in general in advanced capitalist societies.

The inertia of the masses cannot be comprehended on a purely objectivistic level. No matter how relentless may be the social structures that culminate in a net of economic domination, one is yet left with the question: why do some – perhaps most – people knuckle under, while others resist? In other words, there is no quantum of social coercion. Whatever is set up to exert such coercion – and this would include the entire output of the culture industry, the educational apparatus, etc. – has to act through an individual subjectivity that, multiplied without end, comprises the mass. It has to *mean* something to that subjectivity; and, depending on what it means and how the specific subject is constituted, coercion either produces compliance or resistance. Viewed from this end of the process, the 'inertia of the masses' can be rephrased as the failure of an *historical* subject to develop from the *individual* subject. To study this failure, one must examine the historical emergence of that individual subject, in all its weakness and reproducibility. And one must study it in light of the notion of administration, for it is by this mode that history is delivered to the individual, much as medicine is administered to a patient.

What unites all the elements of social coercion in an historical totality is their formal subjugation to the administrative mode, their gathering by the tentacles of a universal bureaucracy. Ultimately, this inhuman process is made by and for humans. If the revolutionary spirit is gone, its elements have been seized and held hostage by administration. Adorno's phrase, 'The totally administered society', arid and impersonal as it may appear, nevertheless strikes a chord of terror. There is something both desolate and diabolic about the idea. We know that this is the heart of the matter: a heart of heartlessness, an icy rationality that paralyses the will and numbs the senses. What we are not able to comprehend is the point of historical mediation between a labyrinth with its endless chambers, their lurid green walls pasted over with yellowing memoranda, their flickering fluorescent lights, stacks of forms and pockmarked bakelite counters – and the humans who line up quiescently behind them and succumb to its will.

For present purposes I shall use a set of congeneric terms, e.g., administrative mode, bureaucratic rationality, etc., to describe a peculiar way public life is delivered to persons within the terms of contemporary capitalist society. The mode is no discrete form, but a dialectical compound of an established reasonableness and fairness on the one hand, and a certain mysterious inexorability on the other. It is designed to be sensibly pleasant but never totally gratifying, to provide a rationalized type of stimulation and a notion of order. And, finally, it seems perfectly transparent and banal, yet invariably gives the impression of unseen forces at work. This is partly the result of a high degree of technological elaboration, and partly the function of the extreme degree of alienation and division of labour characteristic of bureaucratic rationalization. The notion is not confined to bureaucracies as such, but pervades mass media, health care, and other facets of contemporary life. The mode, in short, is superficiality of style with a deep hidden content. Although the bureaucratic mode serves the economic requirements of capital

– notably by exerting some predictable control over the productivity of the work force and by regulating the consumption of commodities – there can be no doubt that it exerts a systematic cultural influence that transcends mere economistic considerations. Indeed, administration infiltrates every pore of personal existence. And by personal existence we mean life with other people, beginning with the family.

As Walter Benjamin[2] pointed out, one is never left in doubt that Kafka's fathers are right and have reason on their side – no matter how monstrous, filthy, seedy, and stupid they also happen to be. The capture of desire completes the triumph of administration. For after K.'s melancholy conclusion, he wearies of disputation and paces alongside the Priest, fearful of becoming 'utterly dependent' upon him. The priest tells him how to leave the cathedral – and now K. panics. ' "I can't find my way about in this darkness . . . don't you want anything more from me? . . . you let me go as if you cared nothing about me . . . " "I belong to the Court," replies the Priest. "So why should I want anything from you? The Court wants nothing from you. It receives you when you come and it dismisses you when you go." '

In love, the weaker is the one who loves the more. Administration wants nothing from anybody; hence it remains the stronger so long as a glimmer of desire comes toward it from the human subject who is its object. And administration wants nothing because it is constituted by the negation of desire. Desire presupposes a subject. It is the vector between the subject and some lost portion of the object world – real or imagined. Bureaucracy, however, is created insofar as subjectivity is wrung out of social intercourse. It is what is left behind: 'rationalization,' if one takes an ahistorical view; administrative domination if one thinks dialectically.

As Heydebrand has recently argued,[3] bureaucratic organizations, far from being the 'abstract march of functional rationality', always embody the fundamental contradictions of capitalist society even as they raise those contradictions to new historical levels. From this standpoint, bureaucratic rationalization always has one superordinate meaning, namely, to increase the productivity of labour. Consequently, it drags along with it all of the contradictory moments inherent in the notion of productivity and the labour process.

In order to turn labour into a commodity, the worker must be objectified so that his activity can be placed into a calculable set of relations out of which surplus value can be extracted. At the same time, some modicum of subjectivity must thrive in order for value to exist at all. In concrete terms, workers must retain enough of a mind so that they may sell labour-power on the market as well as exercise some degree of choice in the consumption of commodities. Without these two ends of the economic process, capital would cease to circulate. Consequently the existence, not to mention the expansion, of capital depends upon the combined maintenance of a ruthless objectification and the cultivation of a certain degree of subjectivity. But such a combination is inherently explosive. For, by permitting the coexistence of subjectivity and objectification, capital becomes vulnerable to the adventitious development of genuine rationality as well as transcendent desire. In other words, capital necessarily permits the germination of what, sufficiently developed, could destroy it. Nothing is more important for its survival than the thwarting of such a development. But this cannot be done automatically. People will not spontaneously accept the cultural terms of capitalist expansion; nor can anything so irrational be taught directly. The terms must be mediated so that stunted forms of human development can be passed off as the apex of human nature. In this struggle, administration becomes capital's stoutest legion.

Bureaucratic rationalization may then be read as the more or less continuous attempt to manage the inter-relationship between the subjectivity and the objectification required by capital. It does so by mediating its peculiar brand of rationality – one that strips desire from subjectivity, as it 'humanizes' objectification, i.e., tries to make it fair and equitable, while retaining a semblance of rational objectivity. Since the instruments of bureaucracy are constituted by the elimination of desire while the human subjects to whom they relate remain passionate, the conditions for bureaucratic domination are therefore automatically established. The question remains as to how these conditions become invested with desire, terror, and necessity.

In the immediate experience of life, the notion of necessity is rooted in the family – to be more exact, in those primitive intra-familial images of self and others that congeal into the matrix of subjectivity. And since as Kafka held, everything must merely be accepted as necessary for bureaucratic domination to exist, the alignment of the matrix of family relations must be secured within the prevailing conception of necessity.

The notion of necessity described here is quite phenomenologically distinct from that allowed by ordinary consciousness and factored into political economy. The latter is experienced as an imperative stemming from the outside world; it is rooted in an appreciation of the self's relation to that outer world; and it is felt in a framework of linear, sequential time, no matter how brief the interval. The structure of such necessity is generally of an 'if-then' nature. 'If I wish to survive, then I had better step out of the way of that oncoming truck.' Or, from the economic sphere: 'If I wish to retain my unemployment benefits, then I had better see to it that I am paid under the table for that free-lance job.' The logic of this form of necessity varies from reflex to calculation; it can be readily assimilated into the prevailing reality principle.

But this notion of necessity is not what Kafka's Priest had in mind; nor is it sufficient in itself to lock people into the order of things. There is another, more primary experience of necessity that does not arise from the outer world, although, significantly enough, it may be projected onto the outer world and be experienced as arising there. It rather emerges from a stratum of 'deep' subjectivity – 'deep' in the sense of being 'thing-like', beneath verbalization, without 'if-then' qualities, outside ordinary time sequence and essentially unconscious, although with a certain degree of determinable structure. The pressure of this stratum into consciousness – and hence its phenomenological surface – is experienced as a murky yet peremptory urging; and the structure of this urging is given by the archaic mental traces of original caretaking others as they had been experienced by the infant through his or her body. Since this quality of necessity is suffused with desire for an outer source of power, and since the model for such a power was once a parent, it may be said that the family supplies a trans-historical substructure for the possibilities of domination. One says *trans-historical* because the structure is an outcome of a universal human disposition: in this case, infantile helplessness and the need for attachment. To this extent, we are introducing 'biological' considerations, although we are dealing with a piece of nature that confers no determinancy and, indeed, sees to it that the nucleus of the human psyche is imaginary.

The family, then, is no 'base' for historical domination. History neither abolishes nor is based on the trans-historical but is a continual transformation of it. If it should turn out that transactions with the mother are responsible for the primary experience of necessity, this does not make mothers responsible for historical domination (although it might help account for the profound and decisive fear of women which enters into the history of patriarchal domination).[4] Similarly, though men in fact rule in patriarchal-dominative orders up to and including capitalism, this does not make fathers as such responsible for the woes of family life. A much more complex account is needed to comprehend the relations between the personal microsphere and the societal macrosphere[5] than has yet been forthcoming from radical thought. Certainly, Marxism continues to flounder for lack of such an articulation.

Marx recognized that the self is an 'ensemble of social relations',[6] and that we construct our beings out of the ways we are with others, but he did not appreciate – and this became a particularly weak point in his system – that the self does not spring up all at once like Athena, but passes from an undifferentiated primordium through a number of intermediary stages, all of which are dragged along and play vital roles in later developments. The first apprehension of self is of the reflection made by the infant in the eyes and gestures of the primary caretaking parent – an object that, for historical as well as biological reasons, generally happens to coincide with the mother. Before there is a well-structured 'I' who can position him or herself with respect to the outer world and so enter the realm of economic necessity, there is the proto-self composed of the initial products of differentiation from the primordium. We may regard these products as comprising an elementary contradiction between the nameless urging that stems from the activity of the infant's organism, and the named construction that stems from incorporating the other's recognition. The former is a matter of sensation, the latter of an internalized perception; the energy comes from within, the form from without; and though they do not go together in nature, it is the job of the nascent self to put them together in its own realm, that of the psyche. In this fashion the primary or narcissistic self arises, the self as other, the self in which the subject fuses itself from a thing-like element drawn from its own bodily urge and an elementary word, or name, that belongs to the other.[7] When this fundamental elaboration of the self begins, individuals are readied for historical participation; insofar as it is ever completed, they become full historical agents.[8]

We may study the primitive manifestations of this organization with the aid of psychoanalysis which, by withdrawing the object of inter-subjective dialogue from view, succeeds in decomposing the screen of ordinary language and in revealing the fundamental structures of subjectivity. Based upon these findings we can generalize that, for each human subject, there is a level beneath which the person can re-experience the empty unstructuredness of an original craving fused with the assignment of agency or structure to an unspecified other. Now this is a frightening and risky position, and in ordinary waking experience, tends to become sealed off – i.e., repressed – rather quickly. The mode of repression is itself a historically specific act which reflects the individual's internalization of the prevailing mode of social relations.[9] From a somehat different angle, this means that repression achieves a synthetic unity between the most elementary properties of the self and the externally established system of domination: in this case, bureaucratic administration. Between these faces of the unity lie the intermediary structures of everyday life and their subjective correlates – more specifically, subjective registration of the family, which coincides, in the most general sense of that term, with the Oedipus complex. In other words, no individual can react to any social force without bringing in all the particulars of his or her individual history. No matter how ant-like the denizens of an administered society may essentially be, each ant moves according to a 'physiology' which is given by personal history. Within any concrete historical situation, all these elements are involved, although the particular conjunction of historical forces may bring one or another feature to the fore.

A brief psychological digression may be in order here. One is accustomed in psychoanalysis to distinguish between two broad phases of infantile mental development, the preoedipal and the oedipal. The former generally coincides with the oral and anal stages of psychosexual development, and the latter, with the phallic and genital phases. However, the essential nature of preoedipal and oedipal phases does not reside in the sexual sphere as such, but rather in the orientation between the self and others in the world. In brief, preoedipal relations are *dyadic* in quality, while those of the oedipal period are *triangulated*. In the former, the self is related to another (generally the mother) into whom it can be more or less fully absorbed. As a corollary to this, the subjective boundaries of the preoedipal self are blurred *vis à vis* the world and its own body.[10] By contrast, the oedipal child has achieved a reasonably clear distinction (subject to numerous lapses throughout life) in relation to the body. Further, the other becomes *others*: there is always a third (classically, father alongside mother) – and beyond this third, an endless elaboration of others in increasingly intricate patterns. It is for this reason that the Oedipus complex can be said to be the subjective registration of the family as well as the mediation between infantile life and social existence. However real the distinction between preoedipal and oedipal phases, of equal importance is their interpenetration: the more deeply one studies an individual, the more problematic becomes any discrete segregation of mental elements into one phase or the other. In particular, one becomes impressed with the tendency of what seems oedipal to dissolve into its preoedipal forerunners. It often seems as if real participation in the world of discrete individuals – i.e., civil society – is necessary to keep the individual from sliding backward into a narcissistic pool of merger with an undifferentiated other. In any case, people seem considerably more vulnerable to manipulation around this point than had previously been realized by psychoanalytic students of society, who had made the Oedipus complex the *alpha* and *omega* of psychosocial transactions. There is a sense in which they were right, since oedipal relations remain the point of intersection between the individual and the many discrete figures of society. However, once entry into subjectivity has been attained, a dialectic between oedipal and preoedipal takes over in which it often seems as if the more primitive layers are the decisive ones.

In other words, the Oedipus complex does not in itself account for the subjective mediation of domination, but is joined with, and indeed rests upon, a more fundamental preoedipal mental organization that has to do with the origins of the psyche itself out of object loss. It is this original function that supplies the universal – i.e., 'biological' or trans-historical – quality to the situation; whereas the oedipal configuration is the inward reflection of the given historical state of the family and of relations of production in general. The Oedipal structures are no less critical for being yoked to more primitive preoedipal functions. But their importance is linked with that of history itself as well as with the previously outlined universal and trans-historical core of subjectivity. Viewed from the angle of history, the Oedipal structures are the shadow cast by the fathers who seized control of society at the dawn of historical time. Viewed from the angle of a transhistorical subjectivity, however, Oedipus, his forebears and his descendants are all hedges against self-dissolution and merger. Combining the two views, we may say that historical domination has been supported and reinforced by what it negates, i.e., a return to certain anxieties attendant upon the primary condition of the self.

These considerations do not make the real position of mothers irrelevant, either as transmitters or victims of historical process. Aside from their position in the oedipal configuration (which is where children generally learn the key lessons about the role of the sexes in society), the actual behaviour of the mother in the preoedipal phase plays an enormous role in the future development of the child. The seeds of resistance as well as acquiescence are sown in the first phase of life. Indeed it seems to me that the refusal of history, which is after all the fount of the revolutionary impulse, is instituted in the preoedipal – and presymbolic – experience of fusion with the mother. Being presymbolic, this experience belongs to the transhistorical, i.e., is removed from the historical system of significations. But the transhistorical is no more an absolute category than the historical. Beyond good and evil, it still only survives under specific historical circumstances, as babies only survive in a given family which shapes and is shaped by them.

It is not easy to pinpoint the central attitude of capitalist society, to say when it began, when it achieved hegemony, or whether it is still in a process of development. For present purposes let us agree to see it as a more or less ruthless universalization of an objectifying attitude. This, finally, is responsible for the mystique of productivity and economism since, by stripping the world of value, it leaves human activity nowhere to go than to work upon lifeless matter. What most critics of this development have overlooked, however, is its irrational core and mediations in everyday life. Despite appreciation of the irrationality of the attitude in its overall historical context, it is somehow assumed that objectification is itself a position rationally chosen and held. There is a confusion here between a transhistorical need to objectify, i.e., to realize needs and subjective wishes by transforming the historical world, and the perversion of this function which occurs under capitalism and is specific to it.

In terms of the above discussion concerning the deeper structures of subjectivity, it may be possible to make some headway into the problem through a consideration of the history of the family under capitalism. Here one essential development stands out as characteristic of the entire era in its effects upon personal life: the relentless separation between so-called productive work and domestic life.

This is not the place, nor have I the qualifications, to develop the history of the bourgeois family in any detail. Let me state as a matter of definition that by the bourgeois family I mean a mode of familial existence specific to capitalist society as a whole, and imposed upon all who contribute to that society. There are important differences between the families of the working and the ruling classes; but all of them are stained with the mark of the totality.

The only point I wish to pursue here is the family's location within the central contradictions of capitalist society. It is perhaps not too sweeping a generalization to claim that the split between productive work and domestic life has cast a longer shadow across personal life than any other historical factor of the entire era.[11] The split has been necessary from the economic side as a means of developing the economic sphere and the primacy of production as such. It was the only way to develop a work force that could be inserted into a calculable system of wages and commodity relations. So long as production had been organized locally and in contact with the rest of personal life, no class hegemony could be established along the lines of economic domination. Once work had been broken from the hearth, however, it could be universalized, along with all its other cultural accoutrements: for example, social mobility, a technical attitude, etc. And once these factors existed at large, they could become the signifying elements for the rising bourgeoisie.

But the bourgeoisie did not pre-exist outside Western history like some nation of Goths hammering on the Roman gates. Rather, it created itself from within European society. Bourgeois self-generation drew on antecedent elements in Western culture; but its specific qualitative distinction did not arise until work had been split from the home. The character of the class – and of subsequent class struggles – became defined by the scission between work and domesticity. To put it slightly differently, it is not productivity as such, or objectification as such, that characterizes the bourgeoisie, except in a symptomatic way. The class has rather drawn its historical dynamic from the dialectic of two aspects of social existence, work and domesticity, that became severed in order that the bourgeoisie might arise.

Focusing for the time being on the domestic side, we can observe several remarkable and contradicting features. First of all, the bourgeois family was from the beginning a *decomposition* of older extended kinship systems that belonged to a precapitalist unity of work and domestic life. This decomposition began in feudal times and is by no means complete. In fact, if one recognizes capitalism's more or less systematic demolition of sustaining features of family life, for example, local rootedness, religious justification or economic necessity, an essential feature of bourgeois society has been to destroy the family as such. If one were to look only at the exigencies of the pure accumulation of capital, the family would be wiped out as an institution – except for those brute 'biological' considerations having to do with the reproduction of the work force that Marx was able to describe in a purely economic way within the framework of *Capital*.[12] Nor can the reality of this destruction be denied: look at any nursing home and see the outcome of family life for those who no longer have their role to play in the circulation of capital.

And yet the bourgeois age is the age of the family in a very real sense – not simply the family as a decayed fragment of metabolic breakdown, but the family as centrepiece of the personal world, the family as location of a desire and intimacy that were not conceptualizable in precapitalist formations, the family that has been called 'nuclear' in the two-fold sense of being the cellular module of social organization and the heart of human emotional life. This latter functional trend inherent in the bourgeois family is no sentimental trifle, nor is it reducible to economic terms – i.e., it cannot be explained simply as a manifestation of the need to stimulate commodity consumption or to develop a highly educated and differentiated work force. If these elements were economically reducible, the capitalist state would not have to worry about its legitimation function – i.e., it could collapse legitimation into accumulation. Instead, the state is beset with a never-ending political struggle based upon the irreconcilable contradiction between those functions, a contradiction in which legitimation is always the weaker, yet never an erasable, element so far as the state is concerned. Hence, the political nature of the struggle.

The legitimation functions are real; they are grounded in bourgeois family existence and they represent the impression made by love on political economy. Splitting work from domestic life did far more than permit the development of a fantastic level of wealth, i.e., of objects of desire: it freed the family from some of the constraints of precapitalist domination.

At the same time, it burdened this new institution – and, in particular, the women within it – with the unmet needs peculiar to the capitalist mode of work, with its systematic alienation. It should be noted that alienation, and not mere brutalization of work, is involved here; and that alienation does not involve a simple degradation of the work process but a more complex function that includes the promise of a higher level of development along with frustration and mystification. In other words, alienated individuals have been exposed to a certain degree of stimulation; they feel at some level the promise of entitlement to better things; and yet they are systematically cut off from any real agency in public or workplace existence. It is this individual who turns to home for the fulfilment of unmet – and historically expected – needs. Typically, this has consisted of the man attempting to reflect the domination experienced at the workplace onto the others at home, while at the same time seeking consolation from his wife. With both power and nurturance alienated away from the workplace, the family has to pick up the cheque at the cost of the woman's individuality. Eventually, the costs are passed all around, appearing at length as neurotic crippling and in character types suitably twisted to conform to capitalist society. There are several themes and innumerable variations, but the basic story remains the same: the conjunction of the historical and transhistorical under capitalism devolves through the family to produce a host of damaged individuals.

And so the bourgeois family is assailed with profound contradictions from the moment of its inception. Its prominence is a product more of these intense contradictory demands than of any supposed 'nuclear' structure it is said to have. A close look at the experience of the bourgeois family would probably disclose that the solidity connoted by the term 'nuclear' is at most a meta-stable resting point in the history of its development; and more likely, just another piece of propaganda. Whatever the duration of the family's stability, it is plain that the forces to which it is subjected would tear it apart if the state did not undertake substantial interventions to patch things up.

One of the casualties of this development deserves some attention: the role of the father, or of patriarchy in general. The classic bourgeois family is patriarchal and it was in such a context that Freud observed the configuration of the Oedipus complex. Yet, at least for the past two centuries, the patriarchal quality of the bourgeois family has been no more than an outer shell steadily hollowed out from within.[13] In this respect, bourgeois patriarchy is like a house nibbled away by termites: it looks fine for quite a while, but then collapses all of a sudden. The hegemony of capital, with its fluid objectification, sounds the knell of patriarchy, even though those who retain power appear for some time to be in the lineage of kings. Capital's ethos of calculating rationality, epitomized in the notion of administration, is antithetical to the spirit of myth in general, and to the Oedipal myth in particular. The arbitrary and capricious will of patriarchy, descended from Abraham and Isaac, yields to fairness, the fact-finding board, and peer review. When Louis XIV boasted that he was the state, he was already protesting too much: the mere fact of having to remind his audience of the identity signalled that a defensive posture was about to be taken toward impersonal administrative forces. Since capital began to win, the real figure of the father has steadily receded. Kafka represents the last gasp of its hold over the imagination, a cry of longing for one who has passed through the door. And with Kafka, the father disappears from Western literature.

What then is the role of the Oedipus complex, and why does patriarchy persist? Is the Oedipus complex, as Freud suspected, ultimately a biological residuum that makes its claim in the face of the historical whittling away of its objective base? Or is there a Lacanian *nom du père*[14] that persists in the structure of language and cognition itself? From extended observation of neurotic and psychotic people, it is clear that oedipal dynamics continue to play a compelling role in their inner mental life; and this role continues to determine a good measure of their active relation to the object world. However, as previously noted, oedipal dynamics cannot be regarded as the exclusive organizing principle of the deeper state of subjectivity. Indeed, with respect to the psyche, they are in a relation homologous to that between patriarchy and administration on the social level: the Oedipus complex being the outer (i.e., closer to consciousness) aspect concealing a more basic and decisive preoedipal organization.

Whether this represents a real historical shift from Freud's time has to remain somewhat speculative at present. Early psychoanalytic formulations, as we know, were almost exclusively oedipal; and Freud himself seemed quite remarkably obtuse on the subject of mothers in general, and the preoedipal relations with mothers in particular.[15] Was this a reflection of that portion of psyche offered up to psychoanalytic investigation at that particular time? And was this a real historical variation or a superficial change? Or did it merely manifest the bias of the analysts, which is itself a historical phenomenon? The question is impossible to answer fully at present (since it begs as well the ever-present factor of the narrow class basis of psychoanalytic discourse).[16] However, whatever the precise contours of the shift in psychoanalytic interest from oedipal to preoedipal dynamics, it seems that a historical force has been at work; and that this force, in its broadest outlines, has had to do with the weakening of actual parental influence in a social order that has remained structured by patriarchy.[17] The early 'oedipal' neurotics Freud studied were by and large people in rebellion against actual fathers who could no longer hold them in check; while today's 'narcissistic' neurotics (who have added to and not replaced the former category) reflect a more general fragmentation of relations with both parents. And as for the bias of the analyst, this has always been a historical factor. It should be recalled for example, that the intense interest in the mother-infant bond did not simply emerge from intrinsically scientific deliberations, but followed the political fortunes of women. As Juliet Mitchell has observed,[18] it was only after World War II allowed great numbers of women access to the public sphere that psychoanalysis began to turn its eyes toward primary human relations.

Freud pointed out that instincts were urges to return to earlier states of things.[19] While this insight was meant in a strictly biological sense, it can only be fully appreciated with respect to the historical – transhistorical dialectic. What is 'instinctual' is a manifestation of that which is transhistorical clinging to what is historically passing away. Given the persistence of patriarchal structures along with the waning of immediate paternal influence, children, from their transhistorical position (which includes somatic givens as well as nurturant familial bonds), conjure up the oedipal parents and relate intrapsychically to them. The instinctual structure stands in an inverse relation to the objective one; and an object is instituted in the mind after it has been lost in reality. Once established intrapsychically, instinctual structures propel the individual to re-find the object in reality. The installation of the Oedipus complex contributes therefore to the persistence of patriarchy. Preoedipal formations, by contrast, are less capable of objective restoration on a social scale, although they structure much of the psychology of love, including its subversiveness. This is because of their dyadic, self-dissolving and protosymbolic qualities.

The loss of real parental influence is associated with an oedipal configuration of fantasy that is intense but incapable of serving as a platform for more mature development. Indeed the individual becomes all too readily suffused with preoedipal fantasy and subject to experiences of personal disintegration. The oedipal fantasies which articulate with these strata of mind are not the classical 'positive' ones of conquest but the 'negative' Oedipus complex of passive yearning for authority.[20] A further propping up by reality is required; and this support both replaces the missing parental influence and articulates symbolically with the negative oedipal fantasies as well as deeper preoedipal ones. It is into this space that administration is inserted, ostensibly a rationalization of the objective disorder of the world, but no less a correlative of the most primitive and thinglike strata of the inner mental world. And it is the conjunction of extremes of rationalization and irrationality that lends administration its sense of mysterious inexorability. It is as though the shadow of love were cast by a most loathsome and heartless suitor.

The essential mode of relation between individuals and the bureaucracy is that of the self toward an undifferentiated other – i.e., it is a relation desired from early infancy, of the self with its primary caretaking object. The triangulation of the oedipal situation yields to the dyad of an original bond; and *capital*, in becoming *post-oedipal*, does so by marshalling that which, in the family, is preoedipal.

Such a development does not take place in a state of happiness. Immediate observation confirms this truth in a compelling way. In its essentials, family life in advanced capitalist society is psychotic. The combination of heightened needs for nurturance with the loss of a material human presence for delivering these needs leads to a situation where the basic tie between the generations is one of psychotic fusion. The essential relation is lack of distinction between the self and other. In an age when increasing individuality is the ruling trend, the child is seen less and less as an individual within the family. The parents are forced to expend huge amounts of emotional energy toward children; yet, lacking social autonomy themselves, they cannot let them go. Children, from their side, feel craving but no structure: in order to preserve sanity, a premature and violent rupture with parents has to be made. The older generation is disparaged and jettisoned, ostensibly with contempt but actually out of fear; for when the parents are approached, ordinary logical relations are suspended and a panicky loss of self, accompanied by extreme hatred, is experienced. Rather than experience this actual state of affairs, a falsified subjectivity arises: the whole panoply of inauthentic personal attitudes that provide the raw material for psychotherapeutic trades.

The distance between generations, combined with a perpetual craving, creates so to speak, vacuoles within personal experience into which the organelles of administration can ever so neatly be inserted. Here at last is a certified source of rationality, not to be valued for itself but as a hedge against madness. The fact that the logic of administration is shadowed by the domination of labour and that it enters as the embodiment of objectification, might make it seem an unlikely candidate for meeting the intense human needs that arise from the crisis of the family. And indeed it is, if needs are taken in a progressive sense, i.e., as what people 'really' need. But in the actual state of disordered subjectivity evoked by contemporary family life, the logic of administration, and the intrusions of the capitalist order in general, play into the given psychological state of affairs.

If the dialectical logic of the unconscious is kept in mind, then someone in the situation outlined above is clearly anything but ready for a full human relation. Indeed, their yearnings, intense as they may be, are primarily a source of anxiety, for they lead back to hatred and to the edge of dissolution. The false subject which represents a lifeline away from this edge demands a false object for its realization; and the instruments of capital, from school curricula and T.V. shows to the bureaucratic logic of corporations and state agencies, are thoroughly tooled to meeting such a need.

The administrative mode provides the objective template upon which the psychoanalytic notion of the *ego* is constructed. This notion, which is a good example of reification in contemporary discourse, depicts the ego as a quasi-independent mechanism capable of mediating – with the ambivalent aid of conscience, or superego – between the 'animal' id within the self and external reality. As recent psychoanalytic critics have pointed out,[21] this idea of the ego is an anthropomorphic fiction that does little justice to the subtleties of mental life. However, although the notion of the ego is extensively reified as a theoretical object, it must be granted that this reification has a certain factual correspondence with personal life within bourgeois society, insofar as the conditions of social existence force upon individuals a profound split between inner and outer life and hence require the development – as a matter of psychological survival – of more or less alienated internal mental agencies. The ego certainly has a mental reality, but it exists as the internalized adaptation to the existing mode of administration. Since it is the imprint of an external social reality that goes its own way antithetical to human desire, the ego (insofar as it can be postulated as a 'thing' within the perimeter of bourgeois relations) is perpetually stretched out to the breaking point between the realms whose mediation it attempts. In this state of crisis, the ego turns to external objects for succour and stabilization; and it is at this juncture that the external social order has seized control. Through the administration of culture, the state sees to it that objects of desire, muted by the pale certification of rationality, are dispensed, whether in the form of muzak, sex-education curricula or professional football. The sign of all these phenomena is the presentation of some deep wish of desire conjugated with the mask of a perfect and ultimate control by an unseen other. A new order of necessity arises. This, then, becomes the fate of the striving for transcendence, which, in unofficial hands, could move toward the revolutionary transformation of society itself.

What we are describing amounts to a *conjugation* between emotional states and objective structures, between desire and instrumental rationality. Each is falsified according to the operation of distinct dynamisms – the dialectic of the family and the commodity, respectively – and each demands of the other respect for its own falsity. Therefore, the conjugation between them is a doubled falsification, the making of 'lying into a universal principle'. The only immediately common feature between the two realms is a sense of power and urgency, Kafka's notion of necessity, not experienced as the apprehension of real relations in the world of space and time but as the inchoate urge towards a distant and receding centre of power. To the extent that such an urge has transhistorical qualities it is reflected in the universal human pull towards transcendence. What characterizes the age of capital, however, is the historicization of the desire for transcendence, its seizure and universalization within a host of material circumstances, from the watching of television to the waiting on line at the neighbourhood bank or supermarket. People are not particularly fascinated by these phenomena. Indeed, what strikes one is the rather low level of libidinal investment characteristic of the conjugation between desire and rationality, compared with more immediate subjective attitudes towards say, one's body or family members. The point is not that people *desire* the administrative mode. It is rather that administration protects them against the desires they cannot stand, while it serves out, in the form of diluted rationalizations, a hint of the desire and power lost to them.

Administrative rationality is nothing that anybody except a small segment of the managerial class is happy about. Indeed, its purpose is not to provide happiness but to offer a dialectical fusion of realistic self-preservation combined with a defence against the deepest anxieties. Since these anxieties are generated by the perpetual crisis of the family, all administration has to do in order to secure a more or less permanently docile population is to keep this crisis going. This task it has undertaken with alacrity, having made the family a prime subject of state concern since the beginning of the century. By thus appearing to be helpful in the human sense, the state manages to destroy the roots of family life and personal autonomy while introducing an endless procession of ego supports in the form of the various helping professions and agencies.[22] The fact that certain individuals may benefit from this arrangement only serves to legitimate it on a large scale – and it is on this large scale that the process of destruction and rehabilitation is carried out.

Thus, administrative rationality has become the great mediating mode between subjective and objective existence. Without creativity, spontaneity, or the capacity to make anybody happy, it becomes the primary glueing force of contemporary culture. As long as it works, there is a rough equivalence between the amount of subjective autonomy it demolishes and the ego supports it provides – and this suffices to keep a reasonably intact population of producers and consumers in line with the prevailing order of things. It is obvious, however, that this state of affairs can never provide more than brief periods of stability for a small segment of the population. And the weakest point is the family. Insofar as the family is so structured as to be unable to match the desires it inculcates with the objects with which it is provided, and insofar as administrative intrusions cannot but in the long run continue the crisis of the family, the present arrangements can be no more than an unstable equilibrium. The system is open to perturbations from any number of angles – from attendant economic shortages to outbursts of unmediable mass-psychological desires and anxieties. In this respect, it should be recognized that the disorders we may expect – the workings on a mass-level of that part of us called id – are the well-springs of resistance no less than acquiescence. The opportunity arises afresh with each child born into the family. For administration, which destroys the autonomy and intimacy that people have become acculturated to need, also continually creates conditions that its own spurious brand of rationalization cannot encompass. By eliminating or otherwise alienating the need for human labour, bureaucratic capitalism leads to an increase in unbound time. It attempts to administer this (mainly through education and the culture industry); but the attempt never succeeds – ultimately because the centre of psychological gravity has shifted to more primitive mental levels. The ground forever erodes under the tread of administration. Watching children watch T.V., one knows they are being dulled, rendered passive, made to numbly accept an unseen administered order . . . but one also senses that the programming never really captures their minds. Some portion of fantasy always escapes, not at all necessarily for better things, but available for something unexpected.

What this will portend I leave to the soothsayers. There are only two considerations for the future I would like to mention in closing. One is the inadequacy of any purely personalistic or family therapy – at least as presently construed – as a way out of the crisis. Whatever individual reconciliation this may offer – and I am not disputing its merit on a personal level – it is plain from the above that no therapy as such can unlock the point of conjugation where the economic order and the state penetrates into personal life. The second consideration follows from the first. It is the necessity of developing a conscious Left strategy, more fully articulated than heretofore, in which the unity of personal and work life can be re-established. This may have to proceed on a concretely microsocial or cellular level for a considerable period of time – time during which an understanding of its generalization to the totality of society can be formulated. The functioning of this strategy is neither to bypass nor reconstruct the family. Neither can be done, for intimate family relations remain a transhistorical given that cannot be avoided, while the notion of reconstruction implies that there once was an ideal family unit to which we must return: a fantasy, understandable in infantile terms, but foreign to a real historical understanding of that perpetually battered foundation of civilization. The job then is not to reclaim but to newly define love, work and the generation of culture free from the tentacles of the state.

Notes

1. Franz Kafka, *The Trial*, p. 243.

2. Walter Benjamin, 'Franz Kafka', in Arendt, ed., *Illuminations*.

3. Wolf Heydebrand, 'Organisational contradictions in public bureaucracies: toward a Marxian theory of organisations'.

4. Cf. Dorothy Dinnerstein, *The Rocking of the Cradle, and the Ruling of the World*.

5. John Fekete, 'Administered society and its culture industry: politics and rationality in science fiction'.

6. Karl Marx, Theses on Feuerbach, VI.

7. Cf. Joel Kovel, 'Things and words'.

8. Lucien Séve developed this concept under the name 'excentration sociale'. Cf. 'Psychoanalyse et materialisme historique', in C. Clement, P. Bruno, L. Sève, *Pour une Critique Marxiste de la Theorie Psychoanalytique*.

9. Wilhelm Reich was the first to pursue this idea systematically. Cf. *Character Analysis*.

10. For a good survey of early self-object differentiation, cf. Margaret S. Mahler, Fred Pine and Anni Bergman, *The Psychological Birth of the Human Infant*.

11. Cf. E.P. Thompson: 'The crime of the factory system was to inherit the

worst features of the domestic system in a context which had none of the domestic compensations.' *The Making of the English Working Class*.

12. Cf. Chapter X, The Working Day, Vol. I, *Capital*, pp. 340–416.

13. Christopher Lasch, *Haven in a Heartless World: The Family Besieged*.

14. Jacques Lacan, *Ecrits*.

15. Philip Slater, *The Glory of Hera*.

16. Michael Schneider, *Neurosis and Civilisation*.

17. Alexander Mitscherlich, *Society without the Father*.

18. Juliet Mitchell, *Psychoanalysis and Feminism*.

19. Sigmund Freud, 'Beyond the pleasure principle'.

20. Sigmund Freud, 'From the history of an infantile neurosis'. See Editor's Note, p. 6, *Standard Edition*.

21. Cf. Merton Gill and Philip Holzman, eds. *Psychology vs. Metapsychology*. Also, William Grossman and Bennett Simon 'Anthropomorphism-motive, meaning and causality in psychoanalytic theory'. The thrust of these critiques is to eliminate biologistic and mechanistic features from psychoanalytic theory. Their hazard is an attentuation of the depth of psychoanalytic discourse; cf. my 'Things and words', *op. cit*. Ego Psychology has come to bear a heavy share of the reification which has crept into mainstream psychoanalysis. In a particularly effective critique of Heinz Hartmann, the main exponent of Ego Psychology since Freud, Roy Schafer pointed out that Hartmann's Ego, rather than the self-subsisting biological agency it was portrayed as being, was more like an endopsychic representation of the efficient Austrian bureaucracy in which Hartmann's father had been a high official. Cf. Roy Schafer, 'An overview of Heinz Hartmann's contribution to psychoanalysis'.

22. For a good survey of this kind of penetration into everyday life, cf. Peter Schrag, *Mind Control*.

References

Arendt, H. ed. (1968). *Illuminations*. Harcourt, Brace and World.

Clement, C., Bruno, P. and Seve, L. (1973). *Pour une Critique Marxiste de la Theorie Psychanalytique*.

Dinnerstein, D. (1976). *The Rocking of the Cradle, and the Ruling of the World*. Souvenir Press, 1978.

Fekete, J. (1978). Administered society and its culture industry: politics and rationality in science fiction. Unpublished paper delivered at the St. Louis *Telos* Conference.

Freud, S. (1918). From the history of an infantile neurosis. *Standard Edition*, Vol. 17, 7–122.

Freud, S. (1920). Beyond the pleasure principle. *Standard Edition*, Vol. 18, 7–64.

Gill, M. and Holzman, P. eds. (1976). *Psychology vs. Metapsychology. Psychoanalytic Essays in Memory of George S. Klein. Psychological Issues* Monograph No. 36.

Grossman, W. and Simon, B. (1969). Anthropomorphism-motive, meaning and causality in psychoanalytic theory. *Psychoanalytic Study of the Child* 24, 78–111.

Heydebrand, W. (1977). Organisational contradictions in public bureaucracies: toward a Marxian theory of organisations. *Sociological Quarterly* 18, 83–107.

Kafka, F. (1925). *The Trial*. Penguin, 1953.

Kovel, J. (1978). Things and words: metapsychology and the historical point of view. *Psychoanalysis and Contemporary Thought* 1, 21–88.
Lacan, J. (1977). *Ecrits* (trans. Alan Sheridan). Tavistock.
Lasch, C. (1977). *Haven in a Heartless World: The Family Besieged*. Basic Books.
Mahler, M.S., Pine, F. and Bergman, A. (1975). *The Psychological Birth of the Human Infant*. Hutchinson.
Marx, K. (1845). Theses on Feuerbach. In *Karl Marx and Frederick Engels Selected Works*. Lawrence and Wishart, 1968.
Marx, K. (1867). *Capital*, Vol. I. Penguin, 1976.
Mitchell, J. (1974). *Psychoanalysis and Feminism*. Allen Lane.
Mitscherlich, A. (1969). *Society Without the Father* (trans. Eric Mosbacher). Tavistock.
Reich, W. (1945). *Character Analysis*, Vision, 1958.
Schafer, R. (1970). An overview of Heinz Hartmann's contribution to psychoanalysis. *International Journal of Psychoanalysis* 51, 425–447.
Schneider, M. (1975). *Neurosis and Civilisation*. Seabury Press.
Schrag, P. (1978). *Mind Control*. Calder and Boyars, 1980.
Slater, P. (1968). *The Glory of Hera*. Beacon.
Thompson, E.P. (1963). *The Making of the English Working Class*. Penguin, 1968.

SCHIZOID STATES AND THE MARKET

Barry Richards

The Unhappy Consciousness

Psychoanalysis has had various historical meanings, and various effects within culture. It has informed different world-views in different ways, and impinged diversely upon social life and upon individual lives. In the midst of its political ambivalences, one of its persistent projects has been the theorisation of unhappiness. This is necessarily amongst its central concerns, as it is based upon clinical practices in which individuals, however ill they may be, attempt to find and to limit the areas of unhappiness which they know, or assume, to be within themselves. So it is not only in its overtly 'political' dialects that psychoanalytic language speaks about modern unhappiness and its sources. In its more general existence psychoanalysis provides a commentary upon social process as this eventuates in particular points of subjective distress.

It has seemed as if this commentary has to be continually retrieved and rearranged if it is to make sense within a socialist problematic, and that has been the concern of the 'Freudo-Marxist' tradition. These secondary operations, however, whatever their value, are not identical with the primary constitution of the terms of the commentary, and attempts to make them so have tended to undermine their own critical aim by impoverishing the terms, cutting them off at source. Perhaps, even, that source is best left alone, as Christopher Lasch implies when he states that 'Psychoanalysis best clarifies the connection between society and the individual, culture and personality, when it confines itself to careful examination of individuals. It tells us most about society when it is least determined to do so' (*The Culture of Narcissism*, p. 34).

The relationship of clinical practice to social comment is thus a contradictory one. On the one hand there is the therapeutic aim of the practice, with its inherent tendency towards concerns with individual happiness. Hence Marcuse's battle against 'neo-Freudian revisionists', and their assimilation, as he saw it, of theory into therapy, so as to produce a 'repressive' theory: 'in a repressive society, individual happiness and productive development are in contradiction to society; if they are defined as values to be realised within this society, they become themselves repressive' (*Eros and Civilisation*, p. 245). American psychotherapeutic Freudianism, about which Marcuse was writing, is a major historical example of one of the social roles of psychoanalysis, the familiar one of support for individualistic ideologies, laying blame upon the shoulders of individual victims of the consequences of capital accumulation. In Britain we can add qualified examples from, for instance, the incorporation of neo-Freudianism into social work theory and practice.

On the other hand, perhaps Marcuse was wrong to equate happiness with therapy, and so reserve illness and negation for theory (or perhaps this is the equation that confronts observers of the American psychoanalytic market-place). To do so overlooks the constant confrontation with unhappiness which is at least available, if not always required, within psychoanalytic experience. Rather, the aim of therapy can be seen, in one sense, to be to expand unhappiness, to pursue and draw it, to differentiate within it, and generally dwell on it. A conceptualisation of this kind is of course a long way from Reichian and other soteriological doctrines of therapy as release or inner revolution. Instead it locates psychoanalysis within a varied enterprise of reflection upon the pains of life, whether specifically of modern life or of human life in a more universal way (the 'transhistorical', as Joel Kovel puts it elsewhere in this book). The latter are also social, in a sense. The core of existential despair may be independent of the process of historical change, but any mitigation of it is available only through quite specific social relations.

So the theorisation of unhappiness contains a moment of social judgement, to which different writers may give different weight and direction. In radical and socialist hands it may frequently be allied with some notion of 'alienation', contributing significantly to the development of that word's meanings. Thus, as Raymond Williams (1976) points out, the Freudian concept of 'repression' has been taken to describe a state in which people are 'alienated' from those parts of themselves which they have repressed. My chapter identifies a characterisation of modern unhappiness which is present in contemporary British psychoanalysis as a successor to the Freudian one, although it may be found to include it, conceptually, rather than replace it; and although it continues the resonance within meanings of 'alienation'.

This characterisation is found in works emphasising the process of splitting rather than repression, and portraying the individual in states of illness as internally split and divided. Contrasted with this is not the classical liberal, legal and economic 'individual' or indivisible agent, but rather the subject whose experience is no longer riven, whose psychic life has acquired a certain degree of wholeness, of communication between and unification of its different parts. 'Integration' is the term most frequently used to refer to this state of relative health, although its connotations and its etymology are too suggestive of purity and of an undisturbed wholeness.

In order to set out this characterisation it will be necessary first to talk at some length within psychoanalytic theory, although I will only be dipping into the very large and very technical literature that is relevant. The next section may then be found difficult by readers who are unfamiliar with the theoretical developments under discussion. The study of these developments is required, though, if a psychoanalytically informed commentary on social processes is to keep abreast of developments within psychoanalysis, and if the claim is to be examined that the prevalent forms of personality organisation in monopoly capitalist society can be adequately described only in the light of those developments.

Accordingly the next two sections of this paper will deal in some detail with psychoanalytic ideas. In the first, the object relations theory of schizoid states is outlined and some of its differences from Freudian theory commented upon. This is necessary in order to spell out how this post-Freudian development can provide a basis for moving on from Freudo-Marxism and its tendency towards millenarian denunciations of the evils of repression and patriarchy (see Lasch earlier in this volume). The move is from a focus on the pathologies of repression and classical neurosis to one on those of splitting and schizoid states. There are a number of obscurities and difficulties within psychoanalytic theory associated with this development, especially with the definition of splitting, and a short Appendix to the chapter highlights some of them.

The second section comments briefly on some American accounts of 'borderline' and 'narcissistic' pathologies, and notes their basic similarity to the main features of schizoid states. The following two sections make a bridge from these psychoanalytic technicalities to cultural analysis. Two American accounts of narcissism in culture are outlined and then some general problems with this use of psychoanalytic categories are discussed.

The rest of the chapter is concerned with indicating how the psychopathological framework which has been presented may contribute to an understanding of everyday life in a society constituted by market relations and by the rationality of exchange and bureaucratic administration. It can be seen that the outer world of consumption and rationality offers some 'solutions' to the problems of living in the schizoid inner worlds described by Guntrip, Khan and others. Such an interpenetration of inner and outer can also help to explain the weakness and corruption of the political process, although some sites in mass culture of possible resistance to the commodification of emotional life are noted.

It is important throughout to sustain the effort to imagine the symbolic levels or experiential modes involved, since these are outside the affective range of most everyday experience, and may indeed be largely pre-symbolic. The imperative to split, for example (see below), is moved by terrors which no conceptual account can properly convey with its ordered positioning of 'Good' and 'Bad', since what is at stake is not a particular arrangement of experience but a sense of existence itself. Continual experiments in intuition are necessary to appreciate mental life at this level.

One way of beginning is to examine the changes over time in the kinds of psychopathology which psychoanalytic practice (and also psychiatry) attempts to define and treat. New emphases and new categories emerge; old ones are displaced or subsumed. Foremost among such changes is the shift away from a concern with the 'classical neuroses' (hysteria, obsessive/compulsive neurosis, anxiety neurosis), in part a shift towards greater concern with psychotic states, which Freud himself left largely unexplored. Analytic consulting rooms, however, are not now full of overtly psychotic patients; in terms of the diagnostic categories of patients, the shift in interest has been towards a group of categories not envisaged by psychiatry's distinction between the neuroses and the psychoses. For perhaps fifty years, reports of analytic work have referred increasingly to patients who do not present primarily with well organised neurotic symptomatology, nor with the massive disturbance of overt psychosis. Their malaise is profound but diffuse. Khan (1966) says: 'The schizoid character disorders are distinguished by the fact that the symptom lies in the way of being' (*The Privacy of the Self*, p. 69).

These diffuse disorders have been described and theorised in a variety of ways. In particularly common usage at present are the terms 'schizoid', 'narcissistic', and 'borderline'.

The Schizoid Condition: Splitting and Withdrawal

One of the seminal theorists of schizoid conditions was W.R.D. Fairbairn who, from his outpost in Edinburgh, made important contributions to psychoanalytic theory from the 1930s until the late 1950s.[1] 'The fundamental schizoid problem', he wrote in 1940, 'is the presence of splits in the ego' (*Psychoanalytic Studies of the Personality*, p. 8). In Fairbairn's theory of psychic development, the neonate ego is pristine and unitary and in a relatively simple relation with its similarly undifferentiated object. The first defensive reaction to bad experience – the completely inevitable frustrations of infancy – is to internalise the object in an attempt to control it and then, again defensively, to split[2] its experience of the object so that several objects are formed. Corresponding bits of the ego must also be split off in order to maintain relations with these split-off objects. Accordingly there develops a series of ego-object couplets, of which Fairbairn identified three.

The Central Ego, which relates to the Accepted Object, is largely co-extensive with the conscious and pre-conscious self of everyday awareness; it is what remains of the original unitary ego after its affective parts have been split-off. Likewise the Accepted Object is what remains of the object after its more arousing parts have been split-off.[3]

All passion and drama are thus separated off into the two other couplets: the Libidinal Ego and its Exciting Object, and between the Anti-Libidinal Ego and its Rejecting Object. The Exciting and Rejecting Objects are, respectively, the alluring and frustrating parts of the primary object (the mother); the Libidinal and Anti-Libidinal Egos are those parts of the ego deputed to maintain appropriate relations (respectively, greedy and hateful) with those part objects.[4] Both of those ego-object dynamic structures are aggressively rejected by the Central Ego – they are repressed as well as split-off. Fairbairn termed this configuration of object relations 'schizoid'; he believed it to be the fundamental, original organisation of psychic structure.

By abstraction from the details and difficulties of Fairbairn's particular formulation,[5] one can discern a tragic characterisation of psychic life in some ways the same as that of the classical Freudian theory against which Fairbairn so earnestly (and cogently) argued on several questions of metapsychology (see below). Both are studies in the inevitability of psychic cleavage in response to threats, deprivations, and dangers. In the course of early development, massive areas of affective life are proscribed from the more socialised parts of the individual. As a consequence, these parts are deeply impoverished, though not infrequently disturbed by forces active within the less socialised parts.

In this respect, Fairbairn's Central Ego/Accepted Object structure, in its relationship of opposition to the Libidinal Ego/Libidinal Object and Anti-Libidinal Ego/Rejecting Object structures may be equivalent to Freud's ego besieged by id and superego. (Fairbairn's discussion in 1944 of the aims of psychoanalysis seems to bear this out – the Central Ego is to be extended and strengthened in much the same way as the Freudian ego.[6]) In both accounts there is a central or surface structure mediating actions in the external world, but created and defined internally by defences and absences.

Yet the differences between Freud and Fairbairn are numerous. For example, the Freudian ego is *produced* by differentiation from the id; the Fairbairnian Central Ego *produces*, by splitting and repression, the subsidiary egos and their objects. Freud's picture tends to be seen as one of a set of homunculiform or anthropomorphised apparatuses; Fairbairn is more clearly talking about internal scenarios, about qualities of phantasy rather than quanta of energy. But common and fundamental to both accounts are images of defensive structural cleavage, of affective proscription and impoverishment.

Thus far it may appear that Fairbairn's main revision is terminological. But there were several substantive innovations in his work such as the transcendence of the energy/structure distinction, the rejection of the concept of the 'id', and the break with instinct theory and the redefinition of libido as object-seeking rather than pleasure-seeking. These metapsychological innovations have been amply stressed by Fairbairn himself and Guntrip in various works. In developmental theory, however, one innovation is particularly relevant here, though it was much less exclusively Fairbairn's. Klein[7] and others took a similar step, though Fairbairn's particular version of it is important. This step concerns the origins and content of the proscribed affects.

For Freud, these were pre-eminently Oedipal and psychosexual. For Fairbairn (1944), 'the role of ultimate cause, which Freud allotted to the Oedipal situation, should properly be allotted to the phenomenon of infantile dependence.' The dangerous affects are not, fundamentally, Oedipal desires, but arise from infantile needs for nurture. Faced with the inevitable imperfections of maternal care, the infant's reactive aggression is dangerous, since it threatens the 'good' mother as well as the 'bad' one. So is his/her primary libidinal need – 'unrequited love' produces shame, impotence, a fear of having destroyed the object through one's love and at worst an experience of psychic death, since an ego can maintain a sense of existence only in relation to an object. Thus, both aggressive and libidinal affect is split-off and repressed and the unconscious object relations described above come into being. Drained of these affects, the Central Ego/Accepted Object relation is threatened by emptiness and purposelessness. A sense of futility (easily confused with depression) is therefore the characteristic schizoid affect.

The second crucial difference between Freud and Fairbairn is harder to clarify. For Freud, the means by which affect was proscribed – the mode of cleavage – came to be conceptualised as repression, and this, as the founding moment of the unconscious, is the key to his whole theory. In Fairbairn's theory, however, it is cleavage conceived as splitting which assumes a dominant role.

Fairbairn observes that Freud's early interest in the splitting phenomena of hysteria was eclipsed when his attention turned to repression and the superego, with guilt and depression becoming the central clinical phenomena. Freud's much later interest in a phenomenon which he termed 'splitting' (e.g., in 'Splitting of the ego in the process of defence') is rather different from the process focused on by Fairbairn. For the later Freud, splitting was typified in fetishism. The fetishist both *knows* that women do not possess a penis, and *disavows* this intolerable knowledge.[8] His ego is thus split into knowing and disavowing parts. (The putting of the fetishistic object in the place of the absent female penis is something of a compromise between these two parts.) Freud suggested that this kind of splitting was involved in psychosis and, indeed, in neurosis as well, but he did not develop the theme.

The splitting of the ego described by Fairbairn, however, is of a diferent order. For Freud, splitting is intrinsically connected with denial of some matter in the external world and thus with repression of that knowledge. Fairbairn owed his concept of splitting of the ego primarily to the work of Melanie Klein. The Kleinian concept brings into focus splitting of the *object*, as well as of the ego, with splitting as a defence by which the experience of the object is split into 'good' and 'bad' parts (see note 2 and Appendix). This is necessary at the start of life in order to protect the good experience (or rather, the good object felt to be the source of that experience) from the destructiveness which the baby feels to threaten from both inside and outside.[9] Splitting in Fairbairnian theory also implies the notion of *withdrawal* from object relations. It thus stands in the train of ideas that have been developed from Freud's formulation of narcissism in 1914, rather than from Freud's own use of 'splitting'.

Guntrip has extended Fairbairn's analysis of the schizoid condition, introducing an additional structural term, and an emphasis on the pathos of the struggle inherent in the schizoid way of being. The splitting process described by Fairbairn does not, of course, solve the problems of bad experience and bad object relations, it merely re-establishes them in the *internal* object world. So there is a second stage of withdrawal:

> in face of the *internal* bad-object world, the same manoeuvre that was made by the whole ego when it sought to withdraw from the *external* bad-object world [is repeated]. It leaves part of itself to carry on such relations as are possible in sado-masochistic terms, with the exciting and rejecting objects of the internal phantasy world, while the traumatised, sensitive, and exhausted heart of it withdraws deeper still (*Schizoid Phenomena*, p. 73).

However, the danger faced in such withdrawal is greater than any faced in the world of bad objects. This is the danger of complete ego-loss, because an ego, a sense of self and existence, can occur only in relation to an object. Regressive escape from the object world therefore threatens annihilation, and the ego struggles to preserve itself in the face of the regressive impulse. Often it can do this only by maintaining bad object relations, which are better than none at all. The regressed heart of the ego thus becomes trapped in a 'structural headquarters of fear', faced on the one hand by the ultimate danger of ego loss and on the other by (at worst) disintegration of the ego under persecution by bad internal objects.

Guntrip's regressed ego has thus retreated in despair from the superficiality of the Central Ego and the bad object relations of the subsidiary egos. It carries with it the yearning and hope for good object relations but lives in fear of any at all. It is particularly fearful not of its aggression but of its need. To quote Guntrip again, 'The frustration of libidinal need for good object relations both causes aggression and intensifies libidinal needs till the infant fears his love needs as destructive towards his objects . . . it leads to the schizoid withdrawal, a simple fear rejection away from the danger of devouring and therefore losing the love object' (*Schizoid Phenomena*, p. 67).

Guntrip thus describes a process of fearful withdrawal in which the proscription of affect and the depletion of the outer ego are at a maximum. In this he draws not only upon Fairbairn but also upon Winnicott,[10] whose concepts of True Self and False Self (Winnicott, 1960) are close, respectively, to those of regressed ego (Guntrip) and Central Ego (Fairbairn), although the latter is a wider term than False Self (see p. 126). While intellectual skills and practical skills, and perhaps Freudian ego-strength, may be seen as vested in the Central Ego, this also consists of mere social skills – conformist, compliant adaptations to an external world which has to be lived in, but which has been written off as a potential source of the most deeply-needed gratifications, that is as a source of reliable and empathic care. Some degree of False Self functioning is necessary and healthy: that required for effective movement in the social world. But in its pathological developments it serves primarily to conceal the True Self, from which it is deeply split. The True Self thus leads a fugitive life within the inner world as a repository of unmet needs. The dangers of affective involvement with the outer world are so great that contact with the False Self is prohibited; the creative as well as the demanding aspects of the True Self are thus excluded from social interchange.

Borderline and Narcissistic Pathologies

The term 'borderline' is now freely applied in psychiatric practice, and frequently with little understanding of its psychoanalytic meanings. (The only justification for this usage is that in both psychoanalytic and psychiatric contexts it refers to a form of personality organisation which is 'borderline' between the neuroses and psychoses.) A systematic formulation of borderline pathology has been developed by the American analyst Otto Kernberg.

In Kernberg's account, the essential characteristic of the borderline personality organisation is the failure to overcome splitting, so that images of both self and object remain inadequately integrated. Influenced by American ego-psychology, Kernberg sees the early division of internalised objects into 'good' and 'bad' not as defensive splitting but as a simple consequence of the early ego's lack of integrative capacity, although this division is later used defensively by the ego to build and protect a core for itself around good introjects. His view clearly contrasts with Fairbairn's picture of the original unitary ego, as well as with the Kleinian stress on the *activity* of splitting.

Psychotics, too, lack such integration, but they have also failed in early ego-development to establish sufficient differentiation between self and not-self. The borderline's reality-testing in this respect is relatively sound. However, burdened with intense rage (which is reactive to frustration but may also be constitutionally determined), s/he cannot bear to admit that good and bad are aspects of the same, whole object. To protect the good object from that rage, primitive idealisations of it reinforce the splitting, as do crude projections of the rage (which can weaken the self's boundaries in the area of the projection and so produce local psychotic effects). The result is a severely impoverished and weakened ego, vulnerable to all kinds of neurotic symptomatology, impulsive episodes and perversions. This ego is capable only of shallow relations with external others, relations which are essentially selfish: as long as splitting predominates, genuine concern for the other as a whole, integrated object cannot develop.

Rosenfeld confirms the primacy, in borderline states, of pathological splitting. He also notes in his 1978 paper the confusion which can result when the needy libidinal self is experienced as causing the rage (when desire unsatisfied has turned to hatred) and is attacked punitively by destructive parts of the self. Confusional states being hard to bear, they are dealt with, he suggests, by further splitting-off of the confused parts of self and object.

There are indeed substantial similarities between these descriptions of borderline personalities, on the one hand, and the Fairbairn/Guntrip picture of the schizoid condition on the other, and Kernberg acknowledges these affinities.[11] Thus without presuming an identity between the two syndromes, one can point to their common descriptive and dynamic features and to the basic importance of splitting processes in both.

The narcissistic personality, according to Kernberg, is a variant upon an underlying borderline (i.e., split) organisation. For Kohut, narcissistic conditions fall into two separate categories, each with greater therapeutic possibilities than borderlines (Kohut and Wolff, 1978). For both writers, however, the defining feature of the narcissistic personality is the presence of a pathological 'grandiose self' – Kernberg here adopts Kohut's term – which is primarily a defence against the rage and helplessness observed to be at the heart of the condition. It is the attempt to do without object relations and their pains by the creation of an omnipotent self which needs nothing outside itself (see, e.g., Rosenfeld, 1964). A facade of object relations may be developed by the projection of this grandiose self, which then relates to its projections of itself.

Implicit in this analysis is the existence, beneath even the very deep delusions of self-sufficiency, of a passive and terrorised inner self, needing to be reached and nurtured. Such themes are less developed in the writings of Kernberg and Kohut than in those of the British object relations theorists. For the Americans, analytic technique is still very much a matter, above all else, of the skills of interpretation. However, in terms of structural and dynamic theory, the American accounts of narcissism remain close to the British theory of schizoid states.[12] Fundamental to the narcissistic personality are massive splitting and withdrawal, as Freud had pointed out in 1914. The grandiose self can be constructed only where the sense of weakness has been completely split-off and where idealisation is untempered by any integrated perception of the object, however incomplete.

All these accounts of schizoid, borderline, and narcissistic pathologies identify a process of withdrawal from object relations. It is seen as the result of a traumatic experience of unmet need in the earliest stage of development, with the subsequent construction of a fabric of relationships in and with the world that conceal, and are cut off from, the inner centres of infantile experience and need. There are splits between these relationships in the outer world, where dread and euphoria frequently pass each other by. And this defensive separation of different elements of experience is the outward sign of the most fundamental split, that between inner and outer, which is the characteristic schizoid manoeuvre.

Excursions into the Cultural Field: Narcissism in Contemporary Capitalism

During the 1970s, a number of analyses of contemporary culture as narcissistic appeared, two of which made some use of psychoanalytic accounts of narcissism. The first was Richard Sennett's *The Fall of Public Man*.

Sennett argues that during the nineteenth century there was a breakdown in the distinction between 'public' and 'private' which had developed during the early expansion of industrial capitalism when the idealised 'private' was constructed as a refuge from the chaos and rapacity of the new order. An 'immense fear of public life . . . gripped the last century', due to collapsing confidence in the security of the boundary between public and private. Participation in public life while maintaining personal privacy came to seem increasingly difficult. There were several reasons for this.

Some developments in the nineteenth century science (e.g. physiognomy, phrenology, Darwin's ethological observations of emotional expression) sought to catalogue the involuntary disclosures of inner character and feeling. More generally, argues Sennett, there was the development of an 'immanent' philosophy, which turned away from the consideration of transcendent meaning and saw the fact and the instant as real and significant in themselves; any appearance might give a clue to meaning. The development of capitalist commodity production also contributed to this trend: as clothes became increasingly machine-made and homogenised, a marketing drive to 'personalise' them got under way. (The extension of commodity consumption in many other fields, as an exercise in personalising the public domain, could probably also be examined to support Sennett's argument and to connect it more deeply with change in the mode of production.)

The result was a withdrawal from public life as a domain of social life clearly distinct from the private, as a region of social interaction in which encounters with others were controlled and distant yet, in their own way, emotionally satisfying. Such encounters were no longer possible, if the soul could be read off from facial movements, garments or bumps on the head. Knowledge of others now came not from intercourse with them but from observation of them. Sennett does not refer to it, but the great interest in blushing as an index of character, which as Skultans describes developed during the 1820s, would be a good illustration of this belief. The only defence against this nightmare of permanent visibility was to withdraw and be silent. Strangers therefore lost the right to address each other; public space was transformed from areas of active interchange into a network of corridors along which isolated individuals hurried from one hopefully private place to another. And ultimately 'the defence against being read by others was to stop feeling' (Sennett, p. 27).

As the private thus became public, so the opposite corruption occurred. If public life was no longer possible on its own terms, it could exist only as a projection of the private. It was in the nineteenth century, Sennett argues, that the concern with the personal 'authenticity' and 'integrity' of politicians emerged. Cults of personality and intimacy invaded more and more areas of public life. Civility, defined as refraining from burdening others with one's conflicts and doubts, became suspect; impersonal convention and ritualised politeness came to seem hollow and hypocritical. Spontaneity and individuality became de rigueur.

The analysis is a suggestive one and, although sweeping, is extensively documented. But Sennett's title is perhaps less appropriate than 'The End of Privacy' would have been. For it is not an aggressive personalism or the expansion of intimacy that in themselves have brought about the disintegration of the public domain; these are *defensive* developments. As Sennett himself shows, it is the erosion of secure intimacy and of privacy, that is, of the conditions for a private, personal life, which is at the heart of things and is the basis of the fear of impersonality.[13] A confident and creative impersonality has to be founded on a secure sense of personal existence but Sennett seems at times to be implying that all effort at intimacy, intensity, and expressiveness is corrupt.

Sennett offers a brief discussion of Kohut's work on narcissism, and a reference to Kernberg, the implication being that their clinical accounts of narcissism have direct reference to the large-scale shifts in personal conduct and attitude which he describes. He says that 'narcissism is now mobilised in social relations by a culture deprived of belief in the public and ruled by intimate feelings as a measure of the meaning of reality' (p. 326). However his definition of narcissism seems to be more social-psychological than psychoanalytic. For Sennett narcissism is a condition pressed on adult individuals by the wider forces of social life rather than a condition originating in infantile experience. It is a later development, which even undoes the positive achievements of early life such as the capacity for play. This he sees in a way opposed to the celebration of play as 'spontaneous'. He notes the highly conventionalised nature of much play and the importance of children's games in enabling participants to develop 'self-distance' – i.e., to learn submission to rules and to experience the satisfactions of regular, limited social encounters. 'Play for the child is the antithesis to expressing himself spontaneously' (p. 315). But 'strengths of playacting developed in childhood are effaced by the conditions of adult culture' (p. 314), and 'the strength to play which the human being had before he grew up and entered "reality" ' (p. 315) is, it seems, relatively easily destroyed – and with it the capacity to act in public, since 'play is the energy for public expression' (p. 316). Whatever the merits of his inverted celebration of play and of his assessment of its relationship to public life, his notion of its effacement by adult culture cannot be squared with psychoanalytic notions about the primacy and resilience of the deposits of early experience. These would encourage him to look instead for the corruption of play and of experience before the entry into 'adult culture'.

A more informed and extensive use of psychoanalytic psychopathology is made by Christopher Lasch in *The Culture of Narcissism*, which builds on his previous work (*Haven in a Heartless World*) on changes in the ideology of, and social possibilities for, family life. It also follows the path indicated by the Frankfurt School writers, especially Horkheimer, in the 1930s. Lasch connects the clinical picture (particularly Kernberg's) of the narcissistic personality with the general development of welfare capitalism.

The growth of dependence on the state and its experts in every sphere of personal life and family life – marital and sexual relations, infant care, the management of adolescents, and so on – has undermined parental confidence and authority, he argues. An increasing bureaucratic and technical regulation of areas of previously personal, moral choice has divested the family of its value as a site of moral instruction and the discovery of commitments. The aesthetic of consumption has made the ethic of family life appear ridiculous; young people now grow up in the market, not at home. Finding one's identity means establishing oneself in a particular niche in the world of commodities; it means putting together, from the available elements, an idiosyncratic style of consumption.

Selfhood is thus increasingly dependent on consumption and less so on secure intrapsychic identifications with other persons. In the psychoanalytic understanding of development, these basic identifications with parents serve to integrate the child's loving and destructive impulses. Love and constraint are combined in the same parental figures, who tolerate the child's rage at the constraints and frustrations they must impose and continue to offer love. This enables the child to tolerate his or her destructiveness and to identify with the parents as imperfect but whole, realistic and loving figures, thus establishing a sense of imperfect but integrated selfhood. If, however, the frustrations and rage are too severe for destructiveness to be mitigated in this way, or if the parents are unable to continue providing both love and constraint, the child cannot carry through processes of building mature, integrated ego and superego structures around basically good parental introjects. Oral rage, i.e., hatred inspired by experiences of failure in basic nurturance, is left to run its own frightful course. One way of attempting to cope with it is to project it, thus bringing into being sadistic, persecutory forerunners or early forms of the superego. (The mature superego is in comparison a basically benign structure, protective and instructive as well as prohibiting.)

In danger, then, of being overwhelmed by aggressive impulses from within and by sadistic attacks apparently from without, the desperate infant psyche seeks refuge in an omnipotent narcissistic self. Unable to identify with the parents as whole, integrated objects, and persecuted by them as bad internal objects, it turns to idealised parental images and attempts to build a self around identification with perfect, omnipotent introjects. The infant's phantasy of omnipotent parent figures thus becomes the adult's phantasy of omnipotent self. The narcissist may appear to be serenely self-sufficient, brilliant, successful, involved in the external world and affirmative of the inner world. But beneath such appearances is buried dread – of frustration, abandonment and rage – and a profound sense of unreality and emptiness, the underside of the phantasised omnipotence. The narcissist, thus understood, is 'self-absorbed' not out of carelessness, or an excess of conceit, but as the only alternative to the disintegration and emptying of the self.

The modern narcissist has thus lost faith in personal relations (a loss sometimes hidden behind cults of 'relationships'), in the past and in the future; a hip instrumentalism of living for the moment becomes the dominant ethic, an ethic of psychic survival in a world where nothing can be expected from others. The narcissist – who to varying degrees is in all of us – protected by 'pseudo self-awareness', is above all concerned to avoid deep commitments and involvements, while at the same time quite possibly making headway and many conspicuous 'relationships' in public and private life. The part of her/him which could bring depth and genuineness to relationships is sealed off, in rage and fear, in some inaccessible inner place.

Thus far we have a broadly consensual psychoanalytic account of the development of the narcissistic syndrome. Lasch goes on to argue that the conditions for this development are precisely those that prevail in contemporary capitalism. Demoralised parents see their efforts to establish permanent, intimate family relations confused by expert advice, undermined by the demands for mobile labour and derided in the clichés of consumption lifestyles. They are incapable of sustaining the depth and steadiness of parenting required for integration in development. Beginning perhaps with a defensive indifference of limited scope and depth, the narcissistic tendency may swell within a generation or two (it is not clear what precise historical period Lasch is describing) into a full-blown cult of irresponsibility and febrile shallowness.

The direct and indirect entry of the state into family life is basic to this development, and both the 'progressive' theorising of social science and the practice of social work and other forms of state intervention are integral to it (the former are assessed by Lasch in the earlier *Haven in a Heartless World*). This is not necessarily to deny that such programmes of intervention have brought real increments in caring and material and emotional benefits to individuals, though Lasch does not perhaps make clear these differentiations and contradictions.

Mine is a somewhat free, but hopefully still faithful, rendering of Lasch's thesis and of his use of psychoanalytic formulations. There are various problems with that usage, to which I will shortly turn, but the evocative scope of his thesis, ranging as it does from psychic primitivity to perhaps epochal historical change, is exemplary. It illustrates how the imperative to withdraw emotional investment from relations with others may be understood historically.

Problems in the Psychopathology of Culture

It may be helpful to try to clarify what kind of venture is being undertaken when we bring psychoanalytic categories to bear on the analysis of culture. What is being said, for example, in the statement that we inhabit a 'culture of narcissism'? In addition to the defensive reactions invoked by psychoanalysis alone, we also have to deal with various sectional investments in the social division of knowledge. For a mixture of reasons, many of those involved in psychoanalysis or in social theory may be wary of the venture. And we cannot cite much oracular approval of it. Freud wrote:

> The present cultural state of America would give us a good

> opportunity for studying the damage to civilisation which is thus to be feared. But I shall avoid the temptation of entering upon a critique of American civilisation; I do not wish to give an impression of wanting myself to employ American methods (*Civilisation and its Discontents*, p. 116).

(Whether American civilisation is the same, in the ways that concern us, as European civilisation is discussed in Chapter 1.) But after stressing the need for caution, Freud conceded that 'we may expect that one day someone will venture to embark upon a pathology of cultural communities'[14] (ibid., p. 144). However, what is a pathology of communities?

One of the simplest meanings we could give to the statement would be an epidemiological one. This could take at least two forms. Firstly, we might be saying that the incidence of narcissism as a clinically recorded condition had increased, such that it now prevailed over all other conditions. In the absence of systematic records of patients in psychoanalytic practice, and of appropriate knowledge of the untreated population, this is of course impossible to substantiate, except impressionistically. Kernberg's impression of borderline psychopathology, for example, is that it has not increased in incidence (Kernberg, 1976). Khan, though, implies that schizoid pathology is now more prevalent, as well as being more visible owing to advances in analytic theory and technique (*The Privacy of the Self*, Chap. 1). Secondly, we might be saying that the sub-clinical incidence of the narcissistic syndrome, or of narcissistic traits, had increased among the general population. Evidence here must be even more impressionistic, though not to be dismissed for that.

Some remarks by Jacoby (1980) suggest that any epidemiological analysis would produce class differences. The 'narcissistic family', he suggests, has appeared in place of the classical bourgeois family and the most narcissistic class is the new middle class, as the cultural vanguard. He also notes that narcissism will have different meanings in different contexts. Its sociopolitical meaning in New York, for example, will differ from that in Southern Italy, where its oppositional potential will be greater.

Lasch also asserts that, independently of their numbers in society, more narcissistic individuals are now in positions of social leadership. While fundamentally an *effect* of a narcissistic culture, which produces leaders in its own image, this would presumably also extend and strengthen the cultural presence of the psychopathology. But again, it is difficult to map out a sound evidential basis for such a proposition, though it would receive some support from Kernberg's comments on the adeptness of narcissistic individuals in leading through the reduction of ideological systems into clichés, and on their appropriateness for positions of either charismatic or bureaucratic leadership (*Internal World and External Reality*, Part 3). In general, however, to convert these observations, or even the whole argument, into an epidemiological question would be to miss the point, which is that the major issue is not about head-counting but about the mode of cultural reproduction.

Sennett's view of what constitutes a narcissistic culture is consistent with his social-psychological understanding of narcissism itself. 'In modern social life', he says, 'adults must act narcissistically to act in accordance with society's norms.' Narcissism is a property or, rather, potential of individuals mobilised by the conditions of contemporary life. This is a relatively clear and limited hypothesis – that we have within us potentials for narcissism as, presumably, for many other pathologies and we live in a world which particularly elicits or potentiates that narcissism. Thus, although Senntt blames a rampant intimacy for the social malaise, his position tends towards sociological determinism. Narcissism for him is not something which individuals bring with them into the adult world from early experience; it is rather something which that world requires of them.

For Lasch, things are more serious (and not that Sennett's judgement is light). Not only do the current conditions of life draw out narcissistic traits, but these traits are also on the increase in individuals prior to their full immersion in the market and bureaucratic relations of the adult world, since those relations have invaded infancy. And here more difficulties for the argument arise: how to establish that links exist between major features of the cultural scene, on the one hand, and, on the other, the specific conditions of parenting that are known, through clinical studies, to generate specific kinds of pathology. There are risks of ending up either with an over-specific account that makes one kind of pathogenesis carry too broad a load – which is the error to which Lasch tends; or with an over-general one which says little more than that ill parents will mediate bad social relations to their children who will thus become ill (some popular derivations from Laing amount to no more than this).

These problems of establishing the right specificity and scope are more serious than any raised by the objections that psychoanalytic inquiry into culture is psychologistic or reductionist. These objections, the stuff of traditional Left and liberal hostility, appear though to be justified by some work in psychoanalytic anthropology. This tradition has yet to be fully examined and assimilated by radical students of culture, although Robinson in *The Sexual Radicals* provided a sympathetic and lucid portrait of its founder,

Geza Roheim. Perhaps it is Roheim's uncompromising psychological reductionism which has helped to limit the influence of his work. Or perhaps the tendency to functionalist liberalism amongst other anthropologists influenced by him, though more widely known than he (e.g., Margaret Mead), has been a disincentive for Left intellectuals to approach this area. A radical appreciation of Roheim and his school may be overdue. In addition to benefiting from a reading of their empirical work, we may find that the theoretical problem of reductionism is not as great as might be feared. We could not endorse Roheim's ontogenetic theory of culture and see culture as the *product* of infantile trauma. But we may nonetheless want to consider ways in which cultural artefacts are used to help us forget, contain, or work through such traumas.

Also, Roheim's view of the basic trauma is close to contemporary psychoanalytic thought. Influenced by Rank and Ferenczi, he saw separation from the mother as the founding crisis of development. He conceived of all cultural enterprises as searches for substitutes for the lost mother, as ways of coping with the pain of the first loss. With a more open-minded approach to the traumatic content, so that the interrelationship between earlier and later traumas can be appreciated, this conception is the basis for a principle of cultural analysis which could be complementary to a materialist history. Psychoanalytic reductionism may at one level be right in its interpretations even while it is inadequate as history. The problem for a socialist critique of culture is how to utilize such interpretations within a politically purposeful perspective. Our difficulties in doing this at present are not to be brushed aside but need not become the occasion for abandoning interpretive work under pressure from a tyrannical pragmatism.

Other objectors may query the apparent transposition of psychopathological categories to objects for which they were not intended and do not fit – institutions, material objects, patterns of social life, etc. Cultural diagnosis may be seen to be premissed upon an organismic view and medical knowledge of society, and to have taken a body politic, or a psyche cultural, as its literal object. This is to some extent a problem of conceptual and methodological clarification. The psychopathology of culture is the study of the qualities of individuals' experience of participation in social life. It claims that social process can legitimately be described in terms of those qualities, as it can also be described – again partially – in terms of the economic or governmental. Perhaps the methodological misunderstandings overlay antipathies linked to a need to ensure that unconscious phantasies, if recognised at all, are kept as interesting exotica in conceptual zoos and not allowed to roam in public and attend the mundane round of Central Ego activities. The gains to understanding made by psychoanalytic studies of work groups and organisations (e.g. Bion, 1961; Menzies, 1970; Kreeger, 1975; Kernberg, 1980) would be foregone if this selective accommodation were allowed.

More obvious hostilities abound. Our ears continue to ring with the accusations that psychoanalysis is bourgeois, Freud a patriarch, etc. And the radical critique of psychoanalysis as normative and authoritarian has now been complemented by the radical critique of psychoanalysis as instrument of power, not in its repressive moment but in its campaign *against* repression, its 'incitement' to sexual discourse. Foucault (in *The History of Sexuality*) hears in it part of the 'great sexual sermon' which has swept through modern society with false promises of liberation. Notwithstanding the merits of Foucault's account, we can also offer some alternative characterisations of the cultural imprints of psychoanalysis. Calls for the lifting of repressions may have found wide resonance in earlier years but rather different rhetorical themes emerge from more contemporary analytic writings. In the tradition of work represented by Balint, Winnicott, Guntrip and Khan, for example, psychoanalysis appears primarily as a statement on the needs and possibilities for nurturance. This work is of course primarily concerned with two interpersonal relations – between mother and baby, and analyst and patient – but the moral and practical address of the work can be taken in relation to social life generally. It is an elaboration from within classical psychoanalysis rather than an importing into it, and yet it also converges upon a central socialist ideal. Rather, it may be providing means to rework and strengthen that ideal, since political conceptions of care and welfare have not had the theoretical and emotional sophistication developed in therapeutic nurturing work.

Nor does the Kleinian tradition appear as an optimistic incitement to desublimation. In its emphasis on innate destructiveness and envy it is more readily presented as a pessimistic meditation upon sin and its convolutions. More deeply, in the theory of the developmental importance of reparation[15] it unfolds a moral discourse within metapsychology and therapeutic technique. In this, and in its strongly relational approach, Kleinian theory is seen by Rustin (1982) as quite deeply consonant with equivalent themes in the socialist tradition.

Finally, there are the complications of cross-cultural differences. The possibilities of differences between the US and Britain in relation to Lasch's analysis are discussed in Chapter 1 of this book, where the case is put that the diagnosis of narcissism, while possibly correct for the US, is not so for Britain. However in the following sections I will try to describe, on the basis of a rather narrowly British experience, some features of a 'pathology of communities' which can be expected now wherever culture is dominated by the capitalist market.

SCHIZOID PROCESSES IN MODERN CULTURE

The analyses of culture as narcissism are an important advance. They have initiated a vigorous debate underwritten by deeper understanding both of psyche and of culture (e.g., the Cortland Conference on Narcissism, reported in *Telos* 44, 1980). However my earlier review of the range of pathologies within which narcissism is located indicates that narcissism may be too specific a diagnosis, if the condensed grandiose self is taken as the defining feature of the narcissistic syndrome, and if pathological splitting is seen as the basal psychic process for narcissism, as for other conditions. I have suggested that 'schizoid' may be a more usefully generic term but this is not to propose a simple alternative diagnosis with which to compete for conceptual sovereignty over the cultural field. Another weakness of the narcissism analysis may be its availability for simplifications in which cultural psychopathology is portrayed as unidimensional. It was certainly a weakness of the Freudo-Marxists that they sought to diagnose capitalism using one or perhaps two of the categories of classical psychoanalytic psychopathology. Thus for Fromm (and later for Schneider) capitalism was anal, for Reich it was genitally repressed, and for Marcuse it was tyrannically genital.

Subsequent developments within psychoanalysis have emphasised the interpretation of different levels of pregenital and genital pathology and have thus rendered this diagnostic mode somewhat problematic. Also, Marcuse's work, in particular, was transitional to a more sophisticated analysis in which the full spectrum of psychoanalytic categories is seen as expressive of psychic life in the present epoch.[16]

Klein's paranoid-schizoid position has to be negotiated by everyone and we carry our failures to pass beyond it as an underlay or core to all subsequent developments. Fairbairn suggests that everyone is, in a sense, schizoid. To identify schizoid processes in culture is not therefore to achieve a subtle differential diagnosis nor to privilege a particular area of mental life but to adopt a way of deploying the whole of psychoanalytic theory. Within this framework of developmental and structural concepts, a problematic of primitive need and dependency can be consistently attended to.

Holbrook's Schizoid Minority

Cultural practices and social institutions may support, elicit, or confirm certain psychopathological characteristics in the individuals participating in them or administered by them. Any discussion of the mobilisation of schizoid pathology by such means has to take account of the work of the English writer David Holbrook, who began, in the midst of the cultural events of the 1960s to describe many of those events, and the literary and artistic phenomena which were central to them, in terms of schizoid pathology. Drawing profusely on the works of Fairbairn, Winnicott, Khan, and Guntrip, Holbrook describes the schizoid personality as one based upon fear of dependency and weakness, a fear which generates hatred of human vulnerability. In particular, hatred is directed at the female element, as representatives of that vulnerability, and there ensues the sexual exploitation of women and the whole variety of means by which sex is 'dehumanised'. (Holbrook, notably, began these analyses before the contemporary feminist attacks upon sexual themes in the media got under way.) There are also the narcissistic regressions which Lasch was later to describe on the American scene and the primitive attacks by the 'avant-garde' on the work of symbol formation in art, since true creativity involving the use of symbols, Holbrook argues (following Segal), is based upon the ability to discriminate between self, object and symbol.

Holbrook does not really offer a theory of culture in itself; he has very little concern for the general nature of cultural processes. Instead he enunciates a set of moral-psychological precepts and, using them as hastily-fashioned weapons, he launches them at specific cultural products in film, theatre, journalism, novels, etc. Despite his haste, he is at his best at the point of impact with his target: his detailed analyses of the unconscious meanings of images are frequently sharp and illuminating. He provides an angry compilation of the appearances of False Self activity in much acclaimed modern culture, both 'high' and 'mass'.

However, his critique stops at the doors of the copy-writers, authors and other celebrities. They are a 'schizoid minority' needing to force their hate and harm into others, in which they are aided by a 'trahison des clercs' – that of the critics who condone and sometimes even applaud perversion and sadism and who abdicate the responsibility of moral judgement. Otherwise the dynamics of the process remain unexplored. There are frequent references to 'commercial pressures' and the drive to sell, but no sense of how such forces might be understood and how they might be related to the familial and psychological conditions of impaired mothering that are the source of the schizoid hatred of dependency. His uncritical use of the object relations writers is made with a similar lack of feeling for context, for the intellectual and ideological locations of the writers he extols. Thus there are frequent untheorised appeals to an essential 'human-ness' as the standard by which to measure the decline of post-war society (though, additionally, the time of onset of the problem is not clearly identified or explained).

There is also his tendency to adopt a campaigning tone with repetitious indictments of pornography, which leave one suspecting that Holbrook is dangerously close to what he would describe as a 'hypoparanoid' response to the problems of which he is often so accurately aware. He certainly has little sympathy for those who, unable to sustain hypoparanoid defences or to construct genuine alternatives, insist that the malaise runs wider and deeper than autonomous moral decay and who produce pessimistic art. Holbrook can envisage 'the point of life' and is agitated by the Samuel Becketts of the world who persist in finding it pointless. It may be said of Lasch that he does not examine the possibility of counter-hegemonic refusal existing in or alongside of despair and absurdity in the avant-garde; but in Holbrook's case the problem is that there is no sense of hegemony, or indeed of any context, and therefore no way in which schizoid futility could be invested with any social meaning.

The Fragmentation of Experience

This meaning may be sought in the ways that splitting processes are initiated, encouraged or sustained by the social relations and institutional requirements of modern life. We would expect that a schizoid culture would be both fragmented (into part object relations) and, distinguishing splitting from repression, desublimated. It is not difficult to find evidence for desublimation. Marcuse's insights into 'repressive desublimation' are confirmed daily, and are as yet unqualified by economic recession and the installation as national leader of a more primitively superego figure than others in recent history (Margaret Thatcher as British prime minister; the psychodynamics of Reagan's election may be somewhat different). Desublimation, though deeply repressive culturally, is of course not 'repression' psychoanalytically. And the multiple pleasures of desublimation afforded to the modern citizen, though united extrinsically under the banner of consumption, are intrinsically fragmented from each other, encapsulated by ideologies of immanent meaning and scattered fortuitously across the invisible totality.

A prevalent tendency is to ignore the possibility of connections between different experiences, such that there operates a monadic ontology of pleasures. The sauna is experienced as ontologically and socially discrete from the hi-fi, and both from the new TV series. They may be hung together along a thin thread of narcissistic self-consciousness, but if that breaks then the individual is vulnerable to the feelings of terrible emptiness, worthlessness or aimlessness which are common today. In this atmosphere to challenge the synthesis-through-consumption by talking (as socialists try to) of a *social* totalisation of experience can seem fanciful or spoiling. Moreover such talk may derive from the tendency to adopt defensive and rigid schemes for understanding the world, such that all experiences become explicable and fused within a few simple categories. (I have in mind the example of the Manichean world-view of sections of the Leninist and Trotskyist Left.) Here the fragmentation is concealed by an intellectual strategy, often a reversal or refraction of the consumption ethic.

The fragmentation of experience is well illustrated by certain aspects of television. After a short series of bright and clamorous advertisements, there may then be a violently sudden return to the feature programme. Where the switch is back to, say, a documentary about disease or torture, we may become angrily aware of the ignorance or heartlessness which is manifest. But whatever the content of advertisements and programmes, there is nearly always a violence, as there is within a series of advertisements alone. The violence is to the 'viewer's' expectations of experience as meaningfully continuous. The intensity and abruptness of the advertisements hammer home that no such continuity is available in the world of consumption, but this message is overlaid by the socio-technical unity of the form – it all comes in the same monovocal blare from the same flickering box. Sometimes there are broadcast moments of silence and immobility, at the end of an advertisement or an announcement. In the space thus afforded for reflection, unease may develop, the television may seem fitful and inadequate and we glimpse the emptiness of it all. We are soon rescued, however, and relieved of the responsibility for establishing a sense of sequence, by being deprived of its possibility.

Our acquiescence in this series of splits and ruptures speaks of a well-recognised feature of tele-viewing: its passivity, its 'orality', technically speaking, although 'viewing' is the mode of incorporation. Amongst the deep structures of experience that are taken in is the violation of any hope or expectancy that experiences and objects can be linked and integrated over time (no matter how nostalgic the images that may be used). Moreover, this attack on the integrity of experience is carried out in a way that embeds and obscures it in social interchange: since we all watch the *same* television, more or less, we can emerge from our private scenes of consumption and pass the time (which is now a series of slots to be filled) in collective discussion of televised life.

Further examples of this phenomenon may be found in the displays of magazines in any well-stocked newsagents, in the silent juxtapositions of pornography, royalty, hi-fi, knitting, business, motorcycles and so on. Thus homogenised in brilliant gloss, these bits of experience are not seen as severely split from one another, and from the social whole. The brilliance of the display obscures the poverty of each in isolation. A similar dazzling, synthetic function is accomplished by the typographical and linguistic unity of the tabloid newspaper. Senseless items of 'interest', splinters of 'news', crude images of the body, of violence and omnipotence, are fused into a voyeuristic world of envy and contempt. The integration of the cultural form thus conceals and complements the lack of psychological integration.

Flights to Reality

We would also expect that psychic life will be characterised by the processes of fearful withdrawal from object relations, and by the development of pathological False Self structures to conceal that withdrawal. Here in particular the emphasis on schizoid states rather than on narcissistic pathology extends our analytic and evocative range.

As a consequence of leaving split-off parts of itself to conduct relations with bad objects, internal and external, and with the neutralised 'Ideal Object' (see Note 3), the remaining core of the ego is faced with the worst danger of all: its loss of all object relations and thus its own annihilation. There thus follows a 'struggle to preserve an ego' (Guntrip), one major defensive form taken by which is the flight to reality: compulsive involvement with external objects in an attempt to stave off or swamp the inner sense of desperate isolation.[17]

Often this flight will be sexualised, in which form it can deploy a maximum of libidinal investment. Khan, in *Alienation in Perversions*, writes of the 'eroticised flight to reality' of the pervert; Guntrip sees the compulsive experience of appetitive needs as one way of extorting an experience of feeling real within the schizoid configuration. In Fairbairnian terms, it is as if the Central Ego for a time delegates executive authority to the Libidinal Ego or appropriates some of the Libidinal Ego's activity. Such a move, regardless of how desublimated the external culture may be, would tend to amplify the retaliatory activity of the Anti-Libidinal Ego and so deepen the cycle of persecution and withdrawal.

In these eroticised flights, there may be a major displacement from the sites of primitive anxiety – as in the case of fetishism – or the flight may serve its defensive function by directly eroticising the anxiety content. A prominent example today of the latter mode would be the photographic cult of the breast.[18] Men (and through a somewhat different and more vicarious process, women) can flee from the bodily site of the most primitive terrors of abandonment, attack, rejection and object-loss without actually leaving the site at all. By regressive revival of other primitive memories of the breast, it is transformed into an object of greedy contemplation. Through this containment of terror by titillation, an embattled Central Ego is able to disregard the intuitions of need and fear from the inner world and instead to enlist that need in the development of a more acquisitive and fascinated deportment in the outer world.

The world of commodities offers endless opportunity for flights into reality, sexualised and other. There is often a manic quality to this defence; Schneider speaks of 'commodity euphoria'. The realities concerned range from the connoisseurship and accumulation of goods (the 'materialism' for which the 'affluent society' is indicted), through hobbies, and scientific and technical interests, to compulsive enagements in social life, in personal and sexual relationships.

These flights may often fail, either because their basic faithlessness to the inner world is sensed or because the object-relational investments they require may reinvoke the schizoid panic at involvement. Fear of sexual, intimate, or competitive relations may, for example, bring them to a halt. Clinical illness is then a likely outcome but there are alternatives. As this schizoid dilemma becomes more widespread and acute, further 'normal' or 'healthy' solutions to it are elaborated within culture. The proliferation of mystical and meditative sects, for example, can be seen in this light. They offer flights from the flight to reality; codified apologies for schizoid defeat which at the same time, through the creation of regressively supportive subcultures, provide a matrix of relations to keep the ego alive. The subversive and creative potentials of inwardness are not likely to be found here in any very healthy condition.

Another mode of flight into reality, and one which requires no dangerous delegations to subsidiary egos, appears as a compulsive rationality[19] in the organisation of experience and conduct. This is the entry of bureaucratic and market rationality into the fine print of individual psychology. As Adorno has written, we 'can expect to encounter disguised administrative categories even in . . . the most finely-nuanced emotions of the individual, in his voice and gestures' ('Culture and administration', p. 104).

We impinge here upon traditional sociological concerns with rationality, as can be seen in Michael Schneider's *Neurosis and Civilisation*. His central hypothesis is that repression, as a psychodynamic phenomenon, is the counterpart to the abstraction of exchange-value from concrete use-values in the socio-economic processes of commodity production and exchange. Under capitalism, Marx's account holds, production is determined not by the possible use-values of products but by their exchange-value, i.e., their value in the market. Exchange-value is an abstraction, something rationally abstracted from the concrete, sensuous, useful properties of products, the use-values of which are therefore 'repressed' in this abstraction process. Similarly, in the psychology of the individual, Schneider argues, the concrete and sensuous needs and satisfactions of bodily life (the world of the Freudian id) are repressed, and from them is abstracted a rational ego which takes its place in the calculating, logical world of the market. The rationality of the ego is thus consistent with the dominance of rationality in the exchange relations of the market, and is opposed to the realm of libidinal 'use-values' in the irrational id.

This analysis is a powerful allegorical address to the contradictions between emotional need and the profound impersonality of the market. But one of its main problems is that it presents a too direct and simple reflection of the mode of production in the mode of psychic formation. Schneider argues that psychoanalysis can grasp the irrationality mediated by family socialisation but not that arising from commodity production. Here he makes the unreasoned assumption that there are two separate modes of psychic formation, that family relations somehow leave some psychic material untouched for later impressions to be made directly by work relations. Moreover, in the light of the post-Freudian developments in the theory of splitting, it is no longer adequate to ground psychoanalytic thought so exclusively on the concept of repression.[20]

The compulsive rationality of the ego, though, can be seen as one mode of defence (to be considered within the wider category of flights to reality), one tactic available in the struggle to preserve an ego. It is perhaps the most available culturally, at least to certain classes or subclasses, of all the contemporary styles of functioning which are adopted by Central Egos. It provides a deep sense of engagement with the world while painting over all vestiges of primitive need for objects in that world.

Any individual act of exchange or of administration may seem wholly rational to its participants but it is enveloped by irrationality in two dimensions. 'Outwards' it is determined by the global chaos of the capitalist market. 'Inwards' it is suffused with unconscious phantasy and symbolism.

In these circumstances there is a strong congruence between intra-psychic defensive need and cultural hegemonic imperative. Knowledge of irrational forces both within and without must be excluded from daily life. We thus develop subjective rationalities of great depth, flexibility and optimism. As a compulsive psychic defence, therefore, rationality is strongly supported externally; for instance, the rational reality of bureaucratic administration nurtures the rational Central Ego in its endeavours to remain engaged with the world. At the same time, through the regressive dependence encouraged by modern bureaucracy in both its employees and subjects, it covertly ministers to the frightened ego behind the rational facade. The two dimensions of irrationality are thus simultaneously obscured – on the one side infantile phantasies of all kinds, but with the 'unthinkable anxiety', as Winnicott called it, of ego-loss and annihilation at the centre; and on the other side, the underlying destructive chaos of the mode of production (and perhaps at a different level, the dread – less irrational – of its collapse). The broad rational consensus of 'common-sense' (as Gramsci described it) in the social world reflects the pooling of these defensive efforts and their consolidation into the ideologies and practices of domination. Thus the rationality of exchange comes to pervade psychic and social life and extensive bans on thinking are ratified.

Along these lines, the analysis of schizoid processes connects with the critique of capitalist market rationality developed by Lukacs, the critical theorists, and others.[21] That rationality is not, of course, without its contradictions. In science and technology we see extensive elaborations of these contradictions in the conflation of domination with potentially liberatory achievements.

Failures in Integration

The psychic defence is likewise contradictory. Khan identifies 'the positive trends that lie buried under the débris of the erotic expertise of the pervert' (*Alienation in Perversions*, p. 16). He speaks of the 'latent affectivity' in schizoid characters and the attempt to mobilise it in polymorphous-perverse body-experiences and object relations. The element of love in perversions may be overwhelmed by hate, but is nonetheless present. The individual may be capable of loving and reparative feelings only towards things, or thing-like persons, but will go to great lengths to express those feelings.

Compulsive rationality may be seen to have this sort of reparative moment. There will be positive trends buried under the administrative expertise of the bureaucrat. In both its obsessional and manic inflections, there may struggle within the rational defence a wish to make amends, to make some contribution to the general good. In this respect administration is a tragic substitute for the public life pictured in its disappearance by Sennett. His analysis of the origins of public expression in play, though with an acknowledgement to Winnicott, misses the importance of the reparative impulse. It is partly through the diffusion into public space of the integrated and loved object that the capacity for constructive public action is developed. Civility, public service and democratic participation all offer possibilities for giving, for making restitutive contributions to a mixed but basically nurturant environment. That these possibilities are now so limited must reflect two levels of development.

Firstly, the more obvious corruptions of politics and the civic sphere render them unworthy, apparently, of reparative work. As the conviction is confirmed that politics, even radical and socialist politics, is for charlatans, self-seekers and fanatics, participation in the political process comes to seem possible only on a delusional or predatory basis. The degeneration of democracy into electoral machination illustrates the absorption of politics into the calculating relations of exchange. Sennett perhaps overstates the case for the importance of the politician's personality; that is but one of a checklist of properties, each commanding various quantities of votes – political 'realism', CV, age, strength of support in the party, etc. The value of a politician is reckoned, necessarily, in the abstract calculus of votes, in just the way that the prices of commodities are established, with the media as the Stock Exchange and as advertising space. And this calculation, daily bread for the rational ego, is inimical to reparation.

Secondly, though, and more fundamentally, these external disincentives to public action must be supported by internal atrophy of the capacity for such action. Winnicott suggests, as we have seen, that a certain degree of False Self development is necessary for adaptive, conventional negotiation of the social world. His use of his term in this way is perhaps rather confusing, but this healthy False Self is the vehicle for the politeness and distance which are now, as Sennett describes, widely regarded as hypocritical or neurotic but which are the modality of public expression. This healthy False Self or Central Ego can develop only on the basis of inner integration and security. In the absence of such conditions there is pressure to develop a pathological and inflated False Self, fluent in the rational discourse, exerting itself in mimicry of reparative involvement.

The hobby, as a component of modern leisure, is another example of this strangulation of reparation. The hobby often commands a uniquely high degree of libidinal investment, e.g., that spent in the preservation or arrangement of cherished objects, or in the loving observation and appraisal of an adored object. People have definite and isolated *passions* for their hobbies which thus function to keep some use-values upon the surface of culture but which are at the same time tragic deflections of love. The hobbyist leaves few traces in the memories of others. The hobby is after all primarily a withdrawal from both public life and intimate relations and so its pursuit is unlikely to contribute to either.

The degeneration of the public realm, then, partly rests upon the immobilisation of the reparative drive through the predominance of schizoid object relations. As long as splitting predominates, and the good object is not also known to be the object of hatred, that drive will either be absent, or present in perverted, imitative, or deflected forms.

At this point, there arises the troubled question of the role of the father in psychic development. For Klein and Winnicott, the existence of the internal *mother* as a damaged good object is, almost alone, of importance. Wisdom, however, argues for the importance of the 'penile introject' in the development of a reparative capacity towards the mother. It is partly through an identification with the father and his capacity to love the mother that the child will develop confidence in its ability and desire to give to the mother-imago. (Wisdom is drawing upon Ferenczi's notion that identification with the father provides an opportunity for regaining some experience of fusion with the mother.)

Chasseguet-Smirgel (1974; 1976a and b), in work that has interested some radicals (Engel; Lasch), has developed the implications of this notion for the theory of the ego-ideal. In the event of failure to identify with the father and to cathect him with some of the lost omnipotence of early babyhood, the ego-ideal will remain attached to a pregenital model, instead of being projected onto the father and his capacities for love and creativity. The only possibilities for regaining the experiences of fusion will then be regressive, through phantasies of direct reunion with the mother, instead of in the direction of greater maturity and autonomy, through identification with parental genitality. The capacity for genital relations may develop but be imitative rather than based on secure identifications – a condition of 'genitality without paternity', as some recent writers have called it (Kernberg, 1980).

If Wisdom's argument is accepted, it raises major questions on a number of fronts. For psychoanalytic theory, it extends the understanding of the working through of the depressive position and the protection therein against regression to schizoid states. And for radical students of psychoanalysis and social change, it suggests some unfamiliar analyses of the importance of heterosexual complementarity in child-rearing. Some recent feminist work based on psychoanalysis (see the Introduction and the chapter by Elshtain in this volume) has used ideas derived from Kleinian theory to portray the sexual division of labour in infant care as disastrous. Dinnerstein is especially eloquent on the sort of splitting that is bound up with our experience of gender roles. Wisdom, Chasseguet-Smirgel and Elshtain indicate ways in which a close scrutiny of psychoanalytic formulations may yield a yet more complex position.

Whatever conclusions, though, are reached regarding the bases of integrative and reparative tendencies, and their relationship to gender, our observations on their present diminution remain. As Kovel says, 'coherence of the object goes by the board in late capitalism' ('Narcissism and the family', p. 96). Such coherence is necessary both in the introjections upon which the sense of self is founded and in the projections which guide our social actions. Without inner coherence, the outer world – from home through public space to world politics – will be incoherent. 'The world view of chaos', as Ewen puts it, 're-enacts the shattered experience of the self on the level of a spectacle, a spectacle to be consumed' ('Mass culture, narcissism, and the moral economy of war', p. 81).

The public domain, if it is chaotic, cannot be constructively approached. Public space is resentfully defiled and disfigured. But there are defences which can be used before the point of nihilistic or vandalistic retaliation is reached. As Rosenfeld observes (see above), the confused self can be split-off and attacked, usually in projected form (e.g., the politician who does not know what he is talking about). Or, with more concerted help from the instruments of hegemony, a unifying vision may be imposed upon the senseless chaos of experience. Ewen suggests that the US is currently experiencing a renewal of militarism to this end – a 'moral economy of war' with which to bind the individual as well as the nation together. The resurgence in Britain of stern Toryism may be of a similar nature. But consistent beneath these fluctuations lies a primitive and resilient phantasy, pared down to its paranoid essentials: the image of world Communism, currently attached almost exclusively to the Soviet Union owing to the belated and well-publicised enchantment of the Chinese leadership with the capitalist way of life. Splitting here is maximal; the destructiveness mobilised against the 'enemy' is as limitless as the terror and rage at abandonment and chaos. Thus paranoid-schizoid object relations are the psychic basis for that aspect of imperialism which Thompson has conceptualised as 'exterminism'.

Amongst those for whom such phantasies do not find convincing expression in the external world and for whom sophisticated False Self functioning is also impossible, the schizoid distrust of the public domain may contain some potential for protest. The combination of visibility and isolation observed by Sennett in the modern office, and perhaps most fully expressed in the car, is an external presentation of the schizoid's internal world and its problems, and so it can never be casually tolerated. The most mundane of everyday relations are deeply problematic for the schizoid; nothing is trivial, since psychic survival is continually on the line. There is thus little scope for the development of complacency; and it is in this way that political protest can be said to originate partly in illness, in the sense of contradictions within a set of defences.

Resistance and Mass Culture

Other sources of protest may be found within a more transcendent resistance to the processes of splitting, withdrawal and depletion characteristic of schizoid defences. ('Resistance' is of course used here in the everyday political sense, not the technical, psychoanalytic sense.) Where in everyday life are there indications of integrative tendencies?[22] Or, at least, when is the lack of integration recognised, and on which occasions are the appeals of the regressed ego allowed to be heard? Psychoanalysis is, we might say, their expression in the realm of theory; and, as clinical practice, it is a highly specialised attempt to respond to them therapeutically. But if schizoid processes are as prevalent as has been suggested, we can look for wider eruptions of the 'latent affectivity' which they entail. And if there are close and mutually supportive connections between defences against that affectivity and the existing social order, then these eruptions will have a socially subversive dimension.

Marcuse wrote:

> With the affirmation of the inwardness of subjectivity, the individual steps out of the network of exchange relationships and exchange values, withdraws from the reality of bourgeois society and enters another dimension of existence. Indeed, this escape from reality led to an experience which could (and did) become a powerful force in *invalidating* the actually prevailing bourgeois values, namely, by shifting the locus of the individual's realisation from the domain of the performance principle and that of the profit motive to that of the inner resources of the human being: passion, imagination, conscience (*The Aesthetic Dimension*, pp. 4–5).

He is arguing here for a positive Marxist theory of aesthetics, but his advocacy of a subversive 'Aesthetic Dimension' need not speak only for art. The domain of intimate relationships, of sexual and familial love, is where inner resources and subjectivity ('passion, imagination, conscience') are, for more people, nurtured, tested and affirmed. And as Jacoby says,

> . . . from Marx through Freud to the Surrealists and the Frankfurt School, unique and individual love and relationships have been seen as elements of freedom, the rejection of a repressive civilisation. The drive to level, to reduce all to identical monads efficient and adept at shifting relationships with anyone or anything is the form of love of late capitalism. Unique love harbours a threat to this indifferent and collective form which is fabricated by bourgeois society or promoted by parts of the left (*Social Amnesia*, p. 144).

In the case of romantic love, we are very familiar with ways in which the 'elements of freedom' have been frozen into the tableaux of 'romance'. These, particularly in books and magazines, induce deep reverie in surprisingly wide sections of the populace. Elsewhere, however, love themes are treated in ways which give substance to Jacoby's claims.

This may be illustrated in relation to pop music, where ideologies of romantic love are endlessly played out. Pop music is a particularly significant subject for cultural analyses. It is a phenomenon of quite unprecedented global dimensions, more ubiquitous than Coca-Cola and in some respects just as uniform and levelling. It surrounds, as only sound can. Also it is fed, with undiminished directness, by forms of music with clear and particular origins in modern oppression, that is, by blues, jazz and their close derivatives.

That oppression was of course initiated by a separation trauma on a massive cultural scale with the violent removal of blacks from Africa. The persistent concern in blues (and thereby in pop) with loss and separation embodies the working through, over generations, of that trauma. It is also the enunciation of a way of life and set of concerns with which to combat the current exigencies of the capitalist world for the slaves and their descendants. The preoccupation with sexual love relations as the only meaningful experiences in an otherwise desolate or oppressive world embodies an ideology of rudimentary resistance to capital, consubstantial with the 'blues' of separation. It may be that the mother-centred forms of the family required in the conditions of slavery and after reinforced the fixation created by the experience of the primary historical separation from the mother-culture and -continent.

The deepest meaning of the clichéd connection between rhythm and sexuality may then be in infantile sexuality, in the bodily experiences of 'baby'. Balint wrote of the 'oral' phase that it contained a great deal more than strictly 'oral' experience:

> . . . we have almost completely neglected to enrich our understanding of these very early, very primitive phenomena by creating theoretical notions and coining technical terms using the experiences, imagery and implications of other spheres. Such spheres are, among others, feelings of warmth, rhythmic noises and movements, subdued, non-descript humming, the irresistible and overwhelming effects of tastes and smells, of close bodily contact, of tactile and muscle sensations especially in the hands (*Primary Love and Psychoanalytic Technique*, p. 135).

The musical language of the blues and its derivatives carries such memories of the first relationship and its sensuous-nurturant values, into the bleak separation of the social and capitalist world. That language also, however, embodies the experience of that modern world and its relations of production, through various inputs to the sources of blues and jazz (e.g., work discipline in the field songs, military organisation in marching band music). Blues and jazz thus affirm separation and modernity, while resisting modern denial of inner need.

This resistance necessarily has a tendency to regression: examples are the reggae/Rastafarian ideal of return to Africa and the transcendent mysticism embraced by a number of avant-garde jazz musicians.[23] But in some contexts, of course, regression can be progressive and therapeutic. This is when it is in the long-term service of greater integration and autonomy. Pop music may offer something of this sort to adolescents in developmental crisis. For the regression to be therapeutic, however, there must be some form of supportive parental presence and if the adolescent does not have access to such a presence, either external or internal, pop music may express more of the disintegrative pressures. In the context of culture as a whole, the best of pop music, in its chords, harmonies, timbres, lyrics and so on, may evoke regressive protest in terms which are social and critical as well as individual-developmental. In an area of the most frenzied commodification, some contact with elementary emotional need is thus kept, alongside a recognition of the modern world and its oppressions. The split between a worldly False Self and an inner locus of sensitivity may thus be lessened.

This kind of dialectic between commodification and resistance may be traced in other areas of popular culture, such as clothing.

Adorno provides a picturesque analogy: 'In an effort to preserve a feeling of contrast to contemporary streamlining, culture is still permitted to drive about in a type of gypsy wagon; the gypsy wagons, however, roll about secretly in a monstrous hall, a fact which they themselves do not notice' ('Culture and administration', p. 101). In the case of clothing, we are encouraged to wear gypsy styles and indeed all other ethnic and historical variations, but all the clothes are to be bought from the same vast boutique. Periodically, in a brief pre-'fashion' moment, there is an attempt to *create* clothing. The Punk style in England was partly of this nature.[24] The use of plastic rubbish bags and cardboard as fabrics, of safety pins and film as adornment suggests an attempt to transcend the commodity form, i.e., to define and manufacture clothing styles independently of the global boutique. It is also suggestive of aggression, albeit mixed with humour, e.g. in the mutilations implied by the pins and by the tearing of clothing. This self-abasement implies a defence by reaction-formation against narcissistic impulses, by making oneself as horrible as possible, e.g., the general associations to rubbish, the extreme ugliness of style. Notable here is the ease with which the defence passes over into the impulse, e.g., the transition from spiky, brat-like hair into multi-coloured plumage, or from pastiness of face into theatrical powdering.

It may be possible to generalise this kind of analysis to other cultural phenomena; its three points are relation to the commodity form, impulse expression and defensive function.[25] The latter two are inevitably closely related, as in the instance described above, and within impulse expression there may be complex combinations of needs. Many fashions in music and clothing speak aggressively: they are loud, dirty, sharp, or unkempt. In the case of Punk, this appears to have been interwoven with a more pleading stance – Punks apparently need to be fed, washed, and have their clothes mended – rather than with genital strivings.[26] This rather chaotic mix of aggressive and sexual phantasies, with pleas for lost or absent care or affection, is generally typical of adolescence, when schizoid object relations are widely reactivated, although at a new level and around new questions of separation. Different cultural phenomena (trends in music, styles of clothing, etc.) fix the chaos in different configurations of meaning. The degree of commodification will not show any simple relation to this psychic meaning: depending upon the content of the impulse and the choice of defence, either the impulsive or defensive aspects of a particular cultural product may carry the greatest potential for resistance to commodification and for overcoming splitting.

Schizoid States in Infancy

We have so far looked at ways in which contemporary culture may mobilise, support, encourage and reflect a number of intrapsychic processes characteristic of schizoid pathology – splitting and fragmentation, desublimation, flights to reality, quasi-reparative endeavours. We have not yet asked whether it might be possible to link the development of schizoid pathology with specific conditions of infant care and thus with wider social conditions.

Lasch sees the origins of narcissism in the 'deterioration of child care'. In the absence of secure and loving ties to the parents, early impressions of the mother assume overwhelming importance in phantasy. The absence of the father intensifies the over-dependence on the mother, so that fear of maternal abandonment becomes central and is the motive for withdrawal and splitting. Lasch's only explicit uses of Klein's work serve to elaborate this point. Mitigating experiences of the actual parents are necessary to modify archaic phantasies about them, to overcome rage and splitting. If the parents are not sufficiently involved in love *and* discipline with their children, splitting will persist and intensify. The withdrawal into defensive identifications with idealised parental imagos will become dominant. And this is where Lasch can open out his analysis into a wider one, for he has already traced the collapse of authority, confidence and commitment within the family to the 'proletarianisation of parenthood', the establishment of dependence on experts and on the State. Narcissism, in one sense the logical endproduct of individualism is also, therefore, the characterological consequence of total administration.

As already noted, there is an over-specificity in this account, in its attempt to connect a very wide range of cultural phenomena with what sounds like a very advanced and distasteful state of decomposition of the American family. Yet at the same time that decomposition is only sketchily portrayed; the account has the shadowiness that it attempts to describe in the parents.

Moreover it is the *general* conditions of parenting that Lasch emphasises, while clinical accounts of the aetiology of schizoid and related conditions tend to focus on the quality of mothering alone. Guntrip, following Winnicott, sees two major causes of schizoid withdrawal: deprivation and impingement. Deprivation is the result of 'tantalising refusal', rejection, or neglect of the infant and its needs by those responsible for it; impingement is yet more basic.

> Withdrawal from direct, frightening impingement by the object in the first place is the more primitive . . . Severe schizoid states disclose a total fear of the entire outer world, and deprivation

and impingement combine. The world is a frightening emptiness when it does not respond and meet the infant's needs, and a frightening persecutor when it actively and hurtfully impinges. The infant cannot develop a secure and strong ego-sense either in a vacuum or under intolerable pressure and he seeks to return to a vaguely remembered earlier safe place, even though in fact he can only withdraw into isolation within himself (*Schizoid Phenomena*, p. 68).

Responsibility for meeting needs and protecting against impingement is of course primarily the mother's. These two functions are expressed by Winnicott (1963) as the object-mother and the environment-mother; the deficiencies of the latter in particular have been frequently discussed in the clinical literature. The environment-mother must manage the baby's experience of the outer world so that it comes in 'small doses' (Winnicott, 1964), so that the baby will not be forced into precocious experience of its own separateness and dependence. It will release omnipotence gradually, at a pace appropriate to its developing ego-strength. Khan develops Winnicott's approach into the concept of the mother as a 'protective shield',[27] persistent breaches in which will cause 'cumulative trauma' to the infant. In a similar vein, Grotstein talks of the Primary Background Object; and Rosenfeld (1978) discusses the importance of the mother's capacity to introject the infant's projections. The vulnerable nascent ego is thus received, held and confirmed by the mother's empathy and own inner security.

Different clinical reports stress different aspects of this protective, holding, containing environment-mother. Modell, discussing narcissism, points to the mother's failure to accept her baby's separateness, thus generating a fear, in the infant, of maternal intrusiveness, which ends in some cases in a denial of need for the object. Adler and Buie, writing of borderline psychopathology, see the absence or failure of the sustaining object, or holding environment, as particularly important during the second year of life, when empathic maternal responses are necessary as the toddler fluctuates between independence and clinging. Khan (1979), in his explorations of the schizoid basis of perversions, finds a pattern of seductive maternal collusion with the regressive omnipotence of the infant, confirming a theme put forward by Chasseguet-Smirgel (1974). Kohut and Wolff list several kinds of failure – failure to respond, to offer integrating responses, to offer calmness; and excessive or premature responsivity. Holbrook (1972), pursuing a theme in Winnicott's writings, blames the mother whose 'False Male Doing' continually disturbs the baby and prevents it from acquiring a secure, peaceful sense of its own Being. All these failures are chronic and cumulative; thus, Kovel (1980) observes the lack of specific, isolated trauma in the family histories of narcissistic patients.

It should be clear, then, from this diverse sample of aetiological observations, that we cannot trace a single clear path from societal process, to infantile experience and pathology, through a specific mode of maternal care, or mis-care. This is not surprising, though, and it brings us back to the point that the argument is about a general formulation of psychoanalytic theory rather than the identification of a specific type of pathology.

As the earlier discussion of Freud and Fairbairn showed, this formulation is not an optional terminological alternative. It involves substantive innovations and preoccupations, which are concerned with the responsibility of maternal care to provide sufficient safety for the infantile ego to gather strength to face the world. Or, with a somewhat different emphasis, it is concerned with the availability of a sufficiently good primal object (Klein, 1957), which, when introjected, can be the basis for strong ego-development, strong enough to survive the attacks upon it from without and within. If these fundamental experiences of safety, and of external and internal goodness, are not sufficiently available to the infant, then dangerous and bad parts of reality, internal and external, will be split-off and thus out of control. To the extent that they are available, a reserve of utopian vision is bequeathed to the adult.

'Whereas in earlier times,' Lasch writes, 'the family passed along the dominant values but unavoidably provided the child with a glimpse of a world that transcended them, crystallised in the rich imagery of maternal love, capitalism in its late stages has eliminated or at least softened this contradiction' (*Haven in a Heartless World*, p. xxiii). It achieves this by devaluing or obscuring that transcendent imagery, and also, Lasch's argument would suggest, by the corruption of its source, by undermining love in the name of 'modernity', i.e., by market values.

Psychic Citizens of Late Capitalism

As we have just seen, the corruption and debilitation of the environment-mother is a many-sided business. Perhaps in the future the relations between historical change and the basic psychodynamics of splitting might be clarified, but at the present time we can more clearly and confidently address the historical constitution of the working out, rather than the origins, of schizoid pathologies. The False Self may, in some way, be a transhistorical structure but its content is historically specific. The cold rationality of exchange, the imperatives to toughness of life in the market, provide the perfect cover for inner withdrawal. The schizoid is likewise the perfect customer (providing he/she remains just this side of clinical breakdown) for the fragmentary experiences on sale in the global market.

Hegemony and defence thus reciprocally invigorate each other. In interpersonal terms, the exchange principle means interchangeability, instrumentalism, and autonomy. The autonomy is illusory in two ways: it is part of the schizoid defence against enormous unmet dependency needs, and it is the individual's hegemonic 'false consciousness' of genuine agency in a world dominated by capital, where the only individual agency permitted is that produced and manipulated within the sphere of commodity consumption. So the only relationships in which people keep their 'independence' are inauthentic and commodified ones.

The psychological disintegration threatened by defensive splitting is warded off by the stultifying cultural pseudo-integration achieved through education, welfare, the media, and consumption. The psychic disorder in turn obscures the domination of capital, which no longer *appears* to organise inner life. With so much chaos, whim and pleasure abroad, it is difficult to imagine that any systematic interests exist, let alone dominate. New populisms on the Left would best be tempered by some understanding of 'the people' in these terms. The False Self is a 'pseudo-adult pattern which masks the frightened child inside' (Guntrip). It is, as a pathological growth within the Central Ego, the typical psychic citizen of late capitalism. These citizens, some resignedly, some in a frightened commitment to happiness, move about their business through the rational networks of sociality in hopeless indifference to the devastation around; they are, as someone put it, deeply shallow.

Acknowledgements

Thanks are due to those who read earlier drafts of this paper and made numerous helpful suggestions: Peter Barham, Karl Figlio, Janet Graham, Les Levidow, Jon Stokes, and Bob Young.

Notes

N.B. Notes with asterisks are those which offer some definition or clarification of terms.

*1. Fairbairn is proposed by Guntrip (1961), at least implicitly, as the principal author of 'object relations' theory, though Guntrip later (1971), in an unusually defensive passage, eschewed talk of a new 'school'. 'Object relations' refers to the organisation of the inner world, to the structure and content of the individual's relations with his or her 'objects'. 'Objects' are the internal representations of the objects of experience. They are usually (perhaps always) derived from external reality, but do not *reflect* current reality – they mediate it. Although internalised, they may be experienced as internal or external, i.e., the subject of an object relation may feel the object to be either inside or outside. Either way, the *representation* of the object is inside.

*2. The concept of splitting is discussed at some length later on and in the Appendix. To begin with, we can take it in this context to be referring to one of the earliest, most primitive means of defence. It is the attempt to preserve good objects by separating the experience of good and bad, so that good objects will not be threatened by the rage felt at bad ones. It is therefore the way of avoiding the guilt and pain of more *integrated* experience, when objects are experienced in a more *whole* way, and aggression must be confronted in the context of love. In splitting, badness is separated off, and prevented from contaminating the rest of experience.

3. The term 'Ideal Object' was introduced by Fairbairn (1951b) to replace 'Accepted Object' and overcome certain inconsistencies, and was not a part of his principal 1944 account of splitting and psychic structure. It seems to be one of the most problematic terms of his theory. If it is divested of arousing qualities it must have a blandness, if not emptiness, which his description of it as 'idealized' does not connote. The difficulties are compounded by Fairbairn's (1951a) suggestion that it may correspond to Freud's ego-ideal.

4. Here seems to be another area of difficulty in Fairbairn's exposition. The Anti-Libidinal Ego (or Internal Saboteur, as he first called it) is said to be libidinally tied to its object. What he means by this is not clear; it seems, rather, to be the case that the Anti-Libidinal Ego adopts an identical rather than complementary attitude to that of the Rejecting Object – i.e., a persecutory, attacking one. A simple structure of subject-object distinctions is thus difficult to maintain.

5. Ignoring, for example, the controversies around his assertions that the primary state of the ego is unitary and that only the bad object has to be internalised (which, amongst other things, makes the subsequent history of splitting more difficult to explain).

6. Overall Fairbairn is equivocal about the relations between his structural account and Freud's. At some points (1949; 1951b) he suggests there is a 'rough correspondence' between the two tripartite systems, but other comments he makes on particular parts of the ego do not always conform to this. Kernberg's (1980) discussion is helpful.

*7. In the genealogy of psychoanalytic systems, Klein's is the progenitor of Fairbairn's, primarily in her concerns with earliest experience, mothering, and the development of the internal phantasy world of object relations. The genealogy is expounded by Guntrip (e.g. 1961; 1971) in a lucid and partisan way. See the References for details of some of Klein's own work; and for accounts by others of her theories see, e.g., Segal (1973; 1979), Meltzer (1978) and Kernberg (1980).

*8. It is intolerable because it testifies to the possibility of his losing his own penis. It may also be intolerable, Chasseguet-Smirgel argues (1974), because it is a statement to the young boy of his inability to be an adequate sexual partner for his mother. The vagina needs an *adult* penis to fill it. If mother has a penis, she does not need father for anything and the young boy can phantasise meeting all her needs.

*9. For Klein, the source of destructiveness is ultimately internal, in the death instinct, though through projection, introjection, reprojection and so forth it is soon felt to be distributed throughout the internal and external worlds. For Fairbairn, Winnicott, and especially Guntrip, the source is primarily actual inadequacies in the external environment. See pp. 156–158.

*10. Use of Winnicott's work is made elsewhere in this volume by Stephen Robinson. It is marked by a quaintly unperturbed advocacy of the sexual division of labour (see especially Winnicott, 1964) and a stress on the quality of external care as the major determinant of psychic development.

11. See his *Borderline Conditions and Pathological Narcissism*. Modell (1975) has suggested a different connection: an equivalence of Winnicott's False Self with the narcissistic syndrome described by Kohut (1971) – see p. 131. This seems erroneous, as the False Self does not necessarily possess the characteristics of grandiosity and omnipotence which are the hallmarks of narcissism. Grotstein (1981) suggests a more complex connection between Winnicott and Kohut, with both True and False Selves represented in the different modes of transference observed by Kohut in narcissistic patients.

12. Rosenfeld, the British analyst whose early investigations of psychotic, borderline and narcissistic disorders have influenced the American work reported here, makes it clear (1964) that he sees narcissistic omnipotence as a defence against the awareness of separation, and so focusses on the inner sense of catastrophic weakness.

13. Lasch (1978) makes this point in his critique of Sennett. As he puts it, 'the cult of intimacy originates not in the assertion of personality but in its collapse.'

14. His follower Wilhelm Reich was of course to begin this work perhaps rather sooner, and certainly less cautiously, than Freud would have wished.

* 15. The reparative wish is the wish to make good the harm which in phantasy has been done to the object. It thus develops as primitive splitting gives way to more integrated experience of the object. It is the means by which the guilt brought by such integrated experience (see Note 2) can be mitigated without regression to splitting and is thus the basis for the development of the capacity for mature and loving object relations. The basic ego-strength founded on identification with the good object is threatened if that object is felt to be irreparably damaged.

16. The extent to which they are also expressive of psychic life in precapitalist societies is a matter for historical and anthropological research, of a kind of which little has so far appeared, as far as I know.

* 17. This defence may embody a general psychic capacity for reversal, as seen in 'reaction-formation' and in 'reversal into the opposite'. In reaction-formation there is a counter-cathexis of a consciously experienced object relation which is *contrary* to the repressed one; in reversal into the opposite there is switching of perspective along the dimensions of activity/passivity and subject/object, within the *same* object relation (see Laplanche and Pontalis, 1973). In flight to reality, however, there is a reversal from a tendency which threatens loss of all object relations into a tendency to engage in *any* object relations (though other factors will introduce some discrimination).

18. Lasch (1977) also links the cult of the breast to the fear of maternal abandonment.

19. This term was suggested to me by Talcott Parsons' 'The Social System', in which he describes a variety of 'compulsive' defences as elaborated within the social fabric.

20. Schneider's method of seeking conceptual equations could equally lead to the linking of exchange with splitting rather than repression. Consider for example the statement of Sohn-Rethel (1975): 'But while exchange banishes

use from the actions of people, it does not banish it from their minds . . . Thus the action and the thinking of people part company in exchange and go different ways' (p. 87). With yet another take on the process of commodity production and exchange, this time focussing upon concepts of reification, we could perhaps find correlates in Marxist economic theory of the psychoanalytic concept of projection. The different meanings of reification clarified by Rose (1978) each echo aspects of projection – the experience that one's products confront one as external things, sometimes as personifications, and usually as out of one's control. However, these conceptual Grand Slams, including Schneider's, can be no more than starting points for historical study of the relationships between psychoanalytic and Marxist discourse.

21. It may also converge upon a theme in phenomenology, expressed as 'morbid rationalism' by Minkowski – see Gabel, 1962.

22. Great care is required to distinguish an integrative affirmation from the schizoid/narcissistic celebrations of 'growth', 'relationships', etc., within which deep resources of panic, rage and envy lie split-off. The difficulty of making these distinctions has led to Aronowitz (1980), for example, hailing narcissism as a progressive cultural development, seeing it as the discovery of a selfhood denied by the outer world.

23. Adorno was particularly critical of the tendency to the 'regression of hearing' induced by modern popular music. In his assessment of jazz, his sensitivity to the contradictoriness of things deserted him, and his elegant melancholy became a defensive crustiness. In the case of the jazz mystics, their artistic excellence and faithfulness to the sentience of blues are usually of much greater significance for their music than are their religions.

24. Unlike the Ted and Mod styles which, as the works of Jefferson (1975) and of Hebdige (1975) indicate, were attempts to find expressive ways of shopping *within* the global boutique, of manipulating the commodity form rather than transcending it.

25. It would be more fully consistent with object relations theory to structure the analysis in terms of subsidiary egos, but this is less important than employing a relational concept of impulses and defences.

26. As in, for example, the apparently more armoured and macho-defended 'Heavy Metal' enthusiasts. Here, though, there are 'head-bangers' in need of protection from themselves.

27. This concept (Khan, 1963) may help us to understand something of the psychic meaning of nuclear weapons, and of the readiness of many people to risk holocaust, even to anticipate it. Arguments for nuclear weapons frequently turn around the need for protection, for preserving the sense of self and the space in which to find it ('way of life' and territory), within the paranoid-schizoid world scenario referred to earlier. Chronic early failure of the maternal shield would be expected to initiate a search for later substitutes. Phantasies of the father may be utilised in this search and rage at the early failure may be projected into the protecting object. Thus a terrible militaristic 'shield' can meet some deep needs; in the midst of splitting there is a basic confusion between explosive destructiveness, and protectiveness, as in the experience of a raging parent.

References

Adler, G. and Buie, D.H. (1979). Aloneness and borderline psychopathology: the possible relevance of child development issues. *Int. J. Psycho-Anal.* 60, 83–96.

Adorno, T. (1960). Culture and administration. *Telos* 37, 93–111, 1978.
Aronowitz, S. (1980). On narcissism. *Telos* 44, 65–74.
Balint, M. (1951). On love and hate, in: *Primary Love and Psychoanalytic Technique*. Tavistock, 1965.
Balint, M. (1968). *The Basic Fault*. Tavistock.
Chasseguet-Smirgel, J. (1974). Perversion, idealization and sublimation. *Int. J. Psycho-Anal.* 55, 349–357.
Chasseguet-Smirgel, J. (1976a). Some thoughts on the ego-ideal. *Psychoanalytic Quart.* 45, 345–373.
Chasseguet-Smirgel, J. (1976b). Freud and female sexuality. *Int. J. Psycho-Anal.* 57, 275–286.
Engel, S. (1980). Femininity as tragedy: re-examining the 'New Narcissism'. *Socialist Review* 53, 77–103.
Ewen, S. (1980). Mass culture, narcissism, and the moral economy of war. *Telos* 44, 74–87.
Fairbairn, W.R.D. (1940). Schizoid factors in the personality, in: *Psychoanalytic Studies of the Personality*. Tavistock, 1952.
Fairbairn, W.R.D. (1944). Endopsychic structure considered in terms of object-relationships. Op. cit.
Fairbairn, W.R.D. (1949). Steps in the development of an object-relations theory of the personality. Op. cit.
Fairbairn, W.R.D. (1951a). Addendum to 'Endopsychic structure'. Op. cit.
Fairbairn, W.R.D. (1951b). Synopsis of the development of the author's views regarding the structure of the personality. Op. cit.
Foucault, M. (1976). *The History of Sexuality. Volume One: An Introduction*. Allen Lane, 1979.
Freud, S. (1914). On narcissism: an introduction. *Standard Edition* Vol. 14, 73–102.
Freud, S. (1929). *Civilisation and its Discontents. Standard Edition* Vol. 21, 64–145.
Freud, S. (1940). Splitting of the ego in the process of defence. *Standard Edition* Vol. 23, 275–278.
Gabel, J. (1962). *False Consciousness: An Essay on Reification*. Blackwell, 1975.
Grotstein, J. (1981). *Splitting and Projective Identification*. Aronson.
Guntrip, H. (1961). *Personality Structure and Human Interaction*. Hogarth.
Guntrip, H. (1968). *Schizoid Phenomena, Object Relations and the Self*. Hogarth.
Guntrip, H. (1971). *Psychoanalytic Theory, Therapy, and the Self*. Hogarth.
Hebdige, D. (1975). The meaning of mod, in: Hall, S. and Jefferson, T., eds., *Resistance through Rituals*. Hutchinson, 1976.
Holbrook, D. (1971). *Human Hope and the Death Instinct*. Pergamon.
Holbrook, D. (1972). *The Masks of Hate*. Pergamon.
Jacoby, R. (1975). *Social Amnesia*. Harvester, 1977.
Jacoby, R. (1980). Narcissism and the crisis of capitalism. *Telos* 44, 58–65.
Jefferson, T. (1975). Cultural responses of the Teds, in: Hall, S. and Jefferson, T., eds., *Resistance through Rituals*. Hutchinson, 1976.
Kernberg, O. (1975). *Borderline Conditions and Pathological Narcissism*. Aronson.
Kernberg, O. (1976). Contribution to panel discussion on 'The changing expectations of patients and analysts today'. *Int. J. Psycho-Anal.* 57, 419–427.
Kernberg, O. (1980). *Internal World and External Reality*. Aronson.

Khan, M.M.R. (1963). The concept of cumulative trauma, in: *The Privacy of the Self*. Hogarth, 1974.

Khan, M.M.R. (1966). Role of phobic and counterphobic mechanisms and separation anxiety in schizoid character formation, in *The Privacy of the Self*. Hogarth, 1974.

Khan, M.M.R. (1979). *Alienation in Perversions*. Hogarth.

Klein, M. (1946). Notes on some schizoid mechanisms, in: *Envy and Gratitude*. Hogarth, 1975.

Klein, M. (1957). Envy and gratitude, in: *Envy and Gratitude*. Op. cit.

Kohut, H. (1971). *The Analysis of the Self*. IUP.

Kohut, H. (1977). *The Restoration of the Self*. IUP.

Kohut, H. and Wolff, E.S. (1978). The disorders of the self and their treatment: an outline. *Int. J. Psycho-Anal.* 59, 413–425.

Kovel, J. (1978). Rationalisation and the family. *Telos* 37, 5–21 (and in this volume).

Kovel, J. (1980). Narcissism and the family. *Telos* 44, 88–100.

Laplanche, J. and Pontalis, J.-B. (1973). *The Language of Psychoanalysis*. Hogarth.

Lasch, C. (1977). *Haven in a Heartless World: The Family Besieged*. Basic Books.

Lasch, C. (1978). *The Culture of Narcissism*. Norton.

Marcuse, H. (1955). *Eros and Civilisation*. Beacon, 1974.

Marcuse, H. (1978). *The Aesthetic Dimension*. Macmillan, 1979.

Meltzer, D. (1978). *The Kleinian Development*. (3 vols.) Clunie Press.

Meltzer, D. (1981). The Kleinian expansion of Freud's metapsychology. *Int. J. Psycho-Anal.* 62, 177–185.

Modell, A.H. (1975). A narcissistic defence against affects and the illusion of self-sufficiency. *Int. J. Psycho-Anal.* 56, 275–282.

Parsons, T. (1952). *The Social System*. Tavistock.

Robinson, P. (1969). *The Sexual Radicals*. Paladin, 1972.

Roheim, G. (1944). The origin and function of culture, in: Muensterberg, W., ed., *Man and His Culture*. Random House, 1965.

Rose, G. (1978). *The Melancholy Science: An Introduction to the Thought of Theodor W. Adorno*. Macmillan.

Rosenfeld, H. (1964). On the psychopathology of narcissism. A clinical approach. *Int. J. Psycho-Anal.* 45, 332–337.

Rosenfeld, H. (1978). Notes on the psychopathology and psychoanalytic treatment of some borderline patients. *Int. J. Psycho-Anal.* 59, 215–221.

Rustin, M. (1982). A socialist consideration of Kleinian psychoanalysis. *New Left Review* 131, 71–96.

Schneider, M. (1975). *Neurosis and Civilisation*. Seabury.

Segal, H. (1973). *Introduction to the Work of Melanie Klein* (rev. edn.). Hogarth.

Segal, H. (1979). *Klein*. Fontana.

Sennett, R. (1977). *The Fall of Public Man*. CUP.

Skultans, V. (1979). *English Madness*. RKP.

Sohn-Rethel, A. (1975). Science as alienated consciousness. *Rad. Sci. J.* 2/3, 65–101.

Thompson, E.P. (1980). Notes on exterminism, the last stage of civilisation. *New Left Review* 121, 3–31.

Williams, R. (1976). *Keywords*. Fontana.

Winnicott, D.W. (1960). Ego distortion in terms of True and False Self, in: *The Maturational Processes and the Facilitating Environment*. Hogarth, 1965.

Winnicott, D.W. (1963). The development of the capacity for concern, in *The Maturational Processes and the Facilitating Environment*. Hogarth, 1965.

Winnicott, D.W. (1964). *The Child, the Family, and the Outside World*. Penguin.

Wisdom, J.O. (1976). The role of the father in the mind of parents, in psychoanalytic theory and in the life of the infant. *Int. J. Psycho-Anal.* 3, 231–239.

APPENDIX: Some Theoretical Difficulties Concerning Splitting

Klein's use of the term is not altogether consistent. On occasion she uses it to refer to the state of ego-fragmentation which may occur when the baby feels its destructiveness to have destroyed the object and torn or broken it to bits (for instance, *Envy and Gratitude*, p. 6). This seems to refer to a state of affairs when defences have broken down. More usually, 'splitting' is the defence by which the object world (and the ego with it) is split into broad but immiscible categories.

There is particular confusion around its relations with repression. In Freudian theory, the two are closely linked, both in the earlier formulations of splitting in hysteria and in the later ones of splitting in fetishism. Fairbairn, while seeking to recover splitting from Freud's early work and re-install it at the centre of psychoanalysis, tends to conflate it with repression. He states (1944) that 'splitting of the ego, on the one hand, and repression of the subsidiary egos by the Central Ego, on the other, constitute essentially the same phenomenon, considered from different points of view' (*Psychoanalytic Studies*, p. 108). Also that 'repression itself is a schizoid process' (ibid., p. 131).

For Klein, splitting and repression are clearly different and separable processes. Splitting is the earlier, more primitive defence (though it has its more mature and less pathological forms); repression comes later, a sign of a stronger ego. Kernberg (*Internal World and External Reality*) criticises Fairbairn for his confusion of splitting and repression, and, on Kleinian lines, himself proposes (1976) a basis for a distinction between the two. Splitting is the defence undertaken by the ego to protect itself against anxiety connected with intrapsychic conflicts between introjects of opposing valences; it consists of a process of 'regressive nucleation'. (To refer to it as 'regressive' implies some original state of ego-splitting or unintegration; otherwise this definition is consistent with the Fairbairnian account of the development of subsidiary egos.) Repression, however, is protection by elimination of the threatening material from consciousness. It thus requires a stronger ego to block the threat. In splitting, no such blockage need occur: opposing affects and phantasies may each find direct expression in consciousness and action.

Of course, the problem is not an ahistorical one; it is not a matter of finding the 'best' definitions for a timeless body of clinical material. The increasing interest in splitting, along with that in schizoid psychopathology, is linked with the growing belief that the most important developmental processes occur in the earliest stages of development. Conceptualising the sources and supports of these theoretical changes is a complex affair. They are not simple responses to changes in the clinical population; nor are they the autonomous, maturational unfoldings of theory fed by 'more evidence'. Psychoanalytic notions of splitting are part of a wider history of the elaboration of a range of meanings concerned with internal states of dissociation, multiplicity, and unconsciousness.

An historical overview of the theory of splitting within psychoanalysis has been offered by Grotstein. The cover of his book *Splitting and Projective Identification* confidently states that 'In its first hundred years psychoanalysis has been a history of the mechanisms of REPRESSION and DISPLACEMENT. In its second hundred years it will be a history of SPLITTING and PROJECTIVE IDENTIFICATION.' Basing himself firmly on the Kleinian tradition, Grotstein develops a highly inclusive notion of splitting, including within it, at its normal end, basic cognitive abilities for discrimination. He thus brings many kinds of distinctions and categorisations, normal and pathological, under the rubric of splitting. He portrays, in the development of psychoanalytic theory, the emergence and clarification of splitting as a concept superordinate to that of repression and the other defences. At the same time, in acknowledging the distinction used by Kohut (1971) between 'vertical' and 'horizontal' cleavage, Grotstein echoes Kernberg's distinction between splitting and repression.

THE PARENT TO THE CHILD

Stephen Robinson

Freud tells us that the child is father to the man.

People react in different ways to the loss of another. To learn from such separations one must be able to be disrespectful. When a valued person is lost, through death or another form of separation, there is always a possibility that our own life may become stuck; it is as if we exist in a kind of living death. This is particularly true where the other has become idealised; if we identify too strongly with such a figure we cannot move away from them and therefore we cannot put them into any kind of perspective. Without some kind of distance between self and object, the object cannot be seen, nor can it be used as we would use other objects external to us.[1]

To distance oneself from another requires the use of aggression, and Freud glimpsed this first. It is implicit in his differentiation between love, the force in life constantly seeking union, and its antithesis, aggression, the force constantly seeking separation.[2] Perhaps this provides us with a clue as to why so many people cannot give up psychically what they have lost physically: they fear by endeavouring to obtain such a distance they will destroy and lose the other for ever.

My feeling is that revolutionaries have identified with Marx too strongly, much more strongly than psychoanalysts have identified with Freud. Let me list some of the 'unkind' things psychoanalysts have said about Freud. The main body of his theory (the Oedipal theory) is a theory of early childhood, but Freud says virtually nothing about infancy and therefore virtually nothing about 'life before words'.[3] Although this is perhaps the major absence in his work, there are many 'smaller' lapses and confusions we might comment upon. For example, Freud provides us with at least two different conceptions of how 'instincts' obtain physical status,[4] changes his classification of the major sets of instincts on at least three occasions,[5] provides us with three different schematisations of the earliest post-natal state[6] and reconceptualises the phenomenon of 'psychic trauma' at least twice.[7] It is not as if these different theorisations are merely the expression of a logical development in Freud's thought. Very often one finds Freud forgetting his own earlier theorisations,[8] or providing us with parallel but contradictory accounts of a single process.[9]

By being critical in this way, have we destroyed Freud? I think not. Freud's work cannot be properly understood unless it is grasped as something partial, fragmentary and, at times, contradictory. Freud, like Marx, provided us with a starting point; therein lies his greatness. But I know of very few Marxists who could be this disrespectful to Marx and yet still feel confident of their Marxism. Marxists' insistence on the completeness of Marx's work has played no small part in contributing to the present fragile condition of Marxism, one in which vitality and development are rarely discernible.

Consider Marxism's relationship to a contemporary drama – Poland. We could say that recent events in Poland provide Marxists with food for thought: Poland spreads itself before us invitingly, daring us to understand it. Whether events in Poland enliven Marxism depends, however, upon whether we are willing to take in all that Poland presents to us, and whether we can use what we have taken in to develop and enrich our general understanding of the contemporary world.

The signs are that many Marxists see only what they want to see in Poland – a 'deformed workers' state' incapable of gradual transformation but lacking a revolutionary party capable of breaking the impasse, etc. etc. Poland tells them little they don't already know, they take from Poland only what they have graciously thrust upon it. They are unable to take in any new material for anything new proves unpalatable or indigestible. Poland is allowed to give them nothing that is uniquely Poland's, and therefore receives nothing in return. Such Marxists feed only off their own products, but then there is a limit even to the self sustaining power of a camel.

It may not have escaped the reader's attention that I have presented the Polish drama as if it were some kind of succulent lemon sole which can be devoured, enjoyed and benefitted from if one so wishes. I have deliberately used a rather oral language to describe the relationship between dogmatic Marxism and its object; this is the language of those psychoanalysts who, by being most 'disrespectful' towards Freud, undertook the creative development of his work, from his initial starting point. Theirs is an oral language because this is the language of infancy and infancy is the major absence in Freud's own work. If, to use his own words, Freud indicated that the child was father to the man, Kleinian and object-relations theorists have indicated that the infant is parent to the child.

Outside psychoanalysis itself, however, the key role of figures like Melanie Klein, Ronald Fairbairn, Michael Balint, Wilfred Bion and Donald Winnicott in the development of psychoanalytic theory and practice is largely unrecognised. Following academia, the left in this country has tended to describe the history of psychoanalysis in bizarre terms: psychoanalysis, after Freud's death, atrophies; few signs of life are discerned, with the exception of the odd revisionist (Fromm, Horney, etc.) abandoning ship. Then along comes a Frenchman, Lacan, who in true fundamentalist fashion rediscovers 'what Freud really said'. Having found itself again, psychoanalysis can now begin to live once more. It is about time this parody was laid to rest.

Life Before Words

It has been widely assumed that psychoanalysis sees human subjectivity as emerging from the Oedipal drama, and indeed Freud's work tends to imply this. The drama is certainly central to the later development and to the virtual completion of a gendered subjectivity. However, in its classical form the Oedipal drama assumes a child relating to, and attempting to use, objects.[10] Kleinians and object-relations theorists have tried to understand what Freud's theory assumes, and have posed the question how do the phenomena 'inside'/'outside', 'me'/'not me', 'self'/'other' and 'agent/'object' become a phenomenological reality during infancy?

Even at the very beginning the infant is not without agency. The infant that turns its mouth away from the breast or pacifier, that spews out the milk that it has just taken in, undertakes the first 'great refusal'. Such an infant does not know what it is it wants, let alone can it say what it wants or act upon its wants, but it can 'say' what it doesn't want, it can say 'no'.

This act of refusal is nonetheless the first affirmation. By turning its mouth away, the infant shows that even it cannot be taken for granted and in this way affirms its self.

Refusal is the only form of agency open to a victim of circumstance. Even as adults, in moments of fearful helplessness, we can still say no. As an object in another's world the infant can only reach out towards the humanity that beckons it by being recalcitrant, but it is not yet truly human: it assumes agency through its negativity but it has not yet acquired positive agency. The infant starts from the position of being 'acted upon'; to become fully human it must also learn to 'act upon'. It will never cease to be an object buffeted by internal and external forces, but it can (to use an analogy of Trotsky and Freud) learn to ride these forces as one would ride a horse.[11]

With a little exaggeration we could say that life spreads itself before the new-born infant in a manner analogous to an army assault course. To become an adult it must first traverse a number of hurdles. The Oedipal Complex is certainly one of these, though we might wonder about the historical specificity of this particular hoop. The point is that for the child to begin to negotiate the difficulty of the Oedipus complex, it must already have a firm sense of its own agency. It can only act upon the world if it has acquired the capacity for object-usage and it can only use objects if it is prepared to acknowledge that they exist separately from itself.[12] These two capacities represent, if you like, the equipment the child had picked up from negotiating two more primitive yet more formative infantile dramas – those of the paranoid-schizoid and the depressive positions.[13] A brief discussion of these concepts is necessary at this point, starting with an evocative simile.

Following Balint we can liken the foetus in the womb to a fish in water. Who can say whether the fish is in the water or the water in the fish? We have an undifferentiated expanse, fish-water. The birth of the human infant changes things only slightly for, although from our point of view the infant is now psychically 'out of its mother', from its own point of view nothing has altered – and not just because of the infant's under-developed perceptual capacity. Things can only be acknowledged as 'different' if the infant is prepared to live with separateness and dependence, and such conditions arouse both fear and hatred. Yet to become a human subject the infant must accomplish this essential task. It must become psychically what it physically and phylogenetically already is, a fish/baby out of water/mother.

Klein's two 'positions' mark major way-stations on this journey, each demanding progressive steps towards a differentiation of the original phenomenologically undifferentiated mother-infant expanse. One could say that the paranoid-schizoid position refers to the earliest phase of infant development during which the environment is sensed but not discovered. There is not yet a 'mother present' and a 'mother absent', for this requires thought; in these earliest phases it is sensation that has primacy. In the absence of the desired breast the infant feels bad, in its presence the infant feels good.[14] This first form of differentiation is one based on value; and the good-bad differentiation provides the terms necessary for psychical processes to begin. Initially, such processes have only one concern: to maintain a maximal psychical distance between experiences which are good and life-giving and those which are bad and threatening. This process is known as 'splitting'. From our point of view it heightens the contradiction within the infant's experience of its environment; from the infant's point of view it ensures the continuation of good experience relatively free from the threat of annihilation.[15] Where anxiety is great and splitting excessive, good experiences are idealised and bad ones threaten to become overwhelming. The paranoid-schizoid position, I feel, properly refers to the situation in which the differentiation 'inside-outside' becomes mapped into the differentiation 'good-bad'[16] in such a way that all that is good is inside and as much as possible of bad is outside. The resulting position is 'schizoid' because it rests upon splitting, and 'paranoid' because the attempt to place all badness 'outside' has long been recognised as a basic technique in paranoia.

If splitting is not excessive, the infant can move on from the paranoid-schizoid to the depressive position. In Kleinian terms this journey corresponds to the process by which the wanted breast is experienced as an 'idea of a breast missing' and not as a 'bad breast present'.[17] In other words, with the depressive position the world upon which the infant depends is first truly lost, and therefore first truly found, and the infant now experiences intense ambivalence rather than contradiction. It must face up to the fact that the depriving figure it sometimes hates and wishes it could destroy is synonymous with the good feeding mother that it loves and seeks to preserve. We could say that all healthy infants wish to bite the hands that feed them; the resolution of this dilemma corresponds to the resolution of the depressive position. The key to the resolution resides in the capacity to experience guilt and the corresponding desire to make reparations to those on which we depend but whom we abuse.

This discovery of separateness and difference does not occur all of a sudden. Indeed the infant is 'partially' losing and therefore 'partially' finding bits of its environment from the start.[18] But the objects that populate such an infantile environment are not the fully differentiated and discrete objects of the adult phenomenal world; they are primitive objects, which Klein calls 'part-objects',[19] apparently unrelated and transitory – a terrifying breast, a reassuring belly, a voracious mouth, etc. It is only with the depressive position that an integration can be made and the various unconnected 'bits' to which the infant relates located within the one person. The depressive position therefore offers the possibility of relationship to 'whole-objects' (mother, father). This is crucial; one can relate to part-objects to the extent that they represent bits of the environment which have acquired value (and thus have become meaningful, albeit a phantastic and wholly subjective meaning), but one cannot use them. As Winnicott notes, 'the object, if it is to be used, must necessarily be real in the sense of being a part of shared reality, not a bundle of projections'.[20] The depressive position therefore allows the passage from the stage of (part)-object-relations to (whole)-object-usage and thus to full human agency.

Envy

> 'It is the green-eyed monster which doth mock the meat it feeds on.' Othello.[21]

Without the infant's experience of its own separateness and dependence object-usage cannot properly begin. Envy bars the path to such experience whilst feeding off it. It is born out of the experience of dependence and lack, but is also the denial of them.

The most primitive experience of loss is equally an experience of lack. Loss refers to the outside, to the experience of 'no-thing', while lack refers to the hurt inflicted by loss upon one's narcissism – one feels lacking (one cannot feel 'lossing'). Envy is centred upon the phantasy of possessing what one does not have, a desperate narcissistic endeavour not to feel lacking. Speaking of Klein, one commentator has proposed,

> She thought that envy appears as a hostile life-destroying force . . . and is particularly directed towards the good feeding mother because she is not only needed by the infant but envied for containing everything which the infant wants to possess himself.[22]

Klein suggests that the envious impulse aims to spoil and destroy the source of all that the infant wants for itself.[23] This 'source' is, in the first instance, the mother and her creativeness, which the infant acknowledges but seeks to destroy and eradicate. The spoiling character of envy is particularly important; through it, all that is good, desired and therefore depended upon is turned bad.

Both Klein and Segal[24] point out that jealousy is a more sophisticated emotion than envy, as only the former refers to relations between three or more 'whole-objects' (i.e. persons). But the nature of envious object-relations are, I feel, not made entirely clear by either author. According to Klein,[25] envy 'implies the subject's relation to one person only'. Segal, on the other hand, suggests envy refers to a relation 'in which the subject envies the object for some possession or quality' and, referring to the infant at the breast, adds that 'the very nourishment that has been taken in, so long as it is perceived as having been part of the breast, is in itself *an object* of envious attacks'[26] (my emphasis).

We have grounds then for considering that, whilst envy may pertain to a relationship with one other person, it is nevertheless founded upon some form of *triadic* object-relation (subject, object, quality or possession of object). This suspicion is confirmed in the illustration that many Kleinians give of envy in the psychoanalytic relationship itself.[27] A person manifesting excessive envy will seek to devalue and destroy any analytic work which has been found helpful; but the patient's attacks are directed at the analysis, particularly at the analyst's verbal productions, and not directly at the analyst.[28] It is not just that the envious person seeks to attack the source of the things that he/she needs; envy attacks and spoils the life-giving offerings themselves.

Let us consider everyday examples. It could be said that, whereas one envies an imaginative person, one nevertheless *desires* her imagination, or that whereas one envies an intelligent acquaintance one nevertheless *desires* her intelligence. According to the psychoanalytic interpretation of envy, however, it would not be correct to say one simply desires another's imagination or intelligence. Psychoanalysis sees envy as referring to the situation where in phantasy one does not need the other's qualities because one already has them (though perhaps others have not yet recognised this). A conscious longing for these qualities may exist, but it is constantly submerged beneath a greater loathing: one hates what one most desires *because* one desires it so. One envies the other only because of what they embody. The other is not a discrete other but 'any other', a generalised other. To take things a step further; the particular quality, say intelligence, upon which one focusses so much passion is itself a 'stand-in', a representative of something more fundamental – one's own imperfection and dependence. Thus, it isn't so much, as Segal puts it, that 'the subject envies the object', rather the subject envies the object's other-ness. One desires and yet abhors a particular quality because it represents one's own lack.

Envy arises when the experience of dependence threatens to break in upon narcissism. It is the denial of dependence and the perversion of need; it is a way of poisoning the material upon which one's life depends. Many ostensible 'men and women of action' in fact rarely effect any change in themselves, let alone their environment, because envy constantly undermines their ability to make use of what they find there. An acquaintance of mine once admitted to me that he had great difficulty in reading any contemporary material on political or cultural theory because of an overwhelming feeling that he should already have written what he was trying to read. He begrudged every insight (and there were few) he obtained from his reading. He poured scorn on potentially challenging perspectives, would exaggerate the incomprehensibility of the text, and so on. He could take in and digest little of the new material and was therefore quite unable to adopt a critical stance towards it – it was all or nothing, and usually nothing.

Envy also undermines objectification, that is, the realisation of human need through the imaginative use of objects. Speaking of this process in his (by now famous) comparison between the architect and the bee, Marx says:

> At the end of every labour process we get a result that already existed in the imagination of the labourer at its commencement. He not only effects a change in the form of the material on which he works, but he also realises a purpose of his own that gives the law to his modus operandi, and to which he must subordinate his will.[29]

The labourer must acknowledge his dependence on the materials with which he works, if objectification is to occur. But envy cannot acknowledge such dependence.

I do feel we are justified in using the term 'envy' to refer not just to relationships between people but also to relationships between a person and the natural environment (as in the example from Marx). To the extent that we endow nature and natural objects with human attributes, it is reasonable to surmise that we could envy them. Consider my acquaintance's relationship to his own productions. He hated the recalcitrance of the piano he played and begrudged every moment involved in musical composition. He often became extremely angry with his piano, for its recalcitrance seemed to suggest it was holding something from him (the possibility of musical expression) and thereby keeping this secret to itself. He continuously abused the instrument he most loved, things got squashed and spilt on it and were never cleared up, he persistently forgot to keep it regularly tuned, cigarette ends left their scorches upon it, etc.[30] On the rare occasion when this friend completed a composition he would be quite unable to alter or develop it, for he identified with his product so completely that he could not treat it as something separate from himself that he could make use of. Thus he was unable to benefit from his own work. He couldn't return to a composition he had completed some months previously and pick up an idea or fill in an absence. There was no space in which his products could talk back to him. He could thus assume a constructively critical distance neither from his own nor another's production.[31]

To summarise. In *Envy and Gratitude* Klein provides a phenomenological account of envy which is probably without precedent. For my own part, I find Klein's account of the origin of envy less satisfactory. She not only insists that it is 'operative from the beginning of life' but, moreover, that it has a 'constitutional basis' and is an expression of the death drive.[32] If this were the case then of course pathological envy and covetousness would have to be seen as endemic to the human condition rather than as a contingency of development towards full human agency.

The Internal and External World

> I think the Viennese would reproach us with estimating the early phantasy life too highly at the expense of external reality. And we should answer that there is no danger of any analysts neglecting external reality, whereas it is always possible for them to underestimate Freud's doctrine of the importance of psychical reality (Ernest Jones, 'Early female sexuality', p. 273).

In 1976 a young man in his twenties, a member of a familiar revolutionary organisation on the British scene, was invited by his father, a prominent businessman, to a businessmen's dinner to be addressed by the chairperson of one of the largest nationalised corporations in Britain. The young man accepted his father's invitation but secretly taped the after-dinner speech in which the guest, believing himself to be in safe company, made a number of racist remarks about his non-white workforce. Within a few days the young man's recording had been released to the national press, the chairperson of the corporation was forced to resign, and the young man's revolutionary organisation proudly presented their 'public-spirited' member to the media. The young man's father was left with his shame, the young man with his pride and his guilt; their relationship, which had never been good, reached its nadir.

I was fortunate enough to get, at first hand, the reactions of a number of political activists and a number of psychotherapists to this familial and political drama. Over dinner in middle-class Hampstead my therapist acquaintances guffawed over the young man's 'obvious' unconscious intent, the re-enactment of his Oedipal struggle, the symbolic castration of the father, etc. Over pints of beer in working-class Wandsworth my Marxist friends expressed hushed respect for the young man's shrewd and unswerving adherence to revolutionary duty. The two groups were worlds apart. One saw only the individual, the internal world containing a timeless, vortex-like, Oedipalised family dynamic. The other saw only the public world, public wrongs and public duties.

Clearly each group would accuse the other of having got hold of the wrong end of the stick – one of having made something political out of what was purely personal, the other of having made something personal out of what was purely political. In reality these antagonists have made two stumps out of a formerly useful stick. One wields its depoliticised stump at the other, the other wields its depersonalised stump in return. The point surely is that so long as the investigators of the internal world neglect external reality, their work is bound to be impoverished, placing myth in the absences and silences that their one-sidedness leaves in its wake. And of course the same holds for the investigators of the external world.

Despite Ernest Jones' attempt to reassure early critics of Klein, there can be little doubt that analysts of virtually all persuasions (but particularly the Kleinian one), have neglected external reality. I have no wish to advocate a reductionism whereby everything internal is ultimately reducible to external factors but, by failing to acknowledge the impact of the external upon the internal, the Kleinians are led to attribute too much power to internal reality.[33] The roots of this unbalanced orientation are to be discerned within the Kleinian notion of unconscious phantasy, to an examination of which I shall shortly turn.

Psychical Representation

The Kleinian theory of unconscious phantasy seeks to give content to a phenomenon that Freud sketched but was unable to develop. We can best describe this phenomenon by outlining Freud's question to which it appeared as a reply. Freud's question was this: What is the nature of the first event in the infant's psychical (as opposed to physical) life? Typically he gives us two answers. In two of the metapsychological papers of 1915[34] he suggests that the first psychical events correspond to the re-presentation (the making present again in thought) of an earlier experience of satisfaction; this he links to the work of the wish.[35] These re-presentations also act as representatives (delegates) of the instinctual impulses: they give psychical expression to somatic events, and are termed 'instinct-representations'. However, in 'Instincts and their vicissitudes'[36] Freud suggests that the instincts present themselves directly within the psyche from the outset; they require no representative. Rather, the instincts are themselves representatives of somatic processes and stimuli. Clearly then the term 'instinct-representation' does not apply to this latter formulation.[37]

Although Freud restated the latter formulation on a number

of occasions[38] nowhere does he give it any more content; it retained a quite abstract and speculative character. The concept of instinct-representation, however, finds its precursor in the *Project*[39] and *The Interpretation of Dreams*,[40] and his account of the construction of this representation is staggeringly simple and rather surprising. The hungry infant experiences satisfaction at the mother's breast. After a while[41] the infant, when hungry, will recathect the memory of the original experience(s) of satisfaction. The hunger instinct will then obtain psychical expression by virtue of this recathexis. The surprising feature of this account is its empiricism – external events leave their imprint upon a passive infant via a simple process of associative learning.

Others were quick to take issue with Freud on this count. Max Scheler, for example, was highly critical of the 'mechanical' process theorised by Freud and proposed as an alternative the idea of an infant having some intuitive knowledge of its own impulses.[42] The Kleinians have taken this approach one step further by suggesting not only that the infant has some intuitive knowledge of its own impulses, but also that this knowledge is 'innate'.[43]

Unconscious Phantasy

The theory of unconscious phantasy constitutes the major distinguishing characteristic of the Kleinian tradition, and the classic statement on this phenomenon has been made by Susan Isaacs.[44] And it is to her paper, together with some more recent supplementary remarks,[45] that we shall turn. Isaacs[46] defined unconscious phantasy as the primary content of unconscious mental processes and thence of psychic life itself. She argues:

> phantasy is the mental corollary, the psychic representative of instinct. There is no impulse, no instinctual urge or response which is not experienced as unconscious phantasy.[47]

Although Isaacs speaks of 'psychic representative', it is clear here that the Kleinians as a whole are unaware of the distinction to be observed in Freud's 1914 and 1915 theorisations. The use of the term 'unconscious phantasy' offers the possibility of transcending Freud's own imprecise, ambiguous formulations. However, it soon becomes apparent that this 'articulation' has begun to stray from Freud's own hazy path. Take the following statement:

> An instinct is conceived as a border-line psychosomatic process. It has a bodily aim, directed to concrete external objects. It has a representative in the mind we call 'phantasy'. Human activities

> derive from instinctual urges; it is only through the phantasy of what would fulfil our instinctual needs that we are enabled to attempt to realise them in external reality.[48]

At first sight it appears to be an accurate presentation of Freud's own argument. However, Freud[49] is quite explicit that the aim and (even more so) the object of the instinct are its most variable and contingent parts. Isaacs fails to mention this, both here and elsewhere, and as we shall see, it is one of the points on which the Kleinians part company with Freud.

Isaacs attempts to consolidate her argument by citing extracts from a contribution by Adrian Stephen to a 1943 discussion within the British Psychoanalytical Society. In an attempt to defend the concept of unconscious phantasy, Stephen argues that in the 'Three Essays' Freud describes instincts as 'having aims and objects'. But things are in fact much more complicated. If one follows the sequence of revisions to the 'Three Essays', it is clear that until 1915 Freud held that the sexual instinct was at first auto-erotic and therefore had no object. In amendments and additions to the text in 1915, relating to the early anaclitic nature of the sexual instinct, Freud does, just once, assert that the infant has an object from the outset 'in the shape of its mother's breast'.[50] On a number of occasions elsewhere in the 'Three Essays', however, Freud specifically denies the possibility of the sexual instinct having, from the outset, its own object.[51] Even if we were to concede that Freud sees the infant as having a sexual object from the outset, we are in no way led to assume that there is therefore some 'inner connection' between instinct and object. Indeed Freud is absolutely insistent on this point throughout the 'Three Essays': the object is the most variable and contingent thing about the instinct.

The Kleinians, however, have other ideas. Isaacs cites Stephen as saying,

> it is difficult to suppose that the instinctual impulses, even in a small baby, are not accompanied by some sort of phantasies of their fulfilment. To suppose this would be really to suppose that a baby can have a wish without wishing for anything . . .[52]

Here is the clear implication that the baby arrives in the world with an already established capacity to know what objects will satisfy its wishes. Although nowhere stated, such an argument supposes the existence of phylogenetic memories such that the infant is capable of having a phantasy of the breast from the moment of birth (irrespective of its experience of real, existing breasts). Moreover the infant's inherent knowledge goes beyond a simple familiarity with instinctual objects. Consider this statement by Isaacs:

> The phantasy that his passionate impulses will destroy the breast does not require the infant to have actually seen objects eaten up and destroyed, and then to have come to the conclusion that he could have done it too. This aim, this relationship to the object, is inherent in the character and direction of the impulse itself, and in its related affects.[53]

In other words the aim of the instinct is no more problematic than the object.

The theory of unconscious phantasy has a number of important implications. First of all, the Kleinian theory has nothing to say about 'drive'. So far I have hardly referred to the concept of 'drive' at all; I must admit that I have misled the reader on a number of occasions by referring to 'instinct' when the term 'drive' would be more appropriate. Laplanche and Pontalis[54] I feel correctly point to a mistranslation of Freud's term 'Trieb' so that English editions of Freud's work speak of his 'instinct theory' whereas they should more properly speak of his 'drive theory'. If we restrict the concept of 'instinct' to its traditional ethological usage then we can envisage it, as with hunger, as a specific need which has both specific objects (nourishment) and a specific means of obtaining satisfaction.[55] Clearly Freud had something else in mind in both the 'Three Essays' and (the mis-translated) 'Instincts and their Vicissitudes', for here Freud was exploring motive forces which have quite *in*determinate aims and objects. Much of the Kleinian theory of unconscious phantasy is therefore in fact a theory of the workings of the hunger instinct[56] and not of the sexual impulse. Indeed this was recently explicitly stated by Grotstein, a leading 'West Coast' Kleinian.[57] Secondly, given that it is a theorisation of instinct in the ethological sense, there is a grave danger that the concept of unconscious phantasy will become merely the psychical correlate of innate, coordinated reaction patterns. From here there is but a short step to the ethologisation of psychoanalysis itself.[58]

Thirdly, consider the frequent assumption that the Kleinians were the first, and perhaps only, group of analysts to take seriously Freud's view of the death drive. As should by now be clear, the Kleinian theory of unconscious phantasy actually rules the 'drive' concept out of consideration. Thanatos (death drive) itself then becomes reduced to the status of an ethological instinct.[59]

By repudiating Freud's concern for the contingency of the object, the Kleinians are led to endow impulse with too much structure whereas Freud endows it with too little. Freud, on the one hand, sees the drive as a wild horse thrusting and twisting in every direction, carrying the initially powerless infant on its back. The horse thrashes about with only the most ill-defined and transitory objectives. Later, as human agency is acquired, the infant/child learns to ride the horse but never fully tames it. We have to use a different analogy to illustrate the Kleinian concept of impulse. We must refer not to the unbound energy of the horse, but the structured energy of the guided missile, as energy having not only direction but also prior knowledge of its target.

The idea of unconscious phantasy is one of the most powerful within psychoanalysis. It plays a key role in the functioning of envy. However, in Kleinian hands unconscious phantasy becomes reduced to an *a priori* or instinctive knowledge. Through the concept of 'projective identification' (see below) the Kleinians describe how an already-generated meaning is modified through contact with external reality, but the problem of how such meaning is first generated through the internal/external interface is neglected.

The theory of unconscious phantasy also leads the Kleinians towards a conception of the infant's (and, for that matter, the adult's) universe which can only be described as solipsistic. Consider the following statement by Isaacs:

> phantasies do not, however, take origin in articulated knowledge of the external world; their source is internal, in the instinctual impulses.[60]

and by Segal:

> reality experience interacting with unconscious phantasy gradually alters the character of phantasies, and memory traces of reality experience are incorporated into phantasy life.[61]

The implication of such statements is profound. The Kleinians' central concern is not to demonstrate how phantasy modifies reality but how reality modifies phantasy. Human experience is basically modified phantasy.[62] This position is most clearly demonstrated in the Kleinian concept of projective identification.

The concept is first introduced by Klein in her paper 'Notes on some schizoid mechanisms',[63] and is used to describe the process whereby split-off parts of the ego are projected into the mother. Leaving aside some ambiguities in Klein's formulation,[64] we may consider the operation of this mechanism in its most oft-cited context, that of the hungry new-born infant. Following Bion,[65] we could say that the absent breast is not yet experienced as 'breast missing' but as 'bad breast present', that is, as the experience that it (the infant) is dying.[66] It seeks to establish a distance between the living (good) and dying (bad) parts of itself by evacuating its dying self through screaming and motility. This process Klein terms 'projective identification'. If the infant is fortunate it will be picked up by a parent who will cuddle it, smile on it and feed it. The parent accepts the feelings the infant cannot think of but wishes to get rid of; the parent returns to the infant both digestible food and digestible feeling. The infant is therefore fed twice, physically and psychically. On the other hand, a parent may pick up the screaming child and scream at it to be quiet; in this instance the infant's phantasy that the parent is terrifying is confirmed. The mother may coldly stick her nipple in its mouth, and the infant may feed (though often it will not). But it will remain psychically undernourished.[67]

The mother therefore acts as an 'auxiliary ego' to the infant; she does its thinking for it until it reaches a stage at which it can begin to think on its own experiences itself. In Bion's terms we could say that the mother acts as a liquidiser rendering indigestible psychical material digestible. I feel the Kleinians have got hold of one of the most important forms of human transaction here, and its significance has been recognised by many who would locate themselves outside the Kleinian tradition.[68] It enables us to understand the processes at work when any one person is asked to carry feelings that another cannot cope with.[69]

Through the concept of projective identification, the Kleinians grant to external reality the power to confirm or disconform phantasy. However, they concede no more to it – the environment may modify ongoing experience but it is not itself the source of experience. It may be objected here that the Kleinians do in fact recognise the impact of the environment because it is the absence of the breast which arouses the bad feelings in the first place. However the Kleinians explicitly discount such a reactive concept of bad experience. Klein for example describes 'privation' as having an internal, constitutional basis as well as an environmental source.[70] Repeatedly in 'Notes on some schizoid mechanisms' she argues that frustration merely reinforces (bad) experiences that are already present.[71] The locus of these experiences is the death instinct, operative from the beginning of life and manifesting itself as the fear of annihilation. As a number of commentators have suggested, Klein is not far here from providing us with a psychological parallel to original sin.[72]

To summarise, according to the Kleinians, bad experiences are either entirely internally generated or partly also reinforced by frustration. To put it the other way around, either the environment is thought to have nothing to do with bad experience or it is held responsible because of what it fails to do (i.e. its failure to provide).

The frightening, terrible mother is a product of the infant's own projections; she may disconfirm these projections but meaning, in the final analysis, remains internally generated.

A traumatic environment

> The study of psychic trauma enables us to compare the relative impact of intrapsychic and external factors, and examine the specific meaning the latter have intrapsychically.
> R. Moses, 'Adult psychic trauma'.

The idea of possession states has long been familiar to religious and spiritualist practices, and more recently to psychiatry and psychoanalysis. Typically an individual is 'possessed' when haunted by some terrifying or disturbing phenomenon, as if some alien force had got inside the person and refuses to leave them alone. Klein's account of this phenomenon is bound up with her theory of projective identification, a mechanism she feels inevitably involves 'the forceful entry into the object (i.e. mother) and control by parts of the self'.[73] Because of its helpless dependence, the infant may reluctantly take the qualities of the mother in upon itself (i.e. introjects her). Then 'this introjection may be felt as a forceful entry from the outside into the inside, in retribution for violent projection – this may lead to the fear that not only the body but also the mind is controlled by other people in a hostile way'.[74] In other words the 'evil spirits' in possession of the infant are of its own creation. Of course what Klein entirely overlooks here is the possibility that there really are frightening and terrifying mothers and fathers who may indeed control children's internal worlds in a hostile way. She lets the infant's environment get away with psychic murder.

It is especially interesting therefore to see Paula Heimann, at one time one of the most important figures within the Kleinian tendency, taking Klein to task on this point by querying whether a terrifying parent figure is always an instance of 'projective identification',[75] and whether the disturbing figures of the child's internal world aren't in fact the outcome of real intrusions of a pathological environment which have forced an entry into the child's psyche.[76]

As I think some writers have guessed,[77] this argument has considerable echoes in Freud's own work. Psychoanalysis properly begins with Freud's studies of hysteria and his theory of psychic trauma. The trauma was conceived of as essentially an environmental event (seduction) intruding upon the victim's psyche and overwhelming it. The seduction theory was abandoned in favour of a schema in which the trauma pertained to the 'strength and urgency of the sexual instincts and the ego's fight against them'.[78] In other words, the location of the trauma shifted from the outer environment to the inner. This reformulation has gained general acceptance within psychoanalysis up to the present day; it is obviously the framework within which the Kleinians work.

However, Freud provides a third and widely overlooked theorisation of trauma in 'Beyond the pleaure principle', one which attempts to refine and develop his first theory.[79] Starting with the example of 'war neurosis', Freud considers a number of examples of trauma, none of which can easily be attributed to the phantasy life of the human organism. Freud in this text considers a traumatic event as one which overwhelms an unprepared ego and breaks through the ego's 'protective barrier'.[80] Now, according to Freud, how does the individual cope with the impingement of such disturbing events? Not, in this instance, by repudiating (projecting) the experience. Freud is quite clear on this point. The individual uses precisely the opposite technique: the experience is embraced and repeated *ad nauseam* ('hysterics suffer from reminiscences').

An example may clarify. A friend of mine once told off a young boy who was attempting to pinch his empty milk bottle stand. Twenty minutes later, whilst he was outside cleaning his car, two men came along and beat him up (one, it turned out, was the child's father). Although he had to receive medical treatment, he was more shaken up psychologically than physically. For days afterwards he went over the situation in his head; as he put it, he just couldn't get it out of his mind. The incident became like a film clip that he would continuously re-run, more often than not in an amended form – one in which he no longer ended up the victim. The hurt to the psyche lingered for several days during which he experienced quite uncharacteristic depression. Although this experience could only be described as mildly traumatic it is probably sufficient to illustrate how bad experiences do begin to haunt us.

Freud explains the 'tendency to repeat' bad experience as an illustration of the death drive at work in human life, for how could repetition of bad experience be compatible with the pleasure principle? My feeling is that Freud's judgement was faulty here. On several occasions within the text[81] he does in fact entertain the possibility that the tendency to repeat may be related to the desire to master disturbing experience, but he eventually appears to reject this argument. I feel it has much to commend it. Yet rather than seeing the tendency to repeat in Adlerian terms (the will to mastery), could we not more usefully place it in the context of the language of orality: as the attempt to digest indigestible material which has forced its way into the system?[82] If you like, we are considering how we deal with experiences that 'stick in the throat' – they assume an alien presence within us; we can neither digest them nor evacuate them, so they haunt us.[83] Clearly from this point of view the tendency to repeat can be seen as a thwarted life-enhancing process, not as something in the service of death.

Freud's third theory of trauma therefore provided us in principle with an important perspective on the impact of the environment on the human psyche. Yet for too long psychoanalysis either ignored the external environment altogether or conceptualised it only in terms of its *absence*,[84] (i.e. in terms of its capacity to deprive and frustrate). There are now signs of change. Starting with the work of Searles, and perhaps also that of Laing, one can detect a growing realisation in non-Kleinian circles that important links need to be made between our disturbed psyches and our disturbing world.[85]

It strikes me that a number of lines of enquiry need to be pursued. First of all, what is the full range of environmental events/contents that can properly be conceptualised in terms of traumatic impingements? A great deal of work has been done on the pathological family,[86] the uniquely pathological culture of the concentration camp,[87] and combat situations.[88] This is but a tiny sample of the full range of possibilities – Fanon's account of the impact of colonisation upon the colonised's psyche,[89] women's experiences of male violence, previous experience of dealing with the threat of 'the bomb',[90] the analysand's experience of an intrusive analyst[91] – the list appears endless.

A second line of enquiry could prove even more rewarding. If the environment is to be recognised in non-passive terms, then it must be understood, for instance, that it is not just the parent who has to deal with the infant's projective identification; but the infant who has also to deal with the parent's.[92] This seems so startlingly obvious that one can only wonder how psychoanalysis has overlooked it for so long. Indeed, virtually all those processes psychoanalysis has considered intrapsychically as 'mechanisms of defence' could be more usefully considered interpsychically.[93] Here, I feel, lies one of Laing's greatest contributions; it is he, more than anyone, who first began to explore interpersonal processes in psychodynamic terms and intrapsychic processes in interpersonal terms.[94] In fact Laing appears to have had some influence upon those (few) within contemporary psychoanalysis who have tried to develop analysis as a discourse whose object is both intrapsychic and interpsychic.[95] It is interesting also to speculate that the discovery of the interpsychic may also have profound implications for the way in which analysis, and particularly the transference and countertransference, is conducted and conceptualised.[96]

The Kantian Frame

We have drifted some way from our consideration of Klein. It is now time to return. I have suggested that the theory of unconscious phantasy is a theory of inherent knowledge, and that this knowledge relates to the infant's instinctual aims and objects. Thus whereas most psychoanalysis would agree that an infant lacking contact and nourishment feels bad,[97] the Kleinians go much further and posit a hungry infant in a phantastic relationship to a bad breast which the infant feels like tearing to bits, scooping out, etc.[98] In other words the Kleinian conception of earliest infantile experience is very different from that of Freud and others who see it as largely structureless.[99] Moreover, by seeing introjection and projection as processes operative from birth, the Kleinians must assume that some fairly well constituted psychic boundary, marking off 'inside' from 'outside', is in existence from the outset.[100]

Segal has followed through these implications in a number of articles. Drawing on Bion[101] she illustrates the way in which the theory of unconscious phantasy resonates strongly with the 'rationalist' tradition within Western philosophy, a tradition which has often counterposed itself to 'empiricism' and its assumption of an initially featureless mind (tabula rasa) which passively acquires its content by reflecting reality. Segal suggests that even in the beginning the infant never innocently approaches reality; rather, it approaches it 'armed . . . with expectations formed by his unconscious phantasy'.[102] Bion, she argues,

> describes the origin of thought in what he calls "a matching of preconception with realisation". He compares this preconception to Kant's concept of empty thought. I would suggest that this preconception is the infant's fantasy, to begin with, that of the good and the bad breast.[103]

Elsewhere Segal has commented on the structural implications of the theory of unconscious phantasy:

> Phantasy-forming is a function of the ego; the view of phantasy as a mental expression of instincts through the medium of the ego assumes a higher degree of ego organisation than is usually postulated by Freud. It assumes that the ego, from birth, is capable of forming, and indeed is driven by, instincts to form primitive object-relationships in phantasy and reality.[104]

The Kleinians are arguing that secondary process (rational, reality-oriented thought) exists from the outset, as does the embryonic ego; here then we have the transposition of Kant's concept of 'empty thought' into psychology. Freud's theory of the wish, on the other hand, suggests that in the very beginning the infant's instinctual striving obtains no representation within the psyche. There is just the id, the seething cauldron of instincts; the mind has no other content, process or structure. This theory of the primacy of the id over the ego is equivalent both to the triumph of Freud's empiricism over his rationalism, and to the ascendancy of the 'economic' over all other principles of mental functioning.[105]

It seems to me that neither the Kleinian nor the Freudian account is particularly satisfactory. One sees the environment as passive, the other sees the infant as passive; one account posits too much ego, the other too little, etc. Neither account gets near to seeing earliest human development in terms of a creative dialectic between internal and external factors.[106] However, the saving grace of both Freud and the Kleinians is ironically their theoretical inconsistency; for each of them puts forward a third conceptualisation of the earliest structural relations – one which gave primacy neither to ego nor to id. This is the theory of the corporeal ego – the idea that in the beginning the ego is neither absent, nor is it to be located within a hypothetical schema of inherent structures of the mind, but rather is to be located *in the body*.

The Mind as Digestive System

From the very first day of life the infant primarily makes contact with the environment through its mouth. If we consider the feeding infant, substances that taste and feel good are taken in and swallowed, those that taste/feel bad are spat out and rejected. The process of accepting and rejecting physical substances by mouth is the earliest form of human judgement, which Freud calls 'oral judgement'.[107] Before we can proceed, however, we must first resolve an ambiguity in Freud's own work.

In his paper 'On negation' Freud implies that these most primitive forms of acceptance and rejection correspond to processes of introjection and projection. The Kleinians also adopt this position – it will be remembered, for instance, how Bion sees the hungry infant as wishing to evacuate its phantasy of the 'bad breast present' and receive the good breast in return.

Elsewhere, however,[108] Freud suggests that processes of introjection and projection occur only after a preliminary period of infant development, and this vital statement opens up a space in which an even more primitive process than introjection can be located. Here Freud seems to be arguing that the newborn infant can take *only* physical materials into the body, for only a physical boundary (the mouth and lips) exists. This is the literal meaning of the process Freud terms 'incorporation' or, if it makes the argument clearer, in-corporealisation. In the very beginning, unless we are to allow for a much greater degree of ego-development than Freud, we must insist that only a physical boundary exists and therefore that nothing can be taken in psychically (introjected). This also appears to be the position of Laplanche and Pontalis, who argue

> We thus have grounds for preserving the distinction between incorporation and introjection. In psychoanalysis the bounds of the body provide the model of all separations between inside and outside. Incorporation involves this bodily frontier literally. Introjection has a broader meaning in that it is no longer a matter only of the interior of the body but also that of the psychical apparatus, of a psychical agency . . .[109]

As they pertinently suggest, 'incorporation' can be seen as the *bodily prototype* of 'introjection'. By insisting that introjection is operative from the beginning, the Kleinians tend to reduce the status of incorporation to the physical support for assumed psychical events.[110] In this way their 'Kantian frame' prevents them from coming properly to grips with the Freudian concept of the corporeal ego. If, on the other hand, we see the first psychical boundary not as a given, but as something which the infant must construct, then it follows that the process of introjection will evolve in a manner appropriate to the degree of 'boundary construction' – at first partial and fleeting, later more substantial and definite. Keeping in mind the connotations of the term 'prototype', we can now say that not only does introjection occur developmentally later than incorporation, but that it is also developed *out of* incorporation.

Incorporation is the first intelligent act of the human infant who, by virtue of this process, becomes discriminating. It discriminates on the basis of value: good things are taken in, bad spat out. So incorporation is not just a physical, instinctual process, it is also an embryonic ego process. As Heimann argues, the infant's first sucking is "neither an id-activity nor an ego-activity; it is both, it is an activity of the incipient ego".[111] The implications are considerable, suggesting that there is a form of intelligence and consciousness which is both pre-verbal and pre-imagery, a 'corporeal intelligence' and a 'corporeal consciousness'. This does not mean that in the earliest phases of development there is no psyche. But nor is there psyche as such: what we have is what I think Winnicott terms 'psyche-soma'.[112] The basis of early infantile experience cannot be phantasy, for with its attendant imagery this properly belongs to the psyche. But clearly the newborn infant must experience something. What, then, does it experience? Essentially a large and varied series of bodily sensations.

Paula Heimann appears to grasp this, and her paper 'Certain functions of introjection and projection in early infancy' leaves the impression of an analyst within the Kleinian tradition who had nevertheless clearly grasped the primacy of sensation in infant life.[113] Take the following statement:

> To begin with . . . it is predominantly through the medium of his sensations that he experiences his objects, and sensory experience forms the matrix of both unconscious phantasy and conscious perception. Since the elementary categories of sensory experience are pleasurable or painful, these are also the primary characters of the infant's object-relation.[114]

I read Heimann as saying here that sensation developmentally predates phantasy and perception, it constitutes their prototype. The Kleinians, however, locate sensation in the same way as they locate incorporation – not as a prototype but as a support. Consider the following statement of Isaacs' in this context:

> At first, the whole weight of wish and phantasy is borne by sensation and affect. The hungry or longing infant feels actual sensations in his mouth or his limbs or his viscera, *which mean to him that certain things are being done to him or that he is doing such and such* e.g. touching or sucking or biting the breast which is probably out of reach. Or he feels as if he were being forcibly and painfully deprived of the breast, or as if it were biting him; and this, at first, probably without visual or other plastic images.[115] (My emphasis.)

It is conceivable that such sensations have some very primitive meaning, perhaps in terms of Lagache's concept of pre-objectal cathexis,[116] that is, 'a tension towards an ill-defined something'. But in Kleinian discourse this 'something' is no longer 'ill-defined'. The meaning of the sensations is not at all elusive or intangible, but refers explicitly to 'the breast', indeed, to a breast which bites back. Once again we return to the Kleinian tendency to impute too much knowledge to the infant – we are back again to the psychological equivalent of Kant's 'empty thought'.

To recapitulate. In the beginning there is an infant-mother expanse, a psyche-soma, some rudimentary but vital body-ego processes and sensations attached both to these processes and to the drives. The key point is that we have a conception of 'mind' as something rooted in the body – the bodily functions of incorporation/excorporation (or expulsion) as the prototype of the mental function of acceptance/rejection; bodily sensation as the prototype of all subsequent psychical content; the limit of the mouth/body as the prototype of the subsequent limit of self;[117] the bodily digestive process as a prototype for the future digestion of all human experiences.

It is in this way that psychoanalysis establishes its claim to provide a materialist theory of human subjectivity. Those who discard such schemas as biologistic[118] and attempt to root human subjectivity in language, should ponder the view of the Kleinian and object-relations theorists that it is only the child who is constituted by language, and (to repeat) that the infant is parent to the child.

Aggression and destructiveness

'The element of truth behind all this, which people are so ready to disavow, is that men are not gentle creatures who want to be loved, and who at the most can defend themselves if they are attacked; they are, on the contrary, creatures among whose instinctual endowments is to be reckoned a powerful share of aggressiveness.'

'I am able to recognize that the psychological premises on which the [communist] system is based are an untenable illusion.' Freud, *Civilization and its Discontents*.

Freud's case against communism, outlined both in *Civilization and its Discontents* and in the *New Introductory Lectures*, rests heavily on the assumed constitutional basis of 'aggressiveness and destructiveness, and so to cruelty as well'. One can only have sympathy with Freud when he criticises the simplistic notion that aggressiveness was created by property. His alternative, however – destructive aggression as a timeless and essential aspect of the human condition – hardly seems any more convincing or attractive.

Psychoanalysis is right to draw our evasive attention to the unsavoury sides of the human personality. But, we shall see, its analysis of destructiveness and aggression has many gaps and inconsistencies. We cannot wait any longer: our nuclear age demands that a more serious analysis of this topic be undertaken, and quickly. The issue, however, is vast and complex. The following pages will attempt an outline of the question; they will not provide many answers.

Freud's most important writings on the issues are to be found in 'Beyond the pleasure principle',[119] *The Ego and the Id*,[120] and *Civilization and its Discontents*.[121] Fortunately he makes several recapitulations of his constantly changing picture of the juxtaposition of the drives,[122] and if we study these closely, a number of questions come immediately to mind.

At first Freud speaks only of aggression, which is seen in his earliest formulations as an aspect of the self-preservative drives. Later, in the theory of narcissism, aggression is considered as an element of narcissistic object-libido along with the sexual drive. Narcissistic object-libido is counterposed to narcissistic ego-libido where the ego itself has been taken as an object of desire. *Beyond the Pleasure Principle* introduces a third reformulation of the drives. Aggressive impulses are now subsumed within the 'death instinct'. Freud can therefore no longer think of any form of 'aggressive libido' because libido is attributed solely to Eros (the 'life instinct'), and the concept of the destructive impulse now finds a place in Freud's writing whereas before it had received no real prominence.[123] We are at once struck by Freud's apparent indecision about whether to subsume aggression within the libidinal forces of life, or to see it as something standing opposed to life.

Let us consider another problem. What is the aim of the drive? Well, one could say that the aim of all drives is to obtain satisfaction. Freud himself admits that this does not take us very far.[124] More specifically, we can detect two lines of thought within psychoanalysis on this issue. The first is best encapsulated within Freud's statement that love 'strives to bring the object nearer' whereas hate endeavours to 'increase the distance';[125] I shall call this line of thought the 'separation/union' dialectic. It is common to Freud's earlier work and we may presume that whereas love corresponds to the sexual drive, hate corresponds to aggression.

In *Beyond the Pleasure Principle* we find the second line of analysis. Following Hering, Freud argues that two basic processes are at work within living substance, 'one constructive or assimilatory and the other destructive or dissimilatory'.[126] Klein later called this tendency to 'preserve living substance and join it together in ever larger units'[127] the synthetic function of the libido,[128] and I shall call this second line of thought the 'construction/destruction' dialectic. A moment's thought is enough to indicate that no obvious link exists between union and construction, nor between separation and destruction; it is just possible that we might be dealing with two distinct sets of processes and not, as psychoanalysis has assumed, two formulations of the one process. If this were the case then 'aggression and destructiveness' could no longer be referred to in the same breath as if synonymous.

For too long now psychoanalysis has used the terms 'aggression' and 'destructiveness' as if they *were* interchangeable; in this way the constructive contribution of aggression to life has been overlooked, as has the destructive contribution of love. Let us take as our starting point the following conundrum. If there is some link between the drive towards union and the life instinct then we should expect confirmation of this link when we consider the most extreme form of psychical union possible – namely, identification. In fact we find quite the contrary. As I pointed out at the start of this essay, excessive identification with objects petrifies psychical life. If one is to live, grow and reach a higher level of integration, one must abandon such identifications and obtain 'emancipation from the object'.[129] In other words one can only use and derive nourishment from a (psychical) object if one can relate to it as separate[130] and this requires aggression. Masud Khan most clearly illustrates the importance of aggression within both the parental and analytic relationships. Parents, he argues, must provide their children with 'the right dosage of aggression', for militantly overprotective anticipation of need 'does not allow any room for aggressive behaviour, which is essential to the crystallization of identity and separateness of selfhood in the child'.[131] The same principle applies to the analytic situation. If the analyst is unable to 'sustain an aggressive distance' from the patient then he/she is unable to obtain any perspective on the client's life and its vicissitudes. Further, without an adequate balance between 'compassionate empathy and aggressive differentiated intellection' the analyst becomes part of the problem rather than part of its solution.[132]

Aggressive differentiation is also vital in the development of the person's internal world. Grotstein puts this splendidly when he argues,

> Thoughts and feelings, like armies, must have room in which to manoeuvre . . . Without separation in time and distance there can be no concept of psychic space and therefore no perception, and certainly no representation. In order to represent, the self must be separated from the object; only then can it re-present it.[133]

The relationship between aggression, 'internal space', and intellectual and emotional development is a fascinating topic which psychoanalysis has barely begun to explore. Moreover the ability to obtain a distance from one's internal and external objects is vital for mature object usage (i.e. for the ability to take effective action).

Let us follow Winnicott[134] in his consideration of the foetal environment. As any mother knows, the foetus is not still but alive and kicking. When the foetus kicks against the side of the womb it experiences[135] opposition. Through such encounters the infant develops the earliest recognition of a 'not-me' world. These foetal movements could be called aggressive if we equated aggression with motility, but on the same basis they could also be called erotic. Winnicott argues that this constant spontaneous activity of the foetus is analogous to the operation of something almost tantamount to a 'life force'. The experience of opposition then effects the conversion of this life force into aggressive potential.[136] The paradox is that the infant must experience contact (i.e. opposition) to become aggressive, and thence achieve separation. Similarly it is only through the experience of separation that the impulse to 'bring the object nearer' can find the conditions necessary for its existence. The terms 'separation/union' would appear thus to qualify as a 'unity of opposites', that is, as a contradiction.

If we pursue the idea that the object world must provide the infant with opposition for aggression to become realised, Marx's concept of productive human action (i.e. labour) is again helpful.[137] Marx suggests that the material upon which the labourer acts is always to some extent recalcitrant. It imposes certain necessities upon the labourer if objectification[138] is to occur; in this sense the material provides opposition to the labourer and his/her intention. Free activity, activity in which one uses the imagination to effect change in reality, is possible only if one used one's aggression to obtain deference from the object, whilst also deferring to the limits the object imposes upon one's desire through its recalcitrance (one cannot make a paper clip out of a piece of stone). The same holds for the infant. If it is to be able to use its aggression in the process of objectification, to become truly creative and effective, it must come to recognize the limits objects place upon its desires. And as we have previously noted it is envy that refuses such recognition and instead seeks to destroy and spoil the object. Envy and aggression therefore stand opposed. Whereas one seeks an imaginative partnership with the object world, the other seeks obeisance to its own terms and finds refuge only in fantasy.[139]

Finally, the concepts of limit and opposition enable us to speculate on the possible relationship between class factors and aggression. If, whenever a child pushes at a limit, the limit gives way immediately, the child will never be able to experience its aggression as real: the aggression will become defused from the rest of the child's desiring life.[140] If, on the other hand, whenever it pushes at a limit, its experience is that the limit will not give in the slightest, then it experiences too much opposition and its aggression will undergo repression. The first is the kind of pathologically permissive environment that has been the object of study for a number of contemporary American cultural critics.[141] The second is a kind of pathological restrictiveness which may be the result of parental pathology, but is as likely to be the consequence of a more general environmental pathology. No job, no money, no time, too many children, no room, no prospects; faced with this much opposition, creative aggression can quickly turn to despair, to the abandonment of hope in object-relating.

What then of the destructive impulse? Again one has to consider that what passes for destruction is very often in the service of life.[142] If, once more, we take the language of orality as our starting point, then clearly the digestion of physical matter is vital for life: we grow physically by destroying living matter.[143] The same holds for the digestion of experience. Take the reading of a text as an example. Some books are like cream cakes which we devour avidly even though they may have more style than content; others are more like slightly undercooked meat, and require a lot of chewing over. To read a text critically we have to be prepared to 'tear into it', to separate out the useful from the useless material, using the former to reach a higher level of integrated intellection. Those with underdeveloped digestion may accept a statement but will have difficulty in cutting underneath the surface content. They will remain at the level of appearances – taking in and using only a little of what is presented. We might say that, rather than being able to take in an argument, they are easily 'taken in' by it. They have a 'common sense' but no 'good sense'.[144]

Destruction, then, can be seen as the necessary preliminary to construction. Indeed, such a notion of constructive destructiveness is central to the idea of revolutionary change. However, such destructiveness, as defined, is not associated with an affective state of hate or rage; on the contrary, it is accompanied by pleasurable feeling, thus betraying its foundation in sexual and aggressive libido.[145] Consider, on the other hand, an infant looking at a brightly coloured block. The infant gazes at it, shows pleasurable affect, starts to salivate, attempts to read the block with its hands and becomes more and more excited. We follow this mounting sequence of excited action for several minutes, during which the infant repeatedly fails to grasp the desired block. At the peak of her activity one notices the first appearance of unpleasurable affect, the excitement quickly turns to rage and destructive impulses are clearly manifested. Such destructiveness is an expression of rage following the frustration of desire; whilst the aim of rage is undoubtedly self-preservative in origin, it is chiefly concerned with 'the inflicting of pain, harm upon, and destruction of the object'.[146] Perhaps we have here a concrete expression of Freud's abstract and intangible death drive?

Further thought convinces us otherwise. Whereas erotic and

aggressive drives are held to exert a near constant pressure, rage is expressed only at moments when the erotic and aggressive drives and the hunger instinct are frustrated. As Parens[147] notes, such destructiveness invariably follows from the experience of unpleasure, the frustration of desire and need. The Kleinians would obviously disagree. From their point of view the infant arrives in the world with a constitutionally based self-destructive instinct. Now whilst one can agree that the hungry infant, like a suffocating adult,[148] may feel as if it is dying (panic, terror, frenzy), it is perverse to attribute such feelings to an assumed desire on the part of the infant to destroy itself.[149] Parens concedes too much on the Kleinians when he argues that the reactive nature of rage does not exclude 'a destructive aggressive impulse from instinctual drive status';[150] we could only grant it such status by undermining the established psychoanalytic concept of drive. But nor, on the other hand, should we conclude that because it is not a drive it is somehow secondary or acquired. Infants show quite clearly that destructive rage is not something they have to learn; it is clearly a part of their constitutional endowment. But if destructive rage does not operate in a manner analogous to the drive, then what is it? What is this thing that manifests itself as the dark side of love, hunger and aggression?

'Bomb Culture' and Life-affirmative Politics

Is it possible to say anything by way of conclusion? Firstly, if we are to equate destructive rage with Thanatos then it is difficult to see how this could properly be described in terms of 'the death instinct'. Whilst it is possible to conceive of 'an object of destructive rage' (this would usually be the object which frustrates desire), it is not at all clear that Thanatos functions in the same concrete fashion. It is something altogether grander, more abstract and intangible than destructive rage. Secondly, how is it possible to speak of the frustration of either Thanatos or destructive rage? Destructive rage is itself a reaction to frustration; can a frustrated reaction itself be frustrated? With regard to Thanatos, clearly the only thing that frustrates Thanatos is life itself, just as death is the only thing that properly frustrates Eros. Eros and Thanatos could only be considered drives if we were to overturn all that Freud said on the nature of such forces in 'Instincts and their vicissitudes' and elsewhere.[151] Lacking the concreteness of a drive that thrusts, Eros and Thanatos could perhaps be likened to tendencies, tendencies which are themselves the consequence of the work of the drives. From this perspective both erotic and aggressive drives contribute in both the death and life-affirmative tendencies in human functioning.

It should by now be clear that I am sceptical about the idea of the kind of 'death drive' invoked to explain our apparent equanimity in the face of the nuclear threat. Rather, of all the psychoanalytic concepts available, the notion of 'envy' has most to offer anyone seeking the psychical correlate of bomb culture. Envy, as denial of dependence, seeks to attack the very life-giving substances upon which the human body and psyche depend. Above all, envy can be visualised in terms of an attack upon the 'natural' element in 'human nature', for it is primarily through this natural element – our body and its physical environment – that necessity makes its presence felt. The association between freedom and necessity, insofar as it suggests the intimate link between human action and human dependence, should not be lightly ignored.

Much of the revolutionary Marxism since the Second World War has careered off in a profoundly voluntaristic direction. Its tendency grossly to underestimate the recalcitrance of the material on which it operates is matched by the narcissistic character structure of its typical recruit – an individual who sometimes seems to deny all personal need for others, or make a virtue out of a monadic unfeeling for other comrades, etc. To this extent revolutionaries do no more than express the dominant psychical structure of the western bourgeoisie, a structure described so well in Lasch's book *The Culture of Narcissism*.[152]

This denial of need, feeling and dependence constitutes an attack on the link between the human subject and the social and physical environment. The latter has been under increasing attack throughout this century via pollution, resource abuse and, more recently, the use of nuclear energy. Nuclear war of course would constitute the final attack upon this link.

It might be objected that an envy-based culture would not be easily reconciled to the prospect of a nuclear war which increases the likelihood of personal death, for after all death is the ultimate necessity that envy struggles so hard to deny. Interestingly enough, however, the more civilisation moves towards collective nuclear overkill, the more it moves us away from an individual encounter with loss and death.[153] If five 20-megaton bombs drop on Britain I have an evens chance of survival – for some time in some form at least; but the chance that I could survive without some form of injury or sickness to self or loved ones, or without some sense of loss for others that I have loved and valued who are now dead, is exceedingly remote. Limited nuclear war, like conventional war, would be a profoundly painful experience. If, however, fifty 20-megaton bombs dropped on Britain (and there exists the capacity for a far greater degree of overkill than this) then virtually no-one would feel any pain. Trying to contemplate such a scenario I am disturbed far less than when contemplating a more limited nuclear exchange. I don't have to grieve over fantasies of my burnt and screaming son because he will have been consumed by the holocaust instantly. I don't have to make plans about moving to New Zealand, nor do I have to harbour omnipotent fantasies of survival in my own nuclear bunker for this would merely exchange a lingering death for an instant vaporisation. Unlimited nuclear war does not threaten us with death or loss but with annihilation – something completely different.

It will be remembered that the infant does not discover loss until it reaches the depressive position. It is only then that it may begin to approach the idea of its own and others' death and will mobilise reparative defences to fight against death anxieties. Before this, it experiences events such as parental absences not in terms of loss, but psychotically as threats of self-annihilation, ceasing-to-be, the only defence against which is splitting. On this analysis, the threat of unlimited nuclear war presents itself (as annihilation) in a pre-depressive modality: that is, in the modality within which it is very difficult to marshal mature (non-psychotic) defences; hence its disabling effect on us. When the great day comes it won't hurt, so why should we get worked up about it?

If this analysis is at all correct then it has some important ramifications. It suggests that overkill is psychically preferable to limited nuclear war; that those living some way from likely nuclear targets are more likely to experience realistic anxiety (as opposed to psychotic anxiety, which is so overwhelming that one is either consumed by or denies it); that there is something neatly congruent about a culture of instant gratification which is also a culture of instant death; and that those of us (and I count myself as one) experiencing psychotic anxiety are going to need to develop some kind of politics which enables us to bring post-psychotic mechanisms to bear upon our existing state of numbness and terror.

In other words, we need to develop a politics and a political culture which is in the fullest sense life-affirmative: reparative, creative, integrative, holistic and constructive. It would be a politics in which both love *and* aggression have a proper place, a politics which acknowledges and celebrates both dependency and the capacity for free human action, a politics which recognizes necessity but also thrills to its subversion. Above all, perhaps, it would need to be a politics with a thorough knowledge of the human subject. Revolutionaries who are on the side of life must begin to take the exploration of human subjectivity more seriously; there is a richness here that could sustain them through their long march.

Notes

1. Hans Leowald, 'On internalisation'.
2. We shall see later that this antithesis should not be confused with that which refers to the relationship between the life and death drives.
3. As Winnicott (among others) notes, the word 'infant' implies 'not talking' (infans). D.W. Winnicott, 'The theory of the parent-infant relationship,' in *The Maturational Processes and the Facilitating Environment*, p. 40.
4. J. Laplanche and J.B. Pontalis, *The Language of Psycho-Analysis*, pp. 364–5.
5. S. Freud, *Civilization and its Discontents*, pp. 117 ff.
6. M. Balint, *The Basic Fault*, Ch. 7.
7. M. Balint, 'Trauma and object-relationship'.
8. Laplanche and Pontalis, p. 364.
9. See Strachey's comments on the vagaries of Freud's libido theory in his appendix ('The great reservoir of libido'), in *S.E.* Vol. 19, pp. 63–66.
10. The concept of the 'psychical object' is central to contemporary psychoanalysis. It refers to any actual, imaginary or phantasic phenomenon which is an object of need or desire.
11. The analogy with the horse underlines the necessary 'plasticity' of Freud's view of the drive.
12. D.W. Winnicott, *Playing and Reality*, Ch. 6.
13. Non-Kleinian analysts usually accept this Kleinian addition to developmental theory though they often reconceptualise such 'positions' in their own terms. See for example, D.W. Winnicott, 'The depressive position in normal emotional development'. In *Collected Papers*.
14. Klein in fact goes further, to insist that the infant doesn't just feel bad but, initially, experiences the presence of a bad breast. I hope to demonstrate later that the Kleinians are assuming too much here.
15. Kleinian and object-relations theorists largely agree that in earliest infancy had experience always tends to become overwhelming. See this chapter p. 180 and note 66; also p. 194 and note 148.
16. Not in fact the Kleinian position, which assumes a considerable degree of 'inside-outside' differentiation existing from the outset of infant life. Again, I feel, this tends to assume too much.
17. W. Bion, *Learning from Experience*, Ch. 12. I would add that successful completion of this journey corresponds to the infant's capacity to tolerate frustration (the experience of 'No-thing'), a capacity the Kleinians feel has a constitutional basis.
18. See note 117.
19. Or, in Winnicottian terms, 'subjective objects'.
20. Winnicott, *Playing and Reality*, p. 103.
21. Cited by Klein, *Envy and Gratitude*, p. 182.
22. Rosenfeld, 'Clinical approaches to the psycho-analytic theory of life and death instincts: an investigation into the aggressive aspects of narcissism', p. 172.
23. Klein, p. 181.
24. Ibid. Also Hanna Segal, *Introduction to the Work of Melanie Klein*, p. 40.

25. Klein, ibid.

26. Segal, pp. 40–1.

27. See, for example, Segal, pp. 42 ff.

28. Speaking of a patient, Segal comments, 'Interpretations which he felt as complete and helpful were immediately torn to pieces and disintegrated, so that it was particularly following good sessions that he would start to feel confused and persecuted as the fragmented, distorted, half-remembered interpretations confused and attacked him internally.' Segal, p. 43.

29. Marx, *Capital*, Vol. 1, p. 178.

30. In its small way I hope this example illustrates the way in which we spoil the environment upon which we (grudgingly) depend through our envious attacks upon it.

31. Although it doesn't apply to this example, W.C.M. Scott's concept of 'self-envy' would appear to provide us with further insight into pathologies in the relationship between the person and her/his productions. See Masud Khan, *The Privacy of the Self*, p. 273.

32. Segal, p. 40.

33. The recent statement by Meltzer, a leading contemporary figure within the Kleinian tendency, does nothing to assuage such feelings. Nothing in his article discourages the assumption that human experience primarily derives its meaning from the 'internal world'. His case example of a South American youth's 'delusion' that torture was being practised in the basement of his asylum made no concessions to the pervasiveness of state terror in most South American cultures. The psychical impact of such traumatic environments even upon 'non-combatants' should not be so easily dismissed. D. Meltzer, 'The Kleinian expansion of Freud's metapsychology'.

34. Freud, 'Repression', and 'The unconscious'.

35. The link between the manifestation of instincts in mental life and the work of the wish is first made in 'The Unconscious' (p. 186) and is then elaborated in Freud's 'Metapsychological supplement to the theory of dreams', p. 116. With further reflection it becomes clear that the intimate relationship between 'instinct' and 'wish' had been posited by Freud long before 1915. For example, Freud's opening statement on 'primal hallucination' in his 'Formulations regarding the two principles of mental functioning' (p. 216) can only be understood in this light.

36. Freud, 'Instincts and their vicissitudes', p. 122.

37. Those interested in charting this terminological confusion are referred to the editor's note to 'Instincts and their vicissitudes' (pp. 111 ff) or to Laplanche and Pontalis, pp. 364–5.

38. For instance, Freud, 'An outline of psychoanalysis', p. 148.

39. Freud, 'Project for a scientific psychology', pp. 319–25.

40. Freud, *The Interpretation of Dreams*.

41. Freud is in fact inconsistent here. In the passage from 'The interpretation of dreams' Freud leads us to assume that a single original 'experience of satisfaction' is sufficient to provide the infant with the mnemic image which can then be re-cathected by the wish. In the 'Project' however Freud appears to hold that a number of such experiences are necessary for the associative link between event and mnemic image to become established. This latter perspective would allow for the possibility of an early stage of infant development which is 'pre-image'. See, for example, H. Benassy and R. Diatkine, 'On the ontogenesis of fantasy'.

42. Max Scheler, *The Nature of Sympathy*, pp. 200–1.

43. In an interesting article Lagache makes a case for the existence of such

'intuitive knowledge' whilst remaining agnostic as to whether this knowledge is also innate. He imputes much less structure and tangible content to such knowledge and seems to stand closer to Winnicott than to the Kleinians. Daniel Lagache, 'Fantasy, reality and truth'.

44. Susan Isaacs, 'The nature and function of fantasy'. In Joan Riviere et al. (eds.), *Developments in Psychoanalysis*.

45. For supplementary remarks, see Hanna Segal, 'Fantasy and other mental processes'.

46. Isaacs, p. 81 ff.

47. Ibid., p. 83.

48. Ibid., p. 99.

49. Freud is consistent on this throughout the 'Three essays on sexuality' and in 'Instincts and their vicissitudes', pp. 122–123.

50. Freud, 'Three essays', p. 222.

51. Op. cit., p. 182 and p. 233. In fact the picture is even more complex. Elsewhere (p. 198) Freud asserts that sexual and feeding activities have the same object, but then in another passage (p. 222) he asserts they have different objects (sexual function – Breast; feeding function – Milk). For my own part I go along with Laplanche in saying that none of these accounts is completely satisfactory. J. Laplanche, Ch. 1.

52. Isaacs, p. 119.

53. Ibid., p. 94.

54. See the well-known discussion of this point in Laplanche and Pontalis, pp. 214–16.

55. Freud terms this the 'specific action'. Laplanche and Pontalis, pp. 425–7.

56. Freud speaks of the ego-instincts or instincts of self-preservation 'which are never capable of auto-erotic satisfaction' as having an object from the outset, Freud, 'Instincts and their vicissitudes', pp. 134–5.

57. J. Grotstein, 'The Kleinian contribution: 1. Instinct theory', pp. 379–380.

58. Grotstein actually advocates this. Op. cit. p. 387 and p. 381. See also his 'The Psycho-analytic concept of schizophrenia: I. The dilemma', Of course such an ethologisation of psychoanalysis has been implicit in the work of Britain's John Bowlby.

59. Grotstein also manages to advocate this. 'The Kleinian contribution', p. 381. 'The Psycho-analytic concept of schizophrenia', pp. 420–1.

60. Isaacs, p. 93.

61. Segal, p. 142.

62. Grotstein, 'The Kleinian contribution', p. 376 and p. 397.

63. Klein, 'Notes on some schizoid mechanisms', in *Envy and Gratitude*.

64. The Kleinian usage of 'projective identification' has been quite inconsistent. First of all, some Kleinians assume the concept refers to the expulsion of bad parts of the self whereas Klein clearly relates it also to the expulsion of good parts. Perhaps we could use Bion's scheme and suggest that some things are unpalatable because they are 'too good to be true' and therefore have to be expelled as if they were poisonous. Secondly, the concept has achieved such status within Kleinian theory that the traditional concept of 'projection' has become passé, but there are still considerable grounds for preserving the distinction between projection and projective identification. Thirdly, the Kleinians often speak of 'projective identification' when they should more properly speak of the re-introjection of projected material. W. Bion in 'Attacks on linking' for instance, preserves this distinction whereas others obscure it (e.g.

D. Malin and J. Grotstein, 'Projective identification in the therapeutic process'). Fourthly, Freud has two usages of the term 'identification': as a cognitive process (viz. 'to identify a wolf in sheep's clothing') and as a cognitive and interpsychic process (viz. 'to feel an affinity with the wolf in the sheep's clothing'). Whilst the Kleinians should presumably only adopt Freud's second usage, they very often use 'projective identification' to refer to the cognitive act only. Useful, though not entirely satisfactory, discussions of the concept can be found in W.W. Meissner, 'Note on projective identification', and in T. Ogden, 'On projective identification'.

65. Bion, *Learning from Experience*, pp. 34–5.

66. 'I have for many years held the view that the working of the death instinct within gives rise to the fear of annihilation and that this is the primary cause of persecutory anxiety.' M. Klein, 'Some theoretical conclusions regarding the emotional life of the infant', in Riviere et al., p. 198.

67. Instructive accounts of this first exchange between parent and infant are provided by Bion, pp. 33–7, and Meltzer, p. 181.

68. See for instance Masud R. Khan, 'The role of illusion in the analytic space and process', in *The Privacy of the Self*, pp. 266–7; and also D.W. Winnicott, 'Hate in the countertransference' in *Collected Papers*.

69. An everyday example of this would be the anxiety felt by someone about or 'on behalf of' a loved one who is ill or under stress but unconcerned about it.

70. Klein, 'Some theoretical conclusions regarding the emotional life of the infant'. In Riviere et al., p. 199.

71. Klein, op. cit., pp. 4–5.

72. See for instance W. Gillespie, 'Aggression and instinct theory', p. 157.

73. Klein, 'Notes on some schizoid mechanisms', p. 11.

74. Ibid., p. 9.

75. 'Many instances of so called 'projective identification' should be defined as the reactivation in the patient of his infantile experiences with his rejecting and intruding mother'. P. Heimann, 'Structural derivatives of object relations', p. 257.

76. Ibid., p. 257.

77. A concern to refine Freud's work on 'psychic trauma' runs through many of the papers in Khan's collection *The Privacy of the Self*. The two most central papers are 'The concept of cumulative trauma' first published in 1963, and 'Exorcism of the intrusive ego-alien factors in the analytic situation and process' first published in 1972. The latter paper is in many respects a pronounced improvement on the former, for whereas in 1963 Khan's focus is on a passive rejecting environment, by 1972 he appreciates much more the way in which the environment is often traumatic because it actively intrudes upon our experience.

78. Khan, 'The concept of cumulative trauma', op cit., p. 43.

79. Concise summaries of Freud's three conceptualisations of trauma are to be found in Khan, pp. 42–44 and M. Balint, 'Trauma and object-relationship', pp. 429–32.

80. Whereas Freud provides us with a somewhat biologistic account of the ego's 'protective barrier' ('Beyond the pleasure principle', pp. 26 ff) Khan, following Winnicott, simply sees it in terms of the protective and regulatory role of the mother or earliest caretaker figure *vis à vis* the helpless infant.

81. Freud, op cit., pp. 14–17.

82. Fairbairn's insistence that the infant does indeed internalise bad experience has long been considered highly idiosyncratic and frankly in contradiction to the 'wish fulfilment' totem. In fact it corresponds perfectly

to the idea that we internalise and repeat bad experience in an attempt to digest it. W.R.D. Fairbairn, 'The repression and the return of bad objects'. In *Psychoanalytic Studies of the Personality*, p. 67.

83. One is reminded of Freud's early case of hysteria in a young woman who had been raised in a tyrannically repressive middle-class family and developed a paralysis of the throat because, as she eventually put it, she just couldn't 'swallow any more'.

84. Even Winnicott, who pays much more attention to the external environment than most, conceptualises environmental impingement essentially as failure in environmental adaptation to infant need. See Khan, pp. 46-7.

85. Certainly in the case of Khan, Searles' work appears to have been a crucial influence. In particular see H. Searles, 'The effort to drive the other person crazy – an element in the aetiology and psychotherapy of schizophrenia'. In Searles, *Collected Papers on Schizophrenia and Related Subjects*.

86. Probably the best known work to British readers is R.D. Laing and A. Esterson, *Sanity, Madness and the Family: Families of Schizophrenics*.

87. W.G. Niederland, 'Clinical observations on the "Survivor Syndrome" '.

88. R. Moses, 'Adult psychic trauma: the question of early predisposition and some detailed mechanisms'.

89. F. Fanon, *Black Skin, White Masks*.

90. Jeff Nuttall's *Bomb Culture* is a vivid account of how the cultural organism first attempted to digest the ultimate in indigestible experience.

91. Searles, pp. 273–83.

92. Of all those who have written on 'projective identification' only Ogden seems to be aware of this. Ogden, p. 360.

93. British and American analysts have considered only the subject in relationship to her/his objects forgetting that this subject is also an object for other subjects. The great strength of the French psychoanalytic tradition is its understanding of this 'dialectic of objectification'.

94. See Laing, *Self and Others* and *Politics of the Family*.

95. See especially, J. Sandler and A.-M. Sandler, 'On the development of object-relations and affects', and J. Sandler, 'Dreams, unconscious fantasies and "identity of perception" '.

96. The counter-transference (that which the patient carries which is properly the analyst's) has not been taken seriously enough by Classical, Kleinian or object-relations theories. Interestingly enough those analysts who take it most seriously are also those who have striven most consistently to recognise the active, intruding role of the environment. See, for example, P. Heimann, 'Counter-transference'.

97. We cannot however go on to say that this infant is hungry. We adults might know that the infant is hungry but, unless we assume the infant had considerable innate knowledge of its own impulses, we cannot attribute to the infant the capacity to know that its sensations and feelings concern *hunger*; it has to learn this. In the beginning an infant may sense a lack but it does not yet experience a need. See I. Ramzy and R.S. Wallerstein, 'Pain, fear and anxiety'.

98. Isaacs, p. 84, pp. 94–5.

99. We might recall that the Kleinians see earliest infant experience structured not only by the familiar instinctual impulses but by other more sophisticated phenomena such as envy, to which they also ascribe instinctual status.

100. 'All that Melanie Klein has described as the dialectic of good and bad, partial and whole, the introjected and the projected, is inconceivable without the first boundary of the ego – however rudimentary it might be – defining

an outside and an inside', J. Laplanche, pp. 80–1.

101. Bion, *Learning from Experience*.

102. Segal, 'Fantasy and other mental processes', p. 193.

103. Ibid.

104. Segal, *Introduction to the Work of Melanie Klein*, pp. 13–14.

105. This 'ascendancy of the economic principle' is expressed in Freud's belief that in all stages of mental life questions of 'quantity' take precedence over questions of 'quality'. Thus, in his discussion of instincts, Freud rejects the idea that they could differ in quality: 'Are we to suppose that the different instincts which operate upon mental life but of which the origin are somatic are also distinguished by different qualities and act in the mental life in a manner which is qualitatively different? This supposition does not seem to be justified . . .' ('Instincts and their vicissitudes', p. 123). This flatly contradicts Isaacs' assertion that different instincts do have qualitatively different aims, qualities 'which are inherent in the character and direction of the impulse itself'.

106. I believe Winnicott's account more closely approaches such standards. Unfortunately space forbids any further analysis of this remarkably rich and provocative theorisation. Readers are referred to his *Playing and Reality*.

107. Freud, 'On negation'.

108. Freud, 'Instincts and their vicissitudes', pp. 135–6.

109. Laplanche and Pontalis, p. 230.

110. P. Heimann, 'Certain functions of introjection and projection in early infancy'. In Riviere et al., p. 143.

111. Heimann, p. 128.

112. D.W. Winnicott, 'Mind and its relation to the psyche-soma'. In *Collected Papers*.

113. 'The first perception of importance must be essentially the sensations of receiving by mouth, sucking, swallowing, spewing', Heimann, p. 127.

114. Ibid., p. 141.

115. Isaacs, p. 92.

116. 'A drive is a motor thrust towards a goal and an object. This thrust is an 'intention', a tension towards an ill-defined something. The plasticity of the goal and the contingency of the object are, within certain limits, compatible with Freud's view of the importance of the economic aspect and the primary predominance of quantity over qualitative discrimination'. Lagache, p. 184.

117. The acquisition of a sense of boundary within which what I call my 'self' resides is the key to the development of subjectivity; the concept of boundary provides the necessary frame within which other aspects of subjectivity – content, structure, process, energy can be articulated.

Freud's reference to the genesis of this psychic boundary is tantalisingly brief (*The Ego and the Id*, pp. 25–6) and we can supplement his remarks with those of Laplanche (p. 81) and Winnicott ('The theory of the parent-infant relationship' in *The Maturational Processes and the Facilitating Environment*, p. 45). The boundary is essentially a psychical projection of the surface of the skin, and Winnicott calls it the 'limiting membrane'. Of course, this frontier exists physically from birth. The infant, via incorporation, makes use of this frontier before having any proper awareness of its existence – it is like a stranger in a foreign land continually making use of a frontier it cannot yet appreciate. The establishment of this boundary is crucial to the process of differentiation; in fact they are two sides of the same coin. At first the infant's psychical environment is entirely undifferentiated (Freud insisted that the first form of object-relationship assumed the form of an identification (i.e. of 'inside' with 'outside')). From a phenomenological point of view the infant's world resembles an undifferentiated ocean. The construction of the boundary is, simultaneously, the establishment of a differentiation – we might liken it to the emergence of a mountain range cutting through the ocean and bisecting it into two domains or seas, one of which becomes 'inner', the other 'outer' Only with the gradual development of its perceptual capacity will the infant be able to register its bodily boundary psychically, and then the discovery will only be partial – at first pertaining specifically to the mouth and lips. To use the analogy of the ocean, the mountain range emerges through the ocean's surface only here and there at first. Thus the outside is at first a 'partial outside' and the inside a 'partial inside'. We are not accustomed to thinking of degrees of 'inside-ness', 'me-ness' or 'object-ness' but this is how we must begin to think if we are to come to grips with the phenomenology of infancy and madness.

118. 'Lacan's point of departure is a critique of those theoretical developments which have taken a biological direction (Klein . . .).' C. Weedon, A. Tolson and F. Mort, 'Theories of language and subjectivity'. In S. Hall et al, *Culture, Media and Language*.

119. Freud, 'Beyond the pleasure principle'.

120. Freud, *The Ego and the Id*, pp. 40–7.

121. Freud, *Civilization and its Discontents*, pp. 108–122.

122. 'Beyond the pleasure principle', pp. 50 ff. *Civilization and its Discontents*, pp. 117 ff.

123. Freud, does, however, refer extensively to hate.

124. Freud, 'Instincts and their vicissitudes', p. 122.

125. Ibid., p. 137.

126. 'Beyond the pleasure principle', p. 49.

127. *Civilization and its Discontents*, pp. 118–119.

128. Klein, 'On identification'. In *Envy and Gratitude*, p. 173.

129. Leowald, p. 15.

130. Hence Winnicott's remark, 'there are many patients who need us to be able to give them a capacity to use us. This for them is the main analytic task.' In *Playing and Reality*, p. 110.

131. Masud Khan, 'Dread of surrender to resourceless dependence in the analytic situation'. In *The Privacy of the Self*, p. 272.

132. Masud Khan, 'On symbiotic ominopotence'. In *The Privacy of the Self*, p. 90.

133. Grotstein, 'Inner space: its dimensions and its coordinates'.

134. Winnicott, 'Aggression in relation to emotional development'. In *Collected Papers*.

135. The infant experiences, that is, in a way which is proper to its stage of development.

136. Winnicott, p. 216.

137. Marx, p. 178.

138. 'Objectification' refers to the process by which an objective is realised through imaginative action. See Lucio Colletti, *From Rousseau to Lenin*, pp. 62–72.

139. Winnicott's distinction between fantasy and imagination is, I feel, a vital but overlooked insight. D.W. Winnicott's 'Dreaming, fantasying and living'. In *Playing and Reality*.

140. Moreover the child will come to believe that all doors will open to its demands.

141. Cortland Conference on Narcissism, *Telos*, Summer 1980, No. 44.

142. There are a number of instances in Klein's 'Notes on some schizoid mechanisms' where she demonstrates how destructiveness operates in the service of life. For instance, where the infant's destructive attacks on early persecutory objects lead to their fragmentation, thus rendering them less terrifying.

143. Panel Discussion on Aggression, *Int. J. Psycho-Anal*. 1972, p. 16.

144. A. Gramsci, *The Prison Notebooks*.

145. Parens calls this 'nonaffective destructiveness'. Henri Parens, 'An exploration of the relationship between instinctual drives and the symbiosis/separation-individuation process'.

146. Ibid.

147. Parens, 'On aggression'.

148. Balint uses the term 'primary love' to describe the way in which the infant takes its environment completely for granted. The infant's need for its social environment is as total and as intense as its need for a supportive physical environment. Balint uses the example of air to illustrate the nature of the infant-parent relationship. When we have air we do not express any particular satisfaction, but deprive us of it and we unleash the most frenzied, terrified reaction. There is more than a passing similarity between this and Klein's notion of the working of the death instinct within. M. Balint, *The Basic Fault*, op. cit., pp. 6–7.

149. O. Fenichel, 'Critique of the death instinct'. In *Collected Papers*, p. 362.

150. Parens, op. cit., p. 53.

151. Fenichel, op. cit., p. 366.

152. C. Lasch, *The Culture of Narcissism*, passim.

153. I claim no originality for the argument that follows: it was first suggested by Jeremy Holmes in a talk given to Radical Science Journal readers in late 1982.

References

Balint, M. (1968). *The Basic Fault.* Tavistock.

Balint, M. (1969). Trauma and object-relationship. *Int. J. Psycho-Anal.* 50, 429–435.

Benassy, H. and Diatkine, R. (1964). On the ontogenesis of fantasy. *Int. J. Psycho-Anal.* 45, 171–179.

Bion, W. (1959). Attacks on linking. *Int. J. Psycho-Anal.* 40, 308–315.

Bion, W. (1962). *Learning From Experience*. Heinemann.

Colletti, L. (1972). *From Rousseau to Lenin*. New Left Books.

Fairbairn, W.R.D. (1952). The repression and the return of bad objects. In *Psychoanalytic Studies of the Personality*. Routledge and Kegan Paul.

Fanon, F. (1967). *Black Skin, White Masks*. Grove Press.

Fenichel, O. (1954). Critique of the death instinct. In *Collected Papers*. Routledge and Kegan Paul.

Freud, S. (1895). Project for a scientific psychology. *Standard Edition* Vol. 1, 295–343.

Freud, S. (1900). *The Interpretation of Dreams. Standard Edition* Vol. 5, 339–623.

Freud, S. (1905). Three essays on sexuality. *Standard Edition* Vol. 7, 130–243.

Freud, S. (1911). Formulations on the two principles of mental functioning.

Standard Edition Vol. 12, 218–226.
Freud, S. (1915). Instincts and their vicissitudes. *Standard Edition* Vol. 14, 117–140.
Freud, S. (1915). Repression. *Standard Edition* Vol. 14, 146–158.
Freud, S. (1915). The unconscious. *Standard Edition* Vol. 14, 166–204.
Freud, S. (1917). A metapsychological supplement to the theory of dreams. *Standard Edition* Vol. 14, 222–235.
Freud, S. (1920). Beyond the pleasure principle. *Standard Edition* Vol. 18, 7–64.
Freud, S. (1923). The ego and the id. *Standard Edition* Vol. 19, 12–59.
Freud, S. (1925). Negation. *Standard Edition* Vol. 19, 235–239.
Freud, S. (1930). *Civilization and its Discontents. Standard Edition* Vol. 21, 64–145.
Freud, S. (1940). An outline of psychoanalysis. *Standard Edition* Vol. 23, 144–207.
Gillespie, W. (1971). Aggression and instinct theory. *Int. J. Psycho-Anal.* 52, 155–160.
Gramsci, A. (1977). *The Prison Notebooks*. Lawrence and Wishart.
Grotstein, J. (1981). The Kleinian contribution: I. Instinct theory. *Int. J. Psycho-An. Psychother.* 8, 375–393.
Grotstein, J. (1977). The psychoanalytic concept of schizophrenia: I. The dilemma. *Int. J. Psycho-Anal.* 58, 403–425.
Grotstein, J. (1978). Inner space: its dimensions and its coordinates. *Int. J. Psycho-Anal.* 59, 55–61.
Hall, S. et al. (1980). *Culture, Media and Language*. Hutchinson University Press.
Heimann, P. (1960). Countertransference. *Brit. J. med. Psychol.* 33, 9–15.
Heimann, P. (1966). Structural derivatives of object relations. *Int. J. Psycho-Anal.* 46, 254–260.
Jones, E. (1935). Early female sexuality. *Int. J. Psycho-Anal.* 16, 273.
Khan, M.R. (1974). *The Privacy of the Self*. Hogarth.
Klein, M. (1975). *Envy and Gratitude and Other Works*. Delta Books, 1977.
Lagache, D. (1964). Fantasy, reality and truth. *Int. J. Psycho-Anal.* 45, 180–189.
Laing, R.D. and Esterson, A. (1964). *Sanity, Madness and the Family: Families of Schizophrenics*. Tavistock.
Laing, R.D. (1969). *Politics of the Family*. Random House.
Laing, R.D. (1971). *Self and Others*. Pelican.
Laplanche, J. (1976). *Life and Death in Psycho-Analysis*. Hogarth.
Laplanche, J. and Pontalis, J.B. (1973). *The Language of Psycho-Analysis*. Hogarth.
Lasch, C. (1978). *The Culture of Narcissism*. Norton.
Leowald, H. (1973). On internalisation. *Int. J. Psycho-Anal.* 54, 9–17.
Malin, D. and Grotstein, J. (1966). Projective identification in the therapeutic process. *Int. J. Psycho-Anal.* 46, 23–31.
Marx, K. (1970). *Capital*. Vol. 1. Lawrence and Wishart.
Meissner, W.W. (1980). Note on projective identification. *J. Amer. Psycho-Anal. Assocn.* 28, 43–67.
Meltzer, D. (1981). The Kleinian expansion of Freud's metapsychology. *Int. J. Psycho-Anal.* 62, 177–185.
Moses, R. (1976). Adult psychic trauma: the question of early predisposition and some detailed mechanisms. *Int. J. Psycho-Anal.* 59, 353–363.
Niederland, W.G. (1968). Clinical observations on the 'survivor syndrome'.

Int. J. Psycho-Anal. 49, 313–315.
Nuttall, J. (1979). *Bomb Culture*. Paladin.
Ogden, T. (1979). On projective identification. *Int. J. Psycho-Anal.* 60, 357–373.
Parens, H. (1972). On aggression. *J. Amer. Psycho-Anal. Assocn*. 28, 89–114.
Parens, H. (1980). An exploration of the relationship between instinctual drives and the symbiosis/separation-individuation process. *J. Amer. Psycho-Anal. Assocn*. 96.
Ramzy, I. and Wallerstein, R.S. (1958). Pain, fear and anxiety. *Psycho-Anal. Study of the Child* 13, 147–181.
Riviere, J. et al. eds. (1952). *Developments in Psychoanalysis*. Hogarth.
Rosenfeld, H. (1971). Clinical approaches to the psychoanalytic theory of life and death instincts: an investigation into the aggressive aspects of narcissism. *Int. J. Psycho-Anal.* 52, 169–178.
Sandler, J. (1976). Dreams, unconscious fantasies and 'identity of perception'. *Int. Rev. Psycho-Anal*. 3, 33–42.
Sandler, J. and Sandler, A.-M. (1978). On the development of object-relations and affects. *Int. J. Psycho-Anal*. 59, 285–296.
Scheler, M. (1970). *The Nature of Sympathy*. Routledge and Kegan Paul.
Searles, H. (1965). *Collected Papers on Schizophrenia and Related Subjects*. Hogarth.
Segal, H. (1964). Fantasy and other mental processes. *Int. J. Psycho-Anal*. 45, 191–194.
Segal, H. (1975). *Introduction to the Work of Melanie Klein*. Hogarth.
Winnicott, D.W. (1974). *Playing and Reality*. Pelican.
Winnicott, D.W. (1975). *Collected Papers: Through Paediatrics to Psycho-Analysis*. Hogarth.
Winnicott, D.W. (1976). *The Maturational Processes and the Facilitating Environment*. Hogarth.

RELATIONAL PRECONDITIONS OF SOCIALISM

Margaret Rustin and Michael Rustin

The purpose of this chapter[1] is to explore the positive conclusions for socialist conceptions of society which can be drawn from those traditions in psychoanalysis which offer insights into the construction of our internal psychic worlds, and which attend to the ongoing relationships between internal and external experience. The works of Melanie Klein,[2] Donald Winnicott,[3] and Wilfred Bion[4] have been particularly rich sources of these ideas. We say the *positive* conclusions deliberately. Much of the appropriation of psychoanalysis by radicals has been critical in its object, and has sought to use psychoanalytic ideas to identify internal and psychological dimensions of social repression. Such 'negative' approaches include work on the authoritarian personality, by Frankfurt School writers[5] in the 1930s; on 'repressive sublimation' when a member of this school, Herbert Marcuse,[6] tried to come to terms with the more liberal sexual climate of the 1960s; Christopher Lasch's work[7] on narcissism as a social and individual pathology; and much Lacanian writing on the misconstructions of gender and childhood unconsciously imposed through the bourgeois family.[8] While we will not dispute the value of these kinds of analyses of the psychoanalytical dimensions of alienation and oppression, we wish to give attention to those indications of the social architecture of a more benign world which can also be drawn from psychoanalytical discovery. We also draw attention to the beneficial forms of social intervention which psychoanalytic observation might suggest.

Conceptions of socialist possibility have many different sources. This is especially so now that mechanistic models of historical inevitability, based on purported invariant economic laws, have been so generally abandoned as a sufficient framework for socialist thinking. The transition from one complex social order to another, whether from feudal to capitalist society, or more speculatively from capitalism to socialism or at least to more socialised forms, is bound to be a complex and multi-dimensional process, and not the simple supersession of one form of power and determination by another. Socialist ideas have emerged from the experience of struggle and endurance by working class communities, and from the institutions they have created in their defence. They have been influenced by memories of an earlier paternalist order which preceded market capitalism, as some of the standards of justice and social responsibility which held at least some sway became grounds for criticism of the impersonality and callousness of market forces. They have also been shaped by some of the better experiences which improved material conditions and even local privilege made possible, experiences which could be extended by writers of altruistic outlook into a vision for a whole society. William Morris' vision of a society based on creative work,[9] in which the division of manual and mental labour would be transcended by generally fulfilling forms of labour, also looked back to the medieval crafts, interpreted through their surviving artifacts.

This medievalist inheritance reminds us of the contribution of Christian moral conceptions to the ethical basis of British socialist thought.[10] Even the material power of transformation of capitalism itself became a condition, for Marx, of the possibility of overcoming human scarcity, and of the attainment of a human world for all. Marshall Berman's recent *All that is Solid Melts into Air*[11] is a forceful presentation of the vision of constant material and cultural transformation as a quintessentially modern experience in a positive sense. From a different point of view, the conception of an 'ecological' or environmental politics, while claiming to be based on an idea of the Natural, is also a highly sophisticated and social rationalism. It requires that the total environment he conceived as a unified system, and that human activities be harmonised with one another through a holistic understanding of economic and political decisions. It depends on economic activity being governed by universal standards and norms, and by very long-term conceptions of welfare and equilibrium.

This variety of influences on socialist thought – some of them contradictory in their immediate conclusions – reminds us that the vocabulary of possibility in the radical traditions both is and needs to be very extensive, and cannot be reduced to one-dimensional formulae. A 'higher' and more advanced form of society has to grow from many current practices,[12] both those conducted in defensive opposition to oppression, and those which already attempt to build alternatives to dominant values. Socialists have to consider which elements of the legacy of bourgeois society they value, and which they reject. It is clear that individual liberty, the rule of law, and even representative democracy, were achieved within capitalist and not socialist states, even if by the pressure of working class movements. Socialism in societies which have experienced these advances in the condition of civil freedom needs to aim for their universal extension and to avoid their unwitting sacrifice in pursuit of other egalitarian ends. While this might on occasion be unavoidable, it is important that such compromises should not be misrepresented in bogus rhetorics of so-called higher or 'socialist democracies' which in fact conceal a clear loss of individual or minority rights.

We shall argue that psychoanalytic thought, and especially the contributions made possible through psychoanalytic work with children and the infantile elements in adults, constitute just such a tradition available to enrich socialist thought and practice. Writers in this tradition, such as Klein and Winnicott, have given emphasis to the potential for and innate thrust towards development in infants and adults, and it is this concept and the understanding of its social preconditions that is valuable for the idea of a socialism of complex societies. They have shown how development in infants depends on intimate relationships between an infant and a mother or other parent-figure who needs to have the security and emotional space to bear the intense (often negative and anxious) feelings of the infant and to modulate its experience of the outside world in balance with its capacity to handle them for itself. Mental growth is held, in this account, to be inescapably linked to undergoing and tolerating the experience of psychic pain and distress. Such pain includes having to share parental love with others; having to recognise what one is not and cannot do; becoming aware of the injuries one inflicts on those one cares for. Emotional development depends on identification, and is especially furthered where those who support growth are able to understand and mitigate the pains of unavoidable limits and deprivation. This should not lead us to set up idealised and persecuting specifications of what are 'good' parents or care-givers. The question should rather be, how are care-givers themselves to be cared for, since their own needs being met is the precondition for their being able to meet the needs of children or other dependants. While it seems that the attention of an individual adult is the most common basis for the satisfactory emotional growth of infants, this is not necessarily an argument for the functions of the biological mother against other kinds of division or sharing of 'mothering' functions among parents or others. What is fundamental is the presence of intimacy and stability in the relationships between infants and a very small number of care-givers.[13] This is compatible with different kinds of family units.

These psychoanalytical findings – supported more recently by a good deal of psychoanalytical observation of mothers and babies in family settings – clarify some basic preconditions or 'building blocks' of individuality, and reveal some of the foundations of the capacities for love and moral discrimination. More specifically, we can clarify the preconditions for the formation of altruistic capacities so important in socialist ideas of humanity. Babies need to have the experience of being cared for adequately, physically and emotionally, if they are to grow beyond a self-centred and narcissistic attitude to their human environment, capable only of making claims and not of contributing. Adequate provision for babies depends on a consistent and not-too-complicated system of care which can very gradually be perceived and understood by the baby. Not too many caretakers and continuity over time are the two important features. If the maximal interdependence of young infants and their caretakers can be tolerated (and this requires a lot of support from the wider adult community) the baby can begin to move beyond the simplest level of using people to satisfy personal needs, towards a two-person relationship in which the separateness and individuality of the mothering person can be recognised. Out of this the baby can enter the wider world of social relations, whether this is seen in terms of the oedipal situation in a family context, where the relationship between the parents and between the parents and other children has to be faced, or whether the perspective is an extra-familial one in which the emotional task of the child will still be that of coming to terms with the sharing of love and care and the giving up of wishes to possess and control the mothering figure. The altruistic feelings evoked by the socialist ideal of fraternity depend fundamentally on a capacity to identify with others who are experienced in the emotional depths as siblings, potential rivals for whatever is available materially or emotionally. Coping with powerful feelings of competitiveness is made much more tolerable for young children, and indeed for all human beings, in settings where there is not an acute sense of deprivation and inadequate resources. We have to distinguish here between externally imputed deprivation and actually experienced deprivation, because these are not the same. A family context, meaning a small social inter-generational group in which there is a reasonable presumption of ongoing dependency, is the best setting for these crucial steps in emotional development. In larger groups, children and adults tend to regress to more primitive modes of relationship, not based on a recognition of individuality and not involving real and differentiated perceptions of self and others.

While the emergence and clarification of this theory of the

preconditions of emotional development of children has been due especially to analytic experience with children, its common practice and acceptance is part of a much wider process of social change in which psychoanalysis has been only one element. The family itself has changed substantially over a period of at least two hundred years, and has developed, initially only in privileged strata, more complex expectations for its emotional life, and for the development of its children. The emergence of 'companionate marriage' among the urban bourgeoisie of the eighteenth century, as Lawrence Stone[14] has described, a conception of childhood as a distinct life-stage with its own perceived preoccupations and tasks, and recognition in particular of the importance of affection and space for thought and imagination as preconditions of this development – these are the main elements of this new conception. The social function of this extended process of family socialisation seems to have been the transmission of cultural capital to members of social strata who depended wholly on their abilities in commerce and in the professions, rather than on inherited property, to advance their social position. This was also its function for members of the bourgeoisie who had acquired some capital but for whom the development of talents and appropriately self-disciplined attitudes was necessary, if their capital was to be increased rather than squandered in luxury and indulgence. These associated ideals of character, family, child-development and education were articulated during the nineteenth century by more liberal elements of the middle class. The writings of John Stuart Mill, Charles Kingsley and Charles Dickens – and of Charlotte Bronte and Elizabeth Gaskell – provide examples of the explicit or implicit advocacy of a pattern of companionate child-oriented marriage, against the grain of dominant patriarchal and authoritarian social practices.

In the twentieth century, with the expansion of a middle class dependent on its sale of skills and 'character' in the labour market, this gentler conception of the family has advanced further. Especially important, as Basil Bernstein[15] has shown, has been the rise of the 'new middle class' based on occupations concerned with work with persons or with symbolic forms such as those of science or the classroom. A dominant order forced to concede many rights and powers to its majority population has had to devise forms of control by consensus, rather than by overt coercion.[16] A number of occupations devoted to interpersonal relationship (e.g. teaching, social work, nursing, medicine, management) have greatly expanded, but perhaps more important than this quantitative growth has been change in the prevailing forms of customary relationship within organisations and between organisations and their clients. Overt discipline and imperative means of control – in schools or workplaces for example – have diminished and control through persuasion, consent, and the subtler manipulations of individuals and groups has grown, with coercive sanctions more in the background. Clearly this is in part the result of a changing balance of power between social classes. The developing 'state of de-subordination' described by Ralph Miliband[17] as characteristic of British society in the late 1960s and early 1970s (and perceived as threatening by the more traditional elements of the middle class) also led to new forms of so-called 'soft' social control,[18] depending on scientific expertise, negotiation, and consent, and less on legal sanction. The social strata most closely involved with these new processes of 'symbolic' and 'human relations' work are those which have been the most active inventors and advocates of these conceptions of child development, education, and personal relationship. Often these ideas, like those of 'progressive education' and indeed child psychoanalysis, have spread downwards from initially highly privileged professional middle-class groups, to a more generalised place in the system of public service provision, in these cases through primary schools and child guidance clinics.[19] The growth of a distinctive children's fiction is another aspect of this process, about which we are writing elsewhere. Posy Simmonds, the *Guardian* cartoonist, provides one ironic guide to the mores of these new social groups.

The values of personal relationship and development, regard for individually fulfilling work, preference for smallness of scale in the immediate environment even while having a cosmopolitan conception of the wider world, thus follow from the experience of these new strata, for whom such outlooks are positively functional in their own life-situation. The blocking of employment opportunities for the highly educated in the recession is the greatest threat to the confidence and security of this class fraction, and this is already manifest, of course, in many individual life-crises.

It is the social groups most exposed to the older and more direct forms of coercive control – whether as its agents or objects – who are most remote from these new cultural and familial attitudes. These will include, for reasons of occupational situation, many manual workers, the subordinates of large-scale bureaucracies, and those opting to exercise authority, as managers, foremen, policemen, within such structures. It is therefore understandable why in certain areas of life, including attitudes to child-development and gender-roles in the family, the new middle class have generally a more developed and advanced culture than classes which are in other material and political respects more egalitarian and communitarian in their outlook.

Critical to the concept of development for which we are arguing here is a distinction between patriarchal and egalitarian family forms. It is the repudiation of patriarchy and father-domination which has made it possible for feeling and imagination to become more central to the idea of human nature. The career of John Stuart Mill, from his rejection of the harsher aspects of utilitarianism in the name of poetry and imagination, to his impassioned writing against male power over women in *The Subjection of Women*,[20] is one eloquent instance of this connection. This has also of course been a leading topic of women's writing, in both fiction and feminist theory. Psychoanalysis developed in Freud's work as the understanding of the unconscious dynamics of the patriarchal family, with its characteristically conscience-driven and repressive personalities, and its distinctive women's pathology of hysteria. Radicals have often elided the critique of the family with the critique of patriarchy as if these were necessarily the same. Alternatives have been sought in the past in hunter-gatherer communities where sex-roles were relatively undifferentiated and childhood apparently a period of relative permissiveness. Or, more relevantly, they have been sought in those early capitalist Puritan or Non-Conformist families in which women's role in domestic production enabled them to maintain some parity of power and function with husbands.

Repeatedly, both in the movements at the turn of the century and in the 1970s, feminists have responded to the subjections of patriarchy by developing cultures of militant celibacy or lesbianism. Such responses to inequality must be respected, not least for their cultural energy and productiveness. But they seem to us to be in the long run less hopeful than change *within* the family, from patriarchy to companionate marriages, from a state of gender subordination to one of differentiation. This is because they are powered by despair and pessimism about the possibilities of more equal relations between men and women. The discovery by Freud[21] that the sexuality of men and women has in each case both male and female elements, derived in part from unconscious identification with parents, makes it possible to acknowledge that different 'divisions of labour' will be sought by each individual and couple. It should enable us to avoid the tyranny of imposed and idealised sexual norms. These findings strengthen the case for the convergence of male and female personality types, especially in regard to female roles in the external and public worlds, and male responsibilities in regard to children and nurture more generally.[22] But it would be realistic to recognise that some general differentiation between male and female roles and personalities is likely to persist in this culture, as a consequence in part of child-bearing functions, in part of family experiences and culture. The experience and exploration of these differences is likely to go on being found by most individuals to be central to their identity. The partial separation of 'male' and 'female' attributes between the sexes is why relations between them are so pleasurable, fulfilling, and necessary for both. Of course it has only become possible to conceive of sexual relationships as a natural fulfilment for both sexes in the context of the repudiation of patriarchy and women's increased power to define their own experience.

Changes in the experience of sexuality can be interpreted in different ways. There have been those, such as D.H. Lawrence and his critical advocate F.R. Leavis,[23] who have argued for a more acknowledged sexuality within the context of whole relationships of emotional commitment. This is also the point of view of the psychoanalytic work we have described, though with the important difference that its viewpoint is no longer predominantly male. The satisfactory or other outcome of sexual relationships will be rarely, in this perspective, a physical matter alone, but will depend on the unconscious meanings with which partners and sexual activities with them are perceived.[24] Sexual well-being is thus likely to be an aspect, not a cause, of good relationships with internal and external objects. It is easy to see that much 'sexual liberation' has been a perversion of human sexual capacities, for example through pornograpy substituting a kind of public masturbation for the private forms current in more repressive societies. Some of the fashionable radical preoccupation with 'desire' and polymorphous sexuality as some kind of idealised infantile state of being, involves some similar misconceptions. This sometimes upholds implicitly solipsistic and also male-centred views of sexual experience under the guise of liberation.

It seems in the end that it is the valuing of the emotional and sexual experience of *women* that is the key issue in making possible a more reciprocal and mutual form of sexual experience. This is denied, implicitly or explicitly, in the attitudes of pornographers, in those of many pro-family conservatives who would in effect make women powerless sexual objects for men once more,[25] and in the outlook of some libertarian radicals. (There are also of course those feminists who dispose of the problem by seeking to dispose of men.) Yet this area of experience, as a result both of greater understanding, and of greater equality between the sexes, has been one of genuine improvement over the last generation, and this is a cause for hope.

Less authoritarian family forms reflect changes in the workplace and in the wider climate of social and political equality, as well as alterations in the balance of power between the sexes *per se*. Brutalisation of men in the workplace was associated with the brutalisation of women and children in the home, and as the former becomes less, so, potentially, does the latter. But a wider social infrastructure has developed to support the activities of the new model family, and public institutions have become the bearers and supporters of some of its key values. We see the development of such institutions, both voluntary and State-provided, as extremely significant in facilitating development for individuals and families, and in making possible a more creative social order. Whereas some critics, such as Christopher Lasch,[26] have seen the development of public and professional services as an invasion and undermining of family authority and functions, we, from the different perspective of the British welfare system, see these institutions as potentially helpful and supportive of individual family relationships. Whether appropriate services are available or not will affect the ways in which families are able to experience different phases in their lives, and may determine whether they can surmount important transitions and crises in ways which allow learning and development to take place. A substantial social infrastructure has been created in support of the new companionate family. An early development was the reform of the education of infants, transferring into the primary school classroom some of the climate of affection and playfulness which was becoming customary in family care. Attention has more recently been given to the process of childbirth itself. Voluntary movements, influenced by feminism, have sought acknowledgement of the emotional and mental dimensions of the experience of childbearing, as a priority to be weighed against technical medical imperatives, and have also won recognition for the role of fathers in supporting their partners through this experience. Researchers in the psychoanalytic tradition have identified the damage caused to young children and their families when separation inadvertently takes place through hospitalisation in sickness or as a consequence of premature birth, and have been able to win recognition of the importance of continuous parental contact to early development.[27] These findings have had some influence on actual medical practice, though this is still far from universal.

The feminist movement has also been influential in the development of more cooperative forms of pre-school care for young children. It has become a more publicly acknowledged fact that the experience of looking after very young children is a difficult one,[28] often producing high levels of depression[29] and anxiety in women who bear the brunt of this work, and that some modern alternatives to the no longer widely available structures of large multi-generational families are desirable. The development of play-groups and other arrangements for the sharing of care between parents has been a significant and positive advance in the social resources available for this stage of life. In this as in other areas, important arguments continue about what kinds of provision are most desirable. Just as there are ideologies of maternal responsibility which are unrealistic about the costs to many mothers of prolonged and unsupported infant care, so there are 'collectivist' positions regarding universal nursery care which neglect the actual relational needs of infants and indeed of their parents, both in the internal organisation of nurseries and in the necessity to limit separations between parents and their children. Clearly there are implications for employment policy and necessary legislation, regarding 'maternity' and 'paternity' leave, and the availability of child care facilities at the workplace, which follow from the proper recognition of children's developmental needs, and a sensitivity to the meaning of parenthood. Comparisons of the standards of child care available to most working class families outside the home, and those which can be obtained sometimes by middle class parents, by reason of superior financial and organisational resources, show considerable class inequalities in provision which probably contribute to more unequal life-chances in later development.

The understanding of the emotional aspects of life-transitions and crises is less advanced in regard to later life-stages which tend to attract less social and state support than childhood. The movement towards 'community care' of formerly institutionalised patients, or old people, has recognised the destructiveness of much institutional care, while so far failing to meet the human and other resource needs of domestic care arrangements. 'Community care' can often mean little more than a cost-saving fiction. We have heard for example of a case where a day-centre for discharged schizophrenic patients was left in the charge of an unsupported student social worker. In states of adult dependency like that of childhood, the support of families by other agencies and resources will usually provide the best available experience. The life-long and relatively unconditional membership provided by familes, and the continuity and identification which this provides between generations, in face of inevitable individual loss, makes family membership an irreplaceable source of meaning and value for most people, surely in any imaginable society. While damaging burdens are now often placed on women as carers by a lack of social and material resources for the old, sick, and handicapped, this is a problem of missing public social provision, not of the role of the family *per se*. There is no more reason in this sphere than in that of childhood for seeing social provision and family responsibility as other than complementary to one another. The experience of old age will often be painful, but pain is best alleviated in conditions of dependable relationship and understanding. Psychoanalytic work on bereavement and loss[30] has been able to suggest what factors may make these life crises moments of emotional depth rather than times of human diminution.

The point of our argument is to show that there is a possible social infrastructure of co-operative and State-supported institutions which can further development among individuals and families in various stages of their life-cycles. In some fields, such as that of childhood and illness,[31] there have been real advances, significantly based on the existence of almost universal and free systems of public provision which have developed high professional standards and commitments. In regard to other areas of life – the social resources available to the old, the provision of educational and developmental opportunities for adults, the transition from school, penal and psychiatric policy – there has been much less progress, though the theoretical conceptions which have influenced the more developed areas have potential relevance here too.

There is an important distinction to be made between the quantity of resources provided in certain instances, and their appropriate quality. The superiority of hospice care for the terminally ill over that of most hospitals does not stem from their greater technical resources, but from the different priority they give to providing a physically and emotionally tolerable experience to dying patients,[32] and from their capacity to hold these issues in mind. The transition from school to work, already a period of difficulty for many even in the period of full employment, has become an area of widespread disaster as employment opportunities of any kind have collapsed for so many of the young. It is clear that a major reconstruction of the educational and occupational arrangements which provide for young people after school is now necessary. Finally, at perhaps the lowest point of social provision is the penal system. Here there has been some token acknowledgement of the social and relational preconditions of rehabilitation of offenders, through some attempt to substitute non-custodial sentences and community service and other reparative programmes for imprisonment. But the main thrust of State penal policy (often against the advice of professional staff) remains an unaltered and brutalising system of imprisonment, whose principal effect is the production of criminals. This is shown by high rates of re-offending, by many reports of the experience of imprisonment, and even by the comments of some prison governors.

The thrust of Thatcherism purportedly to 'support' the family, while actually attacking the social institutions which have developed as its complements and vital resources, is thus completely misconceived. What a system of diminished social provision is likely to produce is a climate of *individual* self-interest, rather than of family solidarity, and large numbers of social casualties of all kinds. Institutions, whether these be the framework of child care, education, employment, or local communities, which provide relationship and support for individuals and families will nurture social feeling and responsibility as a response. Where a society is experienced as merely oppressive or exploitative in its relationship to individuals, individuals will adopt appropriately defensive or predatory strategies of adaptation. In the United States, doctors are frequently sued for negligence; this happens rarely in the National Health Service in Britain. Settled class communities of the past combined a strong network of immediate loyalties to family and neighbourhood, with a wider sense of solidarity and social responsibility. Jeremy Seabrook has written eloquently in *City Close-Up*[33] and elsewhere of the turning of the despair in declining neighbourhoods into the blaming of immigrants to these communities. We have seen similar evidence from a report of community work on an East London housing estate where hostility to newcomers was directly related to the sense that there just was not enough of anything to go round, and the feeling that the authorities would not look after the neighbourhood.

Needs are now more complex, and communities must depend on networks of more specialised and professional institutions, like schools and clinics. But these can engender strong reciprocal feelings of attachment and identification, as those who have experience of good schools and hospitals will know.

Our argument is that psychoanalytic thought, especially in the tradition we have described and its community applications, provides one of the main theoretical bases for a better system of social provision, and also one of the main measures of their adequacy. This approach requires us to think about what happens to individuals in terms of their mental and emotional experience. Physical and even human resources are necessary but not sufficient conditions for ensuring an adequate individual experience. It is not numbers of professional workers, but what they actually do, which will determine what happens in a hospital. A welfare assistant in an infant school who is sensitive to the feelings of children will make it seem safe and secure for them, and will give the process of recovery from minor scratches and scrapes some of the healing and blissful quality that this can have for little children at home. (We have heard about one instance of care so kind that it led to minor grazes being self-inflicted in order to gain access to the treatment.) Whereas one who mainly enjoys the exercise of authority will merely help to induct her charges into an habitual dislike of rules and institutions, if not lead them to actively pass on the mental blows received to some even smaller victims. We want to give two examples at this point of what we mean by 'mental and emotional experience' and to suggest the ways in which we can thereby distinguish between good institutional practices and bad.

The first concerns the experience of a young mother whose first child was born prematurely, at thirty-two weeks. She had gone into hospital expecting to be helped to carry the baby to term, but instead the birth took place precipitately. The baby was not ill, as so many premature babies are. In the hospital unit, the mother and her baby were being observed regularly as part of a research project designed to help in improving the care offered in the unit. In listening to the mother's talk, the striking features were how much she had felt undermined in her identity as a mother by this premature birth – she seemed to feel that if she had not been able to hold the baby inside long enough, how could she possibly be a person who would know how to hold and feed a baby – and secondly how much she wanted to hand the baby over to the safe care of the hospital staff whom she felt had the capacities she lacked. There was a very distressing sequence observed in which the mother, now at home, came to visit the baby and found the incubator empty. She was in a panic, fearing that her baby was dead, not having been prepared for the baby's move out of the incubator into the ordinary hospital cradle in the other part of the nursery. All her feelings that her rhythms and the baby's were out of step were revived by this experience, and she was unable at that point to hold the baby close to her. She was terribly anxious about the idea of taking the baby home, for which she did not feel ready. She spoke of not having any clothes for him, and about her worry whether she could breast-feed. She had been expressing her milk so that the child could be fed by her milk, first by tube, later by bottle. In subsequent observations at home, her acute sense of mis-timing was continually elaborated, mainly in relation to feeding. She felt that she and her baby were never ready at the same time, and her solution was to express her milk and feed from the bottle.

The reasons for this woman's problem in getting over the premature birth were complicated by some factors to do with her own situation and personality, but there was, we think, an opportunity for the hospital staff to intervene helpfully in this crisis. The very limited visiting permitted underlined the mother's conviction that she was incapable of decent mothering. The unthought-out procedures for change in the unit, and especially at the point of discharge from the hospital, left her continually re-exposed to the shock of the unexpected and alarming new development, re-evoking the premature birth. As long as she found no way to feel that her upset state could be noticed and taken into account by the hospital staff whom she experienced as knowledgeable parents, in contrast to her own sense of being a new baby herself, as a mother, she could not really perceive her baby realistically and get in touch with him.

The second example is of a young adolescent boy's response to a move from one children's home to another. This had happened without much preparation, and it was unclear to him and the staff of the home whether it was to be a short-term or a long-term placement. On the first day, he expressed an interest in tadpoles, and went to Hampstead Heath to catch some. With the help of the head-of-home he made a home for them out of an old bread-bin. He seemed much involved in this, made a nice aquarium, and talked a good deal to the woman helping him. The next day she was very shocked to find the aquarium empty and the tadpoles laid out dead in a line alone a rockery wall in the garden. She asked him about what had happened. He explained that he could see that the tadpoles couldn't get used to their new environment. They were upset by the difference from the pond, and so he had taken them out. He seemed not aware of the fact that by taking them out of the water he had killed them himself.

One can see this situation as one in which the boy's anxious uncertainty about his own future entirely invades his capacity to make any realistic observations about the tadpoles. He cannot see them as separate from his own preoccupations. The external world has become confused with the internal world of his own feelings. While the tragedy is total for the tadpoles, the child care worker came to feel in discussion that it was not a statement of despair by the boy, but rather a communication to her about the depth of his fright and confusion, which might help her to understand him, and thus alleviate the loneliness of his position by sharing his anxiety.

The point about these instances is that they show how the process of understanding and thinking about experience is so crucial, both when it occurs and when it does not. Much suffering can be relieved, and energies freed for creative use when unconscious fears are made explicit, and enabled to be tested against reality. Such understanding does not necessarily require the intervention of psychotherapists.[34] One of the points of our examples has been to show how such understanding can often be a crucial part of quite ordinary working transactions with nurses or teachers. The greatest role of psychoanalysis in these contexts is likely to be in providing some more general psychological awareness, and in the training of professionals, and as a clinical service of the last resort only. One of the contributions of child analysis, and the observation of mothers and babies which is now so important a part of its training programmes, is the recognition that the understanding of her infant is one of the most important aspects of the mothering function. This emphasis on receiving and making space to think about unconscious communication is after all no more than a deeper understanding and a wider social application of 'what every mother knows'.

We think it is possible that such forms of understanding of life-anxieties may perform some of the same functions for some people, in providing intellectual meaning or an idea of human value, as beliefs within a religious framework have formerly done (and of course still do). The experience of actual pain and loss has substantially diminished with improvements in standards of life, average life-expectancy, and the control of physical pain. Most individuals in rich societies can look forward, leaving aside the possibility of nuclear disaster, to a life extending into old age, and to the avoidance of the major discomforts of hunger, serious illness, and the loss of children through premature death. In these circumstances the levels of anxieties and personally experienced evils which need to be explained and accepted has become less, and their sources more obviously self-created. A 'religion of humanism' (in Durkheim's[35] sense of religion as the expression of the fundamental values and beliefs of a society) is therefore an understandable development. Such a 'humanism' will have many forms of expression, in the arts, in political ideas, and in theories of human nature. These are unlikely to be unified in a single over-arching system of beliefs, like those of the classical religions. But psychoanalysis, with its emphasis on moral qualities, its particular attention to life-transitions and crises, and its procedures for providing understanding through mediating relationships, can perhaps be understood as performing *some* of the functions alternatively located in religious practice and belief. While secular and humanist in character, it nevertheless involves ideas of fundamental ethical and ontological commitment to certain kinds of personal experience. The tradition of psychoanalysis we have described is characteristically committed to individual experience and understanding, and to the value of the primary intimate relationships of the family. In these ways it is an inheritor of some Protestant and Jewish traditions.

While the stress of psychoanalytic thinking is on individual mental experience and primary relationships, rather than on material resources or social organisation *per se*, there are material and social preconditions which make the individual development valued by analytic ways of thinking more likely to occur. The possibility of individual relationships depends on numbers and proportions of teachers, nurses or care-workers, in any setting, compared with the numbers being looked after. The rejection of a bureaucratic, containment or 'army' model of organisation and a move instead to more personal and developmental conceptions, is the one important condition. Many institutions, including prisons, hospitals, and schools remain organised on a routinised mass-handling basis. Such structures produce insensitivity to mental pain among clients and workers. They also produce systems of defence[36] by which pain is passed on to others by the exercise of authority, or through collusion among victims against the especially weak, in gang-like behaviour for example. Other organisations, like day-nurseries, resort to impersonal care because the needs of their children are experienced as unbearable. This may feel like a situation of engulfment by large numbers, and be responded to by depersonalising routines, even though the numbers are large only relative to the particular context.

At a time when the production of goods is clearly going to require less workers, it seems obvious that greater resources can and should be devoted to work which fosters the development of persons. Much better pupil-teacher ratios in schools, and a greater number of nurses and careworkers available in other conditions of dependency, such as illness and old age, no longer seem utopian objectives. One would expect both the public sector and the market to respond to more complex developmental needs and desires, by creating new institutions and practices. The development of activity-holidays through the market, and school journeys and exchanges in the public sector, is one small example. Increased demand for local arts and arts festivals, for access to the countryside, and for participatory – in contrast with mass-spectator – sports, are others. In all these activities where learning and development can take place, relationships and specific 'activity cultures' can develop around them. A strengthening of many forms of sociability, supported both by government agency and by cooperative and sometimes entrepreneurial activity, is a possible consequence of more educational opportunity, leisure and material sufficiency, and less oppressive experiences of work. The smaller scale of production associated sometimes with new technologies may also be helpful in that they produce greater recognition of individuals in organisations. The move away from mass housing projects and towards a smaller scale of urban design is another sign of the times, and is by no means exclusively to be put down to privatisation and individualism. The 'social architecture' supportive of developmental and creative conditions of life will require a planning framework to ensure that resources are fully and properly used. It also calls for organisational forms that encourage rational deliberation, consensus, and co-operation over social goals.

Considerable progress was made after the Second World War in the development of a more adequate social framework. Where, for the majority, achievements were mainly in terms of basic security and minimum material standards, for minorities more complex ideas of citizenship began to be realised. New social movements such as feminism, a richer conception of childhood and companionate marriage, and public services in health and education which for some began to provide really adequate opportunities, started to show what kind of social provision is conceivable. It is important that these advances, many of them within the public sector, should be extended and made universal, and that their defence should not be inhibited by guilt over continuing inequalities and deficiencies. The emerging social strata most responsible for the intellectual and professional aspects of these developments may yet turn out to be more representative of the possibilities of the future than the *rentier* and philistine business class which has assumed temporary ascendancy with Mrs. Thatcher's Conservative government.

While this argument may seem some distance from psychoanalytic preoccupations, we argue that the developmental ideas which derive from child analysis have a close relationship to the social perspective we have suggested. This cannot be narrowly political in its affiliation; there is, for example, scope for disagreement about whether analytic concepts of development can be realised best through fraternal or parental concepts of social organisation. (Neither dimension can be excluded; they correspond respectively to paternalist and egalitarian ideas of social responsibility.) But the analytic emphasis on development through intimate relationship, on a high quality of individual care, and on decision-making through shared understanding, go strongly against the grain of the regressive politics of individual self-interest and punitive discipline of the 'new Right'. We argue that these psychoanalytic approaches to infancy and later phases of the life-cycle can enrich and deepen a socialist concept of citizenship and shared human needs.

Notes and References

1. An earlier version of this chapter was given as a talk at a conference of the Socialist Society on the 'Politics of the Family' in London in March 1983.

2. See, for example, Melanie Klein, *Envy and Gratitude and other Works*

1946-1963, Hogarth Press, 1975. Also Hanna Segal, *Introduction to the Work of Melanie Klein*, Heinemann, 1975.

3. D. Winnicott, *Through Paediatrics to Psychoanalysis*, Hogarth Press, 1975.

4. W.R. Bion, *Learning from Experience* in his collected papers *Seven Servants*, J. Aronson, 1978. D. Meltzer's *The Kleinian Development*, Clunie Press, 1973, is a good review of the line of development Freud-Klein-Bion.

5. Described in Martin Jay, *The Dialectical Imagination*, Sphere, 1972.

6. H. Marcuse, *One-Dimensional Man*, Sphere, 1972.

7. C. Lasch, *The Culture of Narcissism*, Sphere, 1980.

8. J. Mitchell, *Psychoanalysis and Feminism*, Penguin, 1975.

9. See Morris's essays in *William Morris: Selected Writings*, ed. by G.D.H. Cole, Nonesuch Library, 1934.

10. The most influential statements are R.H. Tawney's *The Acquisitive Society*, Harvester, 1982, and *Equality*, Allen and Unwin, 1965.

11. Marshall Berman, *All that is Solid Melts into Air*, Verso, 1983.

12. Michael Walzer's recent *Spheres of Justice: a Defence of Pluralism and Equality*, Martin Robertson, 1983, argues persuasively for a conception of justice as a due respect for autonomous spheres of social activity.

13. John Bowlby's *Attachment and Loss* (3 Vols.), Penguin, 1981, provides the most substantial account. There is an objective review of this debate in M. Rutter, *Maternal Deprivation Reassessed*, Penguin, 1972.

14. Lawrence Stone, *The Family, Sex and Marriage in England 1500-1800*, Harper, 1979.

15. See the essays in B. Bernstein, *Class, Codes, and Control, Vol. 3*, Routledge, 1977.

16. Ian Gough's *The Political Economy of the Welfare State*, Macmillan, 1979, discusses the function of welfare provision in the post-war period as a means of securing consensus. These issues were also discussed in N. Parry, M. Rustin and C. Satyamurti (eds.), *Social Work, Welfare, and the State*, Edward Arnold, 1978. These developments have recently been viewed as leading to a 'legitimation crisis' as the political system finds difficulty in meeting all the claims made on it. See, for example, J. Habermas, *Legitimation Crisis*, Heinemann, 1976, and C. Offe, *Contradictions of the Welfare State*, Hutchinson, 1984.

17. Ralph Miliband, 'A state of de-subordination'. *British Journal of Sociology* Vol. 29, No. 4, 1978.

18. See especially the essays by Stuart Hall and John Clarke in National Deviance Conference (ed.), *Permissiveness and Control: The fate of the sixties legislation*, MacMillan, 1980.

19. Not that the provision of analytic psychotherapy for children and families in the National Health Service has yet extended much beyond the Home Counties.

20. John Stuart Mill, *The Subjection of Women*, Oxford University Press, 1975.

21. S. Freud, Three essays on sexuality'. *Standard Edition* Vol. 7, 130–243.

22. See N. Chodorow, *The Reproduction of Mothering*, University of California Press, 1978, and D. Dinnerstein, *The Rocking of the Cradle and the Ruling of the World*, Souvenir Press, 1976.

23. F.R. Leavis, *D.H. Lawrence: Novelist*, Penguin, 1973.

24. Donald Meltzer's *Sexual States of Mind*, Clunie Press, 1973, is the most searching exploration of these issues.

25. This would be a possibly unintended consequence of reducing women's work opportunities and increasing their economic dependence on marriage. In fact, however, women's work is continuing to increase.

26. C. Lasch, *Haven in a Heartless World*, Basic Books, 1977.

27. See the *Colloquium on the Care of the Newborn*, in the *Journal of Child Psychotherapy*, Vol. 7, No. 2, 1981.

28. Ann Oakley, *Becoming a Mother*, Martin Robertson, 1979, and *Women Confined*, Martin Robertson, 1980.

29. G. Brown and T. Harris, *The Social Origins of Depression: A Study of Psychiatric Disorder in Women*, Tavistock, 1978.

30. Colin Murray Parkes, *Bereavement: Studies of Grief in Adult Life*, Penguin, 1975. Also Lily Pincus, *Death in the Family: the Importance of Mourning*, Faber, 1981, and *The Challenge of a Long Life*, Faber, 1981.

31. For a recent research study see I. Menzies Lyth, *The Psychological Welfare of Children Making Long Stays in Hospital*, Tavistock Institute of Human Relations Occasional Papers No. 3, 1983.

32. For one personal account of a daughter's terminal illness, see R. and V. Zorza, *The Way to Die: Living to the End*, Sphere, 1981.

33. Jeremy Seabrook, *City Close-Up*, Penguin, 1973.

34. Recent work by psychotherapists in relation to wider settings of care is described in M. Boston and R. Szur (eds.), *Psychotherapy with Severely Deprived Children*, Routledge, 1983, and I. Salzberger-Wittenberg, G. Henry, and E. Osborne, *The Emotional Experience of Teaching and Learning*, Routledge, 1983.

35. E. Durkheim, *The Elementary Forms of the Religious Life*, Allen and Unwin, 1976.

36. Two papers have been especially fruitful in consideration of these issues – Elliott Jaques, *Social Systems as a Defence against Persecutory and Depressive Anxieties*, in M. Klein et al., (eds.), *New Directions in Psychoanalysis*, Maresfield Reprints, 1977, and I. Menzies, *The Hospital Social System as a Defence against Anxiety, Human Relations* Vol. 13, No. 2, 1960.

NOTES ON CONTRIBUTORS

PETER BARHAM is a psychologist who worked for a number of years at the Tavistock Institute of Human Relations, and is now, as Honorary Research Fellow at the University of Bradford, developing a project in the community care of schizophrenics. He has written *Schizophrenia and Human Values* (in press).

JEAN BETHKE ELSHTAIN is Associate Professor of Political Science at the University of Massachusetts. She has written *Public Man, Private Woman* and edited *The Family in Political Thought*.

RAY HOLLAND is a lecturer in sociology at Chelsea College, University of London, and the author of *Self in Social Context*.

SUE HOLLAND is a clinical psychologist and psychotherapist who has developed psychotherapy services to working class communities in Battersea and the White City in London.

JOEL KOVEL is the author of *White Racism, A Complete Guide to Therapy, The Age of Desire, Against the State of Nuclear Terror* and is a psychoanalyst in New York and Professor of Psychiatry at Yeshiva University.

CHRISTOPHER LASCH is Professor of History at the University of Rochester, and was Freud Professor at the University of London in 1981. Amongst his books are *Haven in a Heartless World: The Family Besieged* and *The Culture of Narcissism*.

BARRY RICHARDS is a clinical psychologist who now lectures in the Department of Sociology at North East London Polytechnic. He is a member of the Radical Science Collective.

STEPHEN ROBINSON formerly worked in the Battersea community mental health project in South London and now lectures in urban policy at a British university.

MARGARET RUSTIN is a Principal Child Psychologist in the Department of Children and Parents at the Tavistock Clinic, London, where she does teaching and clinical work.

MICHAEL RUSTIN is Head of the Department of Sociology at North East London Polytechnic. He and Margaret Rustin are currently working on a collection of papers on the psychoanalytic observation of mothers and infants.

INDEX

P

R

S

T

U

V

W

Y

Z